ANCIENT CHINESE BODY DIVINATION

To W. Lloyd Warner

ANCIENT CHINESE BODY DIVINATION

Its Forms, Affinities, and Functions

WILLIAM A. LESSA

Orchid Press

Ancient Chinese Body Divination: Its Forms, Affinities and Functions
William A. Lessa (1908-1997)

First published as *Chinese Body Divination*, Los Angeles 1968.
Second Edition, 2024.

Orchid Press
PO Box 70,
Trinity, NL, A0C 2SO,
Canada

© Orchid Press Inc., 2024. Protected by copyright under the terms of the International Copyright Union: all rights reserved. Except for fair use in book reviews, no part of this publication may be reproduced in any form or by any means, electronic or mechanical, including photocopying, recording, or by any information storage or retrieval system without prior permission in writing from the copyright holder.

Cover image: Physiognomy diagnosis chart, Chinese woodcut illustration from 1817 edition of *Bian que maishu nan jing* [扁鵲脈書難經]. Wellcome Collection. ©

ISBN: 978-1-7782522-3-5

CONTENTS

LIST OF ILLUSTRATIONS vii
LIST OF TABLES viii
PREFACE x

Chapters

  I.   INTRODUCTION 1

         The Importance of Divination 1
         Body Divination Categorized 3
         Body Divination and Supernaturalism 4
         Research Aims and Design 7

  II.   THE LOGIC OF INTERPRETATION 13

         Correlative Thinking 14
         The Microcosmic Principle 16
         The Yin-Yang Principle 17
         The Five Element Principle 18
         The Eight Diagrams 22
         The Theriologic Principle 24
         The Principle of Harmony and the Mean 24
         Ch'i and Li 26
         Residual Principles 27

  III.   THE BODY AS A WHOLE 32

  IV.   THE FACE AND HEAD 39

         The Face as a Whole 39
         The Lines of the Face 51
         The Eyes 56
         The Eyebrows 59
         The Nose 63
         The Mouth 67
         The Lips, Raphe, Teeth, and Tongue 69
         The Moustache, Beard, and Head Hair 71
         The Ears 71
         The Moles of the Face 74
         The Occipital Bone 80

V. THE HANDS, FEET, AND TRUNK 84
    The Hand 84
    The Fingernails 106
    The Foot 106
    The Neck 109
    The Chest 109
    The Belly 109
    The Navel 110
    The Waist 110
    The Back 110

VI. GENETIC CONNECTIONS 111
    The Sources of Sinitic Civilization 112
    Concepts Common to China and the West 117
    Destiny 118
    The Macrocosm-Microcosm 123
    The Doctrine of Signatures 128
    Harmony and the Mean 129
    Theriology 131

VII. EAST-WEST DIFFERENCES 136
    Chinese Concepts Absent in the West 136
    Western Concepts Absent in China 140

VIII. AN HISTORICAL SYNTHESIS 158
    Theoretical Considerations 158
    Donors and Borrowers 159
    Stimulus Diffusion 163
    India 163
    Summary 165

IX. FUNCTION 168
    Personal Divination 168
    Conditions Arousing Concern 169
    Areas of Concern 179
    Functional Parallels in Europe 185
    Recapitulation 194

BIBLIOGRAPHY 197
INDEX 206
ABOUT THE AUTHOR 217

LIST OF ILLUSTRATIONS

Figure	Page
1. The Face Explained in Terms of Six Treasuries, Three Forces, and Three Sections	40
2 The Face Explained in Terms of Four Schools and Eight Schools	42
3 The Face Explained in Terms of Five Planets, Six Stars, Five Mountains, and Four Rivers	44
4 The Face Explained in Terms of Twelve Temples and Five Senses	46
5 The Face Explained in Terms of Thirteen Parts	48
6 The Face Explained in Terms of the Different Ages of a Lifetime	50
7 Lines of the Face (a)	53
8 Lines of the Face (b)	54
9 Lines of the Face (c)	55
10 Type of Eyes (selected)	58
11 Types of Eyebrows (selected)	60
12 Types of Noses (selected)	65
13 Types of Mouths	68
14 Types of Ears	72
15 Moles of the Face (a)	75
16 Moles of the Face (b)	77
17 Moles of the Face (female)	79
18 The Pillow Bones	81
19 Palm Lines Indicative of Wealth and Nobility	86
20 The Eight Diagrams in the Palm	88
21 Some Favorable Lines in the Palm	89
22 Types of Palm Lines	93
23 Types of Palm Lines—*continued*	95
24 Types of Palm Lines—*continued*	97
25 Types of Palm Lines—*continued*	99
26 Types of Palm Lines—*continued*	101
27 Types of Palm Lines—*continued*	103
28 Types of Palm Lines—*continued*	105
29 Types of Palm Lines—*continued*	107
30 Pedomancy: Two Types of Foot Lines	108

31 A Western View of Man as the Microcosm 126
32 Western Theriology: The Ovine Man 133
33 Western Theriology: The Bovine Man 133
34 A Babylonian Birth Omen Tablet.. 135
35 Western Astro-Physiognomy: The Whole Body...................... 146
36 Western Astro-Physiognomy: The Face................................... 147
37 Western Astro-Physiognomy: The Hand 148
38 Western Astro-Physiognomy: The Forehead 151
39 Western Astro-Physiognomy: The Moles 153
40 Western Humoral Physiognomy 155
41 Western Phrenology... 156

LIST OF TABLES

Table	Page
1. Chinese Dynasties (Simplified)...	1
2. The Five Elements and Their Correspondences	20
3. Contemporary Five Element Physiognomics............................	21
4. The Eight Diagrams and Their Correspondences	22
5. Physiognomic Premises according to Various Systems...........	161
6. Areas of Concern As Seen in Physiognomic Responses: Positive	181
7 Areas of Concern As Seen in Physiognomic Responses: Negative	183

PREFACE

Although long interested in physiognomics as the result of research carried on some time ago in the field of human constitution, my first awareness of the Chinese variety came about as the result of a chance conversation with Richard P. Wang, a psychiatrist who directed me to the rich holdings of the Gest Oriental Library at Princeton University. Assisted by Mary Yiu, I was able to extract from there a rich body of source materials. Looking back, I realize more than ever the great talent and patience Dr Yiu brought to bear in abstracting, classifying, and translating these Chinese volumes, and am indebted to Dr Wang for having introduced me to her.

My initial excursion into Chinese physiognomical research ground to a halt when I realized that in order for me to construct a functional interpretation of this mantic art I would have to become more familiar than I was with Chinese history and its social implications. I also felt the need to read more about Chinese philosophy and religion.

Meanwhile, I carried on desultory work in Babylonian, Greek, and Arabic sources with the valued assistance of the late Dorothea Lantos, principally to gain a comparative background for my ultimate interpretations; but these labors were merely a brief resumption that was not to bear fruit until much later.

The third and final phase of my research came about through the encouragement and assistance of Shin-yi Hsu, a graduate student in cultural geography who has recently been awarded the doctorate. Together we learned a good deal about China and taught one another much about the civilization of that ancient country. Our association provided the intellectual catalyst needed to develop the present volume in the form it now takes. I hold Dr Hsu in the highest regard as a research assistant and friend.

While in Taipei in 1966 I was placed in contact with a prominent practicing physiognomist, Shin-ku Chang, through the good offices of Inez de Beauclair and Yih-yuan Li of the Academia Sinica, both of whom were most generous with their time and encouragement. It was a revealing experience to see a physiognomist in action, using today the same basic principles that were so elaborately evolved during the Sung dynasty and the centuries before that.

Libraries and librarians have long been the object of my esteem and I must confess to feeling something of special fondness for them. Consequently, I am gratified to be able to say how much I owe to the staffs of the Gest Oriental Library at Princeton University and of the Oriental Library at the University of California, Los Angeles, for innumerable courtesies extended in the course of my work. At the former institution I was especially assisted by the head of the library, Shi-kang Tung, and the Chinese cataloguer, Lucy Loh. At the latter institution I was similarly helped by the head of the library, Man-hing Mok, and Che-hwei Lin. An added expression of gratitude must go to Robert Vosper, University Librarian on my campus, who generously authorized the purchase of a collection of several hundred Chinese books on divination, many of them dealing with physiognomy.

In conclusion, I cannot refrain from saying that my interest in the Chinese people began as the result of research in physical anthropology conducted in the Hawaiian Islands and Kwangtung Province. After all these many years I have now completed a sentimental journey into another realm of inquiry and trust that it is not without some merit as an interpretation of pseudoscience that has fascinated men for thousands of years, not only in China but elsewhere in the Old World.

WILLIAM A. LESSA
Los Angeles, California
January 1968

Chapter I

INTRODUCTION

In the *Tso Chuan* (左傳), an annalistic history of the state of Lu during its Ch'un Ch'iu or Spring and Autumn period (722–480 BCE), an episode is related to the effect that the Chou king, Hsiang, sent an envoy to the state of Lu to be present at the burial of Duke Hsi. The envoy was Shu-fu, a historiographer of the interior.
> Kung-sun Gaou had heard that he was a master of physiognomy, and introduced his two sons to him. Shuh-fun said, "Kun will feed you; No will bury you. The lower part of Kun's face is large; he will have posterity in the state of Loo" (Legge 1865–96: V, 229).

This is the earliest recorded allusion to physiognomy in China, the year being 626 BCE.

The attempts of men to divine through the human body are old and have important implications not only for social history but comparative sociology as well. Yet these efforts have not aroused much interest among social scientists and students of religion.

Materials for the social analysis of divination of this kind are by no means lacking; they exist in abundance for Europe, the Near East, and China, as well as other parts of the world. The Chinese sources are especially well documented and can serve, as I propose to do, to test hypotheses already advanced in tentative fashion from the European data.

It is my intention not only to make available a descriptive account of classic Chinese body divination and to compare it with that of the West, but also to examine its social context with the ultimate objective of suggesting the individual and social functions that this kind of divination plays in human life.

As chronology has an important bearing on these reconstructions and analyses, a list of Chinese dynasties has been drawn up in Table 1.

The Importance of Divination

Divination as a general phenomenon is an aspect of supernaturalism and enjoys not only great antiquity but almost universal occurrence as well. Written records of course arrived late on the human scene; nevertheless, they show that some forms of divination are of respectable antiquity. Astrology, for instance, was considerably elaborated by the Chaldeans at least 3,000 years ago. The Old Testament makes frequent reference to diviners and various forms of divination, including necromancy and perhaps some kind of sacred dice. The Greeks and the Romans employed highly systematized methods, such as ornithomancy, hepatoscopy, hydromancy, and oracles. As for the Chinese, written records show the use of scapulimancy about 1400 BCE during the Shang dynasty, although we know that it goes even further back in time as a characteristic of the northern China Neolithic.

Indirect evidence would seem to indicate that since the mantic art is essentially a magico-religious art, it may be coterminous in age with supernaturalism itself. The archaeological evidence is such that we may give credence to the belief that some form of religion was adhered to by both Cro-Magnon and Neanderthal man, and perhaps *Sinanthropus* and other earlier hominids as well. This being so, there seems no compelling reason to doubt that divination is equally as ancient.

TABLE 1
Chinese Dynasties (Simplified)

	Shang Kingdom	c. 1520–c. 1030 BCE
Chou Dynasty (Feudal Age)	Early Chou Period	c. 1030–722 BCE
	Ch'un Ch'iu (Spring and Autumn) Period	722–480
	Chan Kuo (Warring States) Period	480–221
First Empire	Ch'in Dynasty	221–206
	Han Dynasty	202 BCE–CE 221
First Partition	San Kuo (Three Kingdoms) Period	CE 221–265
	Chin Dynasty: Western	265–317
	Chin Dynasty: Eastern	317–479
	Northern and Southern Dynasties	479–581
Second Empire	Sui Dynasty	581–616
	T'ang Dynasty	618–906
	Five Dynasties Period	907–960
	Northern Sung Dynasty	960–1126
Second Partition	Southern Sung Dynasty	1127–1279
	Chin (Jurchen Tartar) Dynasty	1115–1234
	Yüan (Mongol) Dynasty	1280–1368
	Ming Dynasty	1368–1644
	Ch'ing (Manchu) Dynasty	1644–1911

Introduction

The antiquity of divination is also implied by its near-universality in the contemporary world, including that of the simpler peoples. Its prevalence in space as well as time implies that the mantic art has occupied an important niche in human affairs. Fortunately, the widespread occurrence of divination is more readily established than its age, for almost all anthropologists and others working with preliterate people have reported some efforts to divine the unknown through supernatural means. The Naskapi of Labrador and the Trukese of Micronesia, the Chukchee of Siberia and the Azande of Africa, the Siuai of Bougainville and the Witotos of Amazonia, have all placed reliance on some form of divination or other. These are only a few societies out of hundreds or even thousands. In the occasional places on earth where it seems to be unreported, as in aboriginal Australia, this may be simply a matter of oversight on the part of reporters.

But time and space are not the only measures of the exalted place of divination in human affairs. When the mantic art is seen in actual action it manifests significant psychological and sociological consequences, both individual and collective, serving to alleviate concern about the unknown. It is an important response to emotional anxiety and cognitive frustration in a situation of uncertainty. Its functional role persists even in contemporary urban societies.

Body Divination Categorized

Some characteristics of body mantic affiliate it with certain methods of divining, while others distinguish it from other kinds. These several attributes enable us not only to define it typologically, but also to establish its unique features.

Just as it has been said that it is possible to wager on the outcome of anything in the universe, it can also be said that it is possible to divine in an infinite number of ways. Geomancy, necromancy, oneiromancy, astrology, hepatoscopy, ornithomancy, dowsing, cartomancy, and tea leaf are among some of the methods of divining known to most people in the Western world, but there are innumerable other methods, many of them peculiar to one society or another.

Sometimes divining is deliberately conducted, as when one sits down to gaze into a crystal ball; at other times it is fortuitous, as when one has a black cat cross his path.

Another way of classifying divinatory practices is in terms of the psychic state of the person doing the divining. Where the answer to a question depends on a change in the psychological state of the individual, it may be said that we are dealing with "inspirational" divination. This is what obtains in mediumship and shell hearing. Where the answer is produced through a dispassionate reading of the signs, we are then dealing with a non-inspirational type of divinations. This is what one encounters in picking daisy petals or rolling bones.

Body divination is always deliberate and non-inspirational, rather than fortuitous and inspirational. What distinguishes it from other methods of divining is its utilization of the human body rather than something external to it.

While a good deal has been written about discrete kinds of body divination, such as physiognomy, chiromancy, ophthalmoscopy, neomancy, and metoposcopy, they have not been studied as a unitary phenomenon. This is a pity, for something of a special nature pervades all efforts to interpret the meaning of human anatomical features for one's past, present, and future. In order to emphasize this common character, as well as to suggest certain implications for its analysis, in 1952 I coined the term "somatomancy" from two Greek words meaning "body" and "divination" (Lessa 1952: 355). It is a word that I shall henceforth occasionally employ as a synonym for body divination.

Body Divination and Supernaturalism

From one point of view the use of the body to read destiny and character may be looked upon as pseudoscience, but to perceive it as such is not to imply that it is not a form of magic or religion. It is necessary to stress that the supernatural element, however much it may be disguised or disowned, it is always present in any kind of divination, even when unusual insight or intuitive perception are credited with its operation. The expression, "physiognomy," is disarming and perhaps even misleading because it does not necessarily imply supernaturalism; therefore, it is generally avoided in this volume except as a loose substitute for body divination.

The reason for raising this question at this point is that in the minds of some there may be a lingering misapprehension as to religiosity of the Chinese, and therefore some skepticism as to the importance of divination, of any kind, in the life of the people. C. K. Yang, in his *Religion in Chinese Society*, has given an explanation for this misconception.

> Great Western Sinologues such as Legge and Giles have emphasized the agnostic character of Confucianism. A later generation of

> Western scholars, who grew up under the influence of Legge and Giles and who became acquainted with Chinese culture through classical studies and through association with the Chinese educated class, assigned a relatively unimportant place to religion in Chinese society, leaving unexplained the universal presence of religious influence (1961: 4).

While recognizing that religion has its non-supernatural elements, Yang insists that in point of fact "the supernatural element has been an outstanding mark of Chinese religious life" (p. 2). Among the major aspects of the Confucian doctrine itself were: "The belief in Heaven and fate, the condoning of divination, the close alliance with the theory of Yin-Yang and the Five Elements, the emphasis on sacrifice and ancestor worship as a basic means of social control, and the lack of thoroughly agnostic and rationalistic attitude towards spiritual matters..." (p. 255).

Similarly addressing himself to the allegation that the Chinese people are not religious, the philosopher Hu Shih has said: "No student of Chinese history can say the Chinese are incapable of religious experience, even when judged by the standards of medieval Europe or pious India" (1934: 80). This famous scholar based his position not only on the long periods when the Chinese were fanatically Buddhistic but also on to the need to define religion without recourse to such Western criteria as "church-going, grace-saying, hymn-singing, and praying," or "the problems of the second person in the trinity, of transubstantiation, of the proper degree of submergence in baptism" (p. 78). He describes the original religion of the Chinese as product of the Shang-Chou cultural combination, consisting chiefly in a worship of their own ancestors, a belief in the spirits and powers of natural forces, a worship of a supreme God or heaven, and a belief in divination, to which was added a belief in the idea of retribution of good and evil. Since this religion lacks a general name he proposed to call it "Siniticism" (Hu Shih 1931: 32–34; 1934: 80–81).

The great preoccupation with magic and religion is clearly seen in the popular religion as recorded by Doré in his huge *Researches into Chinese Superstitions* (1914–38). Of course there are many more works than this, all testifying to the involvement of the people with shamanism, animism, demons, hundreds of subordinate deities, sacrifice, divination, temples, and festivals. Mention may be made of Werner's *Myths and Legends of China* (1922), a work on the beliefs and practices of popular religion, and his *A Dictionary of Chinese Mythology* (1932), a reference work on the gods and demons; Hodous' *Folkways in China* (1929), a catalogue of festivals and other observances and customs of folk religion; Day's *Chinese Peasant Cults* (1940), a study of peasant cults as seen through more than 2,000 paper gods; Reichelt's *Religion in Chinese Garment* (1951), a survey of animistic folk religion in modern China; Burkhardt's *Chinese Creeds and Customs* (1954), a survey of Chinese festivals and other traits of folk religion; and Waley's *The Nine Songs* (1955), a study of shamanism in ancient China (4th century BCE).

Within this medley of ideas one would expect to find concepts significant for the understanding of divination, and indeed one is not disappointed. Thus, the Chinese have long held, since well before the time of Confucius, a belief in *ming*, or fate, governed by an anthropomorphic and anthropopsychic Heaven. Confucius himself often referred to predestination, as did Mencius. It has been erroneously alleged that in his later years, after having experienced considerable frustration in life, Confucius assiduously consulted the *I Ching* (Book of Changes), for its divinatory content, rather than as protoscience. Subsequently, the *I Ching* became the major source of the principle and techniques of Chinese divination that developed in the centuries subsequent to his time. Notwithstanding, it was an obscure book that did not permit unfailing knowledge of fate, and for this reason it yielded considerably to the theory of the Yin-Yang and the Five Elements, which came to hold a strong place in the deciphering of the intentions and predetermined course of Heaven (C. K. Yang 1961: 251–52). This theory fit in with the Confucian doctrine of the interaction between Heaven and man. Much, however, as the Confucians embraced the idea of fate, they did not accept the belief that it was so controlled by supernatural agents that man could do nothing to shape it. On the contrary, man had a share in determining it, for he could plan and exert himself to the utmost of his abilities, even though Heaven would ultimately decree their success or failure (*ibid*. 272–73). In taking this positive view the Confucians placed man with Heaven and earth in a trinity of the universe referred to as *san kang* (三綱), each of the three components sharing a common substance. This made man superhuman and therefore endowed the individual not only with the capacity to determine his own fate through effort but to improve it as well.

Given this pervasive preoccupation with fate, it should come as no surprise to discover that the Chinese, including not only Confucians but others as well, have developed many procedures for dealing with this concept, somatomantic efforts being only one type. These methods are essentially magical in nature and have been recognized as such by most writers who have undertaken to reflect on the matter. This may be seen, for instance, in an article by Su Ting (1953) on fortune telling by means of the Pah Tze or Eight Words. Ting analyzes the reliance placed by this method on the Yin-Yang theory, the Five Elements, and the Pa Kwa, and concludes that this method–also, by inference, other methods of divination using these principles–is "a complex of utterly arbitrary equivalents and a combination of ideas and symbols obtained from various sources," and that it is moreover "a magic complex because it closely follows Frazer's laws, believing in resemblances and taking them to be equivalents, as well as considering related phenomena or facts as having relations of cause and effect or their equivalents" (p. 433).

Research Aims and Design

The study of Chinese body divination or *hsiang shu* (相術) can be directed towards the consideration of questions of concern to both history and social science.

Among the problems on which we shall endeavor to shed some light is the obvious question of the historical relationship between Chinese somatomancy and its counterparts in the West. Is the connection due to diffusion from one to the other, or from a common source, such as Mesopotamia? Or is it the result of chance parallel development?

In deliberating on these matters, it is well to bear in mind that wherever it is found body divination is confined to their higher centers of civilization, being completely absent from the simpler societies except where it has recently been borrowed. Are historical factors or functional ones operative here?

This query leads to a consideration of the motives that have impelled the Chinese to develop and maintain this kind of mantic practice. Was there something conducive in the social milieu? If so, was that same factor present in, let us say, classical Greece and Rome and Renaissance Italy? It is possible that, somatomancy being the intensely personal affair that it is, the importance of the individual as an individual had something to do with it. If all kinds of divination are a response to external pressures creating anxiety and concern, then it is legitimate to ask if the use of the body is linked with special kinds of anxiety and concern, such as those caused by consciousness of self, interpersonal relationships, and social instability. Accordingly, using the assumption that body divination provides a measure of freedom from uncertainty and danger in a world of chaos, some attention will be paid to the kinds of queries that Chinese physiognomy attempts to answer for the client. The aims of course are both predictive and descriptive–predictive in diving future events in the life of the individual, descriptive in interpreting his mental and moral disposition.

The method chosen here to attack these several problems is essentially anthropological in that it combines a descriptive and historical approach with an analytic and comparative one. If we are to shed some light on the ultimate nature and function of body divination we must first have a description of somatomantic theory and practice. I have already in an earlier publication given such a description of its Western manifestations (Lessa 1952) and have completed a preliminary survey of relevant Arabic materials.

Although the present study is essentially an analysis of Chinese body divination, opportunity will be taken to make meaningful comparisons, for only through comparison is the anthropologist able to exercise controls and arrive at the common denominators necessary for scientific generalization. He cannot experiment. This, however, is not fatal, for as someone has pointed out, there are certain branches of natural science, such as astronomy and geology, which are likewise incapable of experimentation. What is inherent in all scientific work is comparison.

Our comparisons will be beset with many drawbacks. They will not be able to achieve any great degree of control because the variables involved are numerous and do not lend themselves to quantification and co-variation. In view of the impossibility of statistical comparison, our research design cannot even begin to approximate the experimental method. Moreover, we cannot always be sure of the comparability of our data. Finally, we shall be confronted with the problem of the uniqueness of some of the historical events and sequences with which we shall deal. As Nadel (1951: 193) has reminded us, uniqueness is the opposite of the repetitiveness sought by science. It is "the appearance of characteristics which are not absorbed in regularities nor reducible to any determinate combination of conditions" and is "merely another word for accident or chance." He says that we must be prepared to allow for chance as well as law. This cannot be avoided. Anthropology is unable to escape the fact that it is forced to be an incomplete or hybrid science, dealing with cultural and social facts which are themselves hybrids born of repetitiveness and uniqueness.

Introduction

Some of our comparisons will be randomly cross-cultural so as to include more than one civilization, all of them more or less unrelated historically. Other comparisons will be internal within one society (China) but at different periods of time.

The aim of all this is to make comparative analyses not only on the descriptive level but the functional as well, so as to establish the relationship between variables and decide if the connection is causal or fortuitous. If the effort is successful it will make a modest contribution to a general theory of divination.

The sources of our data will perforce be published works. Ideally, some amount of field work in the contemporary practice of body divination might have been fruitful but for the most part it would be both inapplicable and impracticable. Between two and three millennia of Chinese history and social change will be encompassed, and here library sources must be used.

The bibliographic works on which I shall draw extend back considerably in time, even though they are mostly secondary and tertiary compilations of manuscript materials. These writings leave much to be desired, for they frequently are no more than a conglomeration of statements by many old authorities, put together in disorderly fashion with innumerable repetitions and many disconcerting contradictions. Often it is dubious that the authorities cited ever made the pronouncements and observations attributed to them. It is unfortunate that despite their tremendous interest in physiognomy and its implications for divination, the Chinese have never made a systematic or scientific study of the matter.

My chief sources, in roughly descending order of importance, have been the following Chinese works:

Shen Hsiang Ch'üan Pien (神相全篇), or "Complete Work on Physiognomy." This was privately collected during the Sung dynasty by Ch'en T'uan (陳搏), also known as Ch'en Hsi-i (陳希夷). He died in 989. The work was revised many centuries later by Yuan Chung-ch'e (袁忠徹) or Yuan Liu-chuang (袁柳庄) (1376–1458) of the Ming dynasty and was published during the Ch'ing dynasty in the year of Ch'ien Lung (乾隆), 1793. The publishing firm was Yun Ching T'ang (芸經堂). The work, which was consulted by the writer in the Gest Oriental Library at Princeton University, consists of 13 volumes, of which one is an index volume. For convenience sake the volumes will be referred to as the *Shen Hsiang*. It should be noted that an earlier edition was published during the Ming dynasty (1368–1644), with the same author and reviser. The preface for both editions was written by

Ni Yüeh (倪岳) (1444–1501), so the time of publication of this early edition may be assumed to be during his lifetime.

Ku Chin T'u Shu Ch'eng (古今圖書集成) or "Complete Collection of Ancient and Contemporary Books." This is a *lei shu* (類書) or so-called encyclopedia, and like other works of its kind consists of materials not expressly written for it but extracted from earlier works, including in this instance the *Shen Hsiang* cited above. The chief compiler of the encyclopedia was Ch'en Meng-lei (陳夢雷), a pardoned rebel who was appointed by the great K'ang Hsi (康熙), the second ruler of the Ch'ing dynasty, to prepare this huge work. The edition consulted by the writer is in the Gest Oriental Library at Princeton University and was published in Peking in 1728, being known as the Wu Ying Tien (武英殿), or "Palace Edition." The encyclopedia consists of 5020 volumes made up of various sections, each dealing with a separate topic. The material on physiognomy is in volume 2982, sections 631, 632; volume 2986; and volume 2987, sections 640 and 642. The text and illustrations are essentially identical to that of the *Shen Hsiang*. The drawings however are so superior that often they have been preferred for reproduction in the present volume. For the sake of brevity the encyclopedia will be referred to as the *Ku Chin.*

Ma-i Hsiang Fa (麻衣相法), or "The Physiognomy of Ma-i." The above mentioned *Shen Hsiang* and its reprinting in the *Ku Chin* owe their source to this book, which has been reprinted in modern times for more or less popular consumption. The *Ma-i*, as it is usually called, was originally titled *Ma-i Shen Hsiang*, and was compiled by the same Ch'en T'uan who is given as the original compiler of the *Shen Hsiang*, which is outgrowth of the 10th century work. According to the editor of the present edition, Ma-i was a nameless hermit who was an expert on physiognomy. Since he concealed his name the people of a later period used the appellation Ma-i or "Mourning Clothes" to refer to him. This same editor maintains that Ch'en T'uan studied under the hermit and then wrote his book. According to Giles (1898: 106), however, Ma-i was actually Ch'en T'uan himself and is known as the Ma-i Tao Jen or "Hemp Clad Philosopher." The present edition is a second reprinting and was compiled and edited by Lu Wei-ch'ung (陸位崇). The publisher is Tsu Lin Book Company (竹林印書局), located in Hsin Tsu, Taiwan. The date is 1958.

Shen Hsiang Hui Pien (神相彙篇), or "Compilation of Physiognomy." This work was compiled by Kao Wei-ching (高味卿), in four volumes,

Introduction

published in Shang Yang (上洋), by Chiang Tso Shu Lin (江左書林), 1843. Kao lived during the Tao Kuang reign period (1821–51) of the Ch'ing dynasty. His work is a compilation from the seventy-three known schools of physiognomy, arranged in concise form so as to make it a readable handbook. The first volume is the most valuable, dealing with morphological units in the conventional manner; the other volumes deal with color; lines, moles, and bones; and behavior patterns. This work was consulted at the Oriental Library of the University of California, Los Angeles.

The authorities who are cited in the preceding bibliographic sources as being responsible for the concepts and statements used in the present volume begin with a time over two millennia ago. Some of them are easily identifiable, others are less well known, and still others can neither be identified nor assigned a chronological position. Those about whom we have some information are:

T'ang Chü (唐舉) of the Epoch of the Warring States. Fl. 240 BCE.

Kuei Ku-tzu (鬼谷子) of the Epoch of the Warring States. Fl. 4th century BCE. He was given the name of the Philosopher of the Demon Gorge but his actual name was Wang Hsü (王詡). He was a famous Taoist and regarded as greatly skilled in divination.

Hsü Fu (許負) of the Earlier Han dynasty. Fl. 206 BCE. The author wrote *Hsiang Te Ch'i Ti-wu* (相德器第五), an important source for physiognomic theories, but the book is lost.

Kuo Lin-tsung (郭林宗) of the Later Han dynasty. He wrote *Hsiang Wu-te P'ei Wu-hsiang Ti-san* (相五德配五行第三).

Kuan Lo (管輅) of the Epoch of the San Kuo or Three Kingdoms. Fl. 3rd century CE.

Chang Chung-yuan (張仲遠) of the Wu dynasty of the Epoch of the San Kuo or Three Kingdoms. Lived CE 222–277.

Lü Tung-pin (呂洞賓) of the Tang dynasty. Also known as Lü Ch'un-Yang (呂純). He wrote *Hsiang Fa Ju Men* (相法入門).

Ta Mo (達摩) or Bôdhidharma of the Epoch of the North and South dynasties. He was the son of a south Indian king who came to Canton by sea in CE 520 or 526. He was the last of the western Patriarchs and the first of the eastern. He is said to have died CE 535.

Sung Ch'i-chiu (宋齊丘) of the Nan Tang dynasty (CE 923–36) of the Five Dynasty epoch.

Ma-i (麻衣) of the Sung dynasty. He wrote the *Ma-i Shen Hsiang*, originally compiled in the 10th century by Ch'en T'uan (陳摶), who may have been Ma-i himself. Whatever his true identity, Ma-i is one of the most widely consulted physiognomists in the history of Chinese body divination and is referred to as an authority even today.

Ch'en T'uan (陳摶) or Ch'en Hsi-i (陳希夷) of the Sung dynasty. Fl. CE 960. He may be the same as Ma-i, above. He is mentioned as being the collector of the *Shen Hsiang Ch'üan Pien*, the chief work on physiognomy consulted in the preparation of the present volume.

Chang Hsing-chien (張行簡) of the Chin (Jurchen Tartar) dynasty (1115–1234). He wrote *Ta T'ung Fu* (大统賦).

Yüan Chung-ch'e (袁忠徹) or Yüan Liu-chuan (袁柳庄) of the Ming dynasty (1368–1644). He revised the *Shen Hsiang Ch'üan Pien*, the edition used in the present volume.

In addition to these men there are certain authorities of unknown dates who are known not by their names but their titles. They are omitted here.

Chapter II

THE LOGIC OF INTERPRETATION

The Chinese explanation of the controlling principles of body divination rests on the idea that the heavenly fate becomes visible in the body and can be seen by inspection of the body.

Paradoxically, an eloquent expression of this belief is to be found in *Lun Heng*, written by the great Han philosopher, Wang Ch'ung (CE 27–97). The work is a rational exposé of the "superstitions" current in his days—days pervaded by magic and mysticism. Yet Wang Ch'ung tells us in his essay "On Anthroposcopy" (or *Ku-hsiang* 骨相) that,

> It is a common belief that fate is difficult to foresee. Far from it, it can easily be known, and by what means? By means of the body and its bones. An inquiry into these manifestations leads to a knowledge of fate, just as from a look at measures one can learn their capacity. By manifestations I understand the osseous configurations (Forke 1907: 304).

After furnishing examples of famous men who had anomalous features—double teeth, eight colors of eyebrows, double pupils, ears with three orifices, double elbows, four nipples, spine curved backwards, horse's mouth—he tells us: "Those who know fate, find out the great folks amidst low people, and discern the miserable among the magnates" (Forke 1907: 304). Then, having given further examples to verify this point he states that it is evident that character and destiny are attached to the body and that "The spirit comes from Heaven, the body grows on earth. By studying the body on earth one becomes cognizant of the fate in heaven and gets the real truth" (*ibid.* 311).

This heterodox rationalist attacked both Confucians and Taoists alike. He exposed the fallacy of the cultic theory of "interaction between Heaven and man," denying that calamities and sufferings were manifestations of Heaven's anger at evil acts committed by men—acts upsetting the order of universal harmony. He did not believe that droughts, floods, unseasonable precipitation, earthquakes, fire, and destruction by lightning were either portents of Heaven's anger or its punishments (Yang 1961: 1939–40). Yet he did not deny the connection between Heaven and the body on earth.

Perhaps his views, however much we may deplore them on other grounds, are not as paradoxical as they seem, for while he did oppose the Confucian anthropomorphic idea of the universe he nevertheless viewed the cosmos and the ordering of human events as thoroughly materialistic mechanisms.

One searches in vain in the tremendously complex network of Chinese physiognomic premises for some semblance of empiricism. Wang Ch'ung's citing of examples among famous men is of course only a spurious use of the experimental method.

It was pseudo-induction of this sort which was the subject of the earlier scathing attack on physiognomy by another Confucian rationalist, the great Hsün Tzu (ca. 298–238 BCE). No narrow Confucian, being known as the "heterodox" champion, he was realistic about the weaknesses of human nature, taking the position that man is by nature bad and acquires his goodness only through training. In his essay, "Against Physiognomy" (Dubs 1928: 67–75), which contains a portion that seems spurious (pp. 71–75), he ridiculed examples given by history as being absurd in their contradictions and claims. For instance, he says, "the Emperor Yao was tall and the Emperor Shun was short," etc. (Dubs 1928: 68). Just as Confucius had objected to having a man's ancestry being used as a bar to his employment, Hsün Tzu protested against a man's features alone rather than his scholarship and purposes being the basis of selection.

In refuting physiognomy, he employed some semblance of empiricism. As one commentator puts it,

> He gathered together, from his knowledge of history, every cripple, hunchback, or dwarf of note, and every notable who had any striking physical peculiarity, to show that figure has nothing to do with ability. He told of men who were extremely thin and long-faced, of those who were bald and those who were unusually hairy (Dubs 1927: 67).

Hsün Tzu sarcastically selected the examples of Ch'ie and Chou, whom he described as very tall, attractive, and handsome, with agile and strong sinews and muscles enabling them to stand up against a hundred men. Yet they were killed and their dynasty destroyed, for they became the greatest criminals in the country. "These evils," he wrote, "were not because they suffered from their features but from a narrow knowledge and low ideas" (Hsün Tzu 1928: 70).

Correlative Thinking

In subsequent sections below, a whole variety of logical principles will be discussed, and it will be at once obvious that they are overwhelmingly arbitrary, symbolic, and unrelated with the real phenomenal world, to say nothing of the human body. They manifest the ancient Chinese passion for a peculiar kind of classification. The question may well be asked if there is any unitary principle linking them together into a consistent whole, and the answer is fortunately in the affirmative.

Several Western writers have addressed themselves to his problem and come up with two kinds of answers. The first, offered by the French philosopher, Lévy-Bruhl, is ethnocentric and overstates the case for Chinese thought as a variety of primitive thinking. Anthropologists and others have generally rejected his views, which were first expressed early in the present century, and they will not be considered here.

The second interpretation of Chinese thought is one ably advanced by such writers as Granet, H. Wilhelm, Eberhard, Bodde, and Jablonski, whose ideas have been assembled and seconded by Needham (1954–: II, 279–303), who makes his own contribution and synthesizes it with those of these others. The next few pages are summaries of what he and these men have had to say, and come from Needham's writings. These authors speak of Chinese thinking as being "categorical thinking," "coordinate thinking," "associative thinking," or, to use Needham's own term, "correlative thinking." They make out a convincing case.

Correlative thinking goes about making associations between things intuitively rather than rationally, and is a thought-form all its own. It does not emphasize external causation at all, for in coordinative thinking conceptions are not subsumed under one another but are placed side by side in a pattern. That is to say, things do not influence one another by acts of mechanical causation but by a kind of inductance. Chinese thought must be understood in terms of order, pattern, and organism. Things behave in particular ways, not necessarily because of prior actions of other things, but because they have position in the ever-moving cyclical universe which endows them with intrinsic natures that make particular behavior inevitable for them. They are parts in existential dependence upon the whole world-organism. They react upon one another more as if by a kind of mysterious resonance than mechanical impulsion (Needham 1954–: II, 280–81).

The idea of resonance is consistent with the Chinese view that the universe of things and events is systematized into a pattern which conditions all the mutual influences of its parts. Things which belong to the same classes, e.g., the five-fold divisions of the Elements or the eight-fold divisions of the trigrams, resonate with and energize each other. What this kind of Chinese thought tries to say is that phenomena have an organic aspect—the universe is a hierarchy of parts and wholes suffused by a harmony of wills (*ibid.* 285).

Chinese coordinate thinking, then, pictures the universe as extremely and precisely ordered, in which things fit exactly. This organization does not come about through fiats issued by a supreme creator-lawgiver, "nor because of the physical clash of innumerable billiard-balls in which the motion of the one [is] the physical cause of the impulsion of the other." It is an ordered harmony of wills without an ordainer (p. 287).

The coordinate or correlative thinking of the Chinese manifests itself in the use of numbers, in what Needham calls a numerology or "number-mysticism." The number has no empirical basis. Needham especially cites Granet's contribution to the understanding of Chinese numerical symbolism, quoting him as saying that the notion of the quantitative played almost no role in the philosophical speculations of the ancients, but that despite this they were passionately interested in numbers. They were preoccupied with "numerical games," says Granet; numbers were manipulated as if they were symbols (p. 288).

The Chinese idea of correspondences finds expression in tables in which time is divided into seasons and sub-seasons and joined to the five regions of space, and these are in turn made to correspond to the elements, etc. Needham quotes Jablonski to the effect that correspondence has great significance and that for the Chinese it replaces the idea of causality. Needham himself expresses the idea most felicitously when he writes: "In such a system causality is reticular and hierarchically fluctuating, not particulate and singly catenarian" (p. 289).

The fact that Chinese organic naturalism was based originally on a system of correlative thinking seems to explain the basic principles out of which the rationale for Chinese physiognomy emerged.

The Microcosmic Principle

Correlative thinking is to be seen in the most important premise on which body divination rests, namely, that man, as a part of the universe, is an image of the universe. Stated in the language used by Western philosophers, man is a microcosm reflecting the universe or macrocosm. About 2,000 years ago Kuo Lin-tsung said in his *Hsiang Wu-te P'ei Wu-hsing Ti-san*, "Man is parallel to the universe; a universe is a man and a man is a universe" (*Shen Hsiang* I, 9b). The head is an image of the sky; the feet are an image of the earth; the eyes are images of the sun and moon; the voice is a semblance of the thunder; the veins are images or rivers; the bones are images of stones and metals; and the hair is an image of the plants (*ibid.* II, 23b). Such statements imply for body diviners that those elements that are desirable in the universe are likewise desirable in a person, and vice versa. If the head is broad and high like the sky, the feet square and thick like the earth, the eyes bright like the moon and sun, the voice clear like thunder, the veins clear like rivers, the bones strong like stones and metals, the nose clear like the outlines of mountains, the hair shiny like plants, then a man will have every good chance of success, wealth, bliss, long life, and honor (*idem*).

Many more correspondences between the human body and the universe than these were constructed by the Chinese. The reader interested in exploring them in all their complex relationships will find them summarized and analyzed by Granet in his *La Pensée Chinoise* (1934: 361–88).

The macrocosm-microcosm doctrine was of course developed independently of the physiognomists and is clearly expanded in ancient writings going back to about 120 BCE. The *Li Chi* (Record of Rites) comes later than this but makes some reference to it, and so does the *I Ching* (Book of Changes). There can be no doubt that throughout the subsequent centuries the universe analogy has continued to hold a central place in Chinese thought.

This broad principle finds more specific and refined expression in the philosophy of Yin-Yang and the Five Elements, which by influencing Taoism and Confucianism was able to gain wide currency and prestige.

The Yin-Yang Principle

The Yin-Yang or two-force theory is frequently associated with Confucius but actually predates him by many centuries. It is present implicitly or explicitly in the many premises used in Chinese divination, being a concept of duality expressed in two principles or modes of energy that constitute everything in life. The Yin is identified with that which is negative and female: Earth, darkness, quiescence, coldness, moisture, and absorption. The Yang, on the contrary, is identified with that which is positive and male: Heaven, light, activity, warmth, dryness, and penetration. All things in the universe result from the interaction of these two forces. Yin and Yang express themselves in activity, and a given object or person is the product of their interaction, the predominance of one activity-mode producing the qualities of one, and the predominance of the opposite activity-mode producing the opposite qualities.

This doctrine exemplifies again the correlative thinking previously discussed. As the two fundamental principles or forces of the universe, the Yin and Yang have assigned to them all things fitting a two-fold arrangement. Some of the basic symbols have been mentioned. Far more could be added. For example, the Yin is identified with the White Tiger of autumn, and the Yang with the Green Dragon of spring, symbolizing the western and eastern quarters of the sky, respectively. Intermeshed with this system of symbolic correlations are the Five Element system and the trigrams and hexagrams, expressing the view that the universe is an organism with all its parts interacting in a mutual service.

Morphological features are clues to the dominance or interaction of these two energy modes within each human being, and it is the responsibility of the physiognomist to identify and interpret their inner meaning from their outward manifestation.

The Yin-Yang school had its origins in the occultists, who in ancient times were known as the *fang shih* (方士), or practitioners of occult arts. In his *History of the Former Han Dynasty* Pan Ku incorporates a six-fold classification of these arts, based on a seven-fold summary prepared earlier by the Confucian, Liu Hsin (c. 46 BCE–CE 23), and in it we find that the sixth and last class of occult art is the "system of forms" and includes physiognomy (Fung 1948: 30, 129). In the days of early Chou feudalism the *fang shih* were hereditary experts attached to all the aristocratic house and had to be consulted when any act of importance was contemplated. As feudalism slowly crumbled away, many of these specialists lost their hereditary positions and spread throughout the country, practicing their arts among the people (*ibid.* 130). From this information it can be inferred that physiognomists go back to at least the Early Chou and that they were already conversant with the Yin-Yang doctrine.

The Five Element Principle

The universe analogy has a variant based on the Five Elements which are believed to constitute the universe and to have resulted from the action of the Yin and Yang. This concept, with which Confucius could not have been familiar as it was originated by Tsou Yen (350–270 BCE)

The Logic of Interpretation

at least one century after his death, is consistent with the generalized belief that in man the whole material of the world, and all the forms and varieties of forms, are reflected. The elements, in the evolutionary order in which they came into being, are: water, fire, wood, metal, and earth. However, as Needham (1954–: 11, 243) has pointed out, they are not so much five kinds of fundamental matter as they are five kinds of fundamental processes, as the generating and destroying capacities described below will demonstrate.

A principle of mutual production, *hsiang seng* (相生) applies to the elements in that one will produce or generate another, in the following order:

>wood produces fire
>fire produces earth
>earth produces metal
>metal produces water
>water produces wood

The process is cyclical. The logic behind this is that wood when burned produces fire; fire, by burning wood, produces ash, or earth; earth produces metals by promoting the growth of metallic ores within its rocks; metal, when melted, gives rise to liquid, or water; water gives birth to trees, or wood. The body diviners, as we shall see, maintain that a person possessing two elements of proper combination will be fortunate. In addition to the first element he must possess a second one capable of producing the first.

Opposed to the above principle is the principle of mutual conquest, *hsiang sheng* (相勝).

>wood conquers earth
>metal conquers wood
>fire conquers metal
>water conquers fire
>earth conquers water

At this point the cycle begins all over again. The logic behind this is that wood, when growing, exhausts the supply of energy in the earth; metal cuts wood; fire melts metal; water extinguishes fire; earth, in the form of a dam, controls water. Persons possessing two elements, one of which destroys the other, are unfortunate.

Not readily apparent in the physiognomic works consulted, but possibly operative as bases for interpretation, are two additional principles deducted from the mutual production order and the mutual conquest order. They have been clarified by Needham (1954–: II, 257–59).

The principle of control, *hsiang chih* (相制) holds that a given process of destruction is controlled by the element which destroys the destroyer. Thus, wood destroys earth but metal controls the process;

metal destroys wood but fire controls the process; etc. This idea is known to have been employed first in fate-calculation, *t'ui ming* (推命), a system of prognostication employing the twelve horary characters or branches, and the ten celestial stems.

The principle of masking, *hsiang hua* (相化) holds that a process of change can be masked by some other process which produces more of the substrate, or produced it faster than it can be destroyed by the primary process. Thus, wood destroys earth, but fire masks the process; fire destroys metal, but earth masks the process, etc.

Pertinent to character reading and fortune telling from the human features is the symbolic correlating of the Five Elements "with almost every conceivable category of things in the universe which it was possible to classify into fives" (Needham 1954–: II, 261). Most of the correlations are of course artificial and arbitrary; only a few are more or less natural. Some of the ones that are relevant for body divination may be seen in Table 2.

TABLE 2

The Five Elements and Their Correspondences

Element	Color	Directions	Mountains	Planets	Sense Organs	Virtue	Form
wood	green	east	Tai-shan	Jupiter	eye	benevolence	long
fire	red	south	Heng-shan	Mars	tongue	propriety	pointed
earth	yellow	center	Sung-shan	Saturn	mouth	sincerity	thick
metal	white	west	Hua-shan	Venus	nose	righteousness	square
water	black	north	Heng-shan	Mercury	ear	wisdom	round

The table shows only some of the correspondences. Over a hundred others have been found in the Chinese literature, among them being: five seasons, tastes, smells, numbers, musical notes, kinds of weather, states, rulers, Yin-Yang combinations, human psycho-physical functions, styles of government, ministries, instruments, classes of living animals, domestic animals, "grains," sacrifices, viscera, parts of the body, and affective states. No better illustration of the correlative type of thinking of the Chinese exists than that afforded by the Five Element system.

Table 3 shows how a recent book on physiognomy published in Hong Kong applies the Five Element concept to body mantic (Tsao 1965: 114–15).

TABLE 3
Contemporary Five Element Physiognomics

Element Type	Morphological Characteristics	Worst Features	Best Features	Special Comments
Metal	Color, white; *ch'i*, bright; ears, normal; eyebrows, regular, eyes, graceful; face, square; lips and teeth, matching; head, even and small.	Head, sharp; nose, sharp; nasal tip, red. (Fire destroys metal.)	Bones and flesh, firm and full. (Earth generates metal.)	By white we mean: the bones are too clear and *ch'i*, is too cold. Cold metal has to be molded with little fire.
Wood	Slim and long; eyes, graceful; beard, regular; lips, red; hand lines, fine and neat.	Color, white; *ch'i*, clear. (Metal destroys wood.)	Color, dark; *ch'i*, calm. (Water generates wood.)	A long and straight body is called the *chia* type of wood. This type of wood has a surplus of wood, only useful when mixed with some metal.
Water	Round, fat, black, soft; ears, eyes, mouth, and nose, all fat; palm, fat and normal.	Yellow, not clear. (Earth destroys water.) Worse when ears are not complete; eyes not sharp; nose not normal; lips not closed (Four rivers flooded.)	Color, white; *ch'i*, clear. (Metal generates water.)	Color, red; no beard; smooth skin and cold flesh. Will have no children.
Fire	Color, bright; red and soft; upper sharp and lower wide; head, red; nose, crooked; ears reveal outline; hair and beard red and scanty.	Flesh, fat; *ch'i*, calm. (Water destroys fire.) Worse when ears, eyes, nose, and mouth big and full.	Body type, slim and straight; beard, regular; eyebrows, graceful. (Wood generates fire.)	Will flourish quickly, but will not reach a million. Noble in military office. Will also have children only when he has luck in economic affairs.
Earth	Fat, heavy, thick; full head and face; thick and large; eyebrows, ears, eyes, nose, and mouth, all thick; belly and back like turtle.	Beard, thick and irregular. (Wood destroys earth.) Bones revealed; flesh, thin.	Color, bright. (Fire generates earth.)	—

Source: Ts'ao Chi-pen, *Hsiang Jen Fa* (1965), pp. 114–15.

The Eight Diagrams

Despite their enormous importance in the *I Ching* (Book of Changes), the Eight Diagrams, or *pa kwa* (八卦), play only a modest role in the art of body divination.

It will be recalled that the *I Ching* explains, often in a mystifying fashion, a mystical system of divination based on the study of combinations of solid lines and lines broken in two. The basic unit of the system is the *kwa*, a trigram of three sets of lines. Eight possible trigrams result from the various combinations of lines, each having a designation as well as certain attributes and correspondences, of which a simplified version appears in Table 4.

When one trigram is placed above another, the two together form any one of sixty-four possible combinations of six lines. These hexagrams, as they are called, each have a symbolism, and while they are the chief subject matter of the *I Ching* they apparently are not used in somatomancy, as are the eight trigrams.

TABLE 4
The Eight Trigrams and Their Correspondences

Trigram	Name	Designation	Image	Influencing Element	Associated part of human body
☰	Ch'ien (乾)	the Creative	heaven	metal	head
☷	K'un (坤)	the Receptive	earth	earth	abdomen
☳	Chen (震)	the Arousing	thunder	wood	foot
☵	K'an (坎)	the Abysmal	water	water	ear
☶	Ken (艮)	Keeping Still	mountain	fire	hand, fingers
☴	Sun (巽)	the Gentle	wind	wood	thigh
☲	Li (離)	the Clinging	fire	fire	eye
☱	Tui (兌)	the Joyous	lake	metal	mouth, tongue

The Eight Diagrams are thought of as images of all that happens in Heaven and on earth, and are in a constant state of change from one into the other, just as there is constant change from one phenomenon to another in the physical world. They represent certain processes in nature.

The book does not appear to be the work of any specific period or one man. The commentaries on it appear to be the work of late Chou and early Han scholars, thus being post-Confucius. Dubs (1927: 69) thinks that Confucius never knew the book because there is absolutely no mention of it in literature prior to the 3rd century BCE. But others, such as Wilhelm (1951: I, xxxiv-xxxv) think otherwise. True, there was a single mention of it by Confucius, stating that he wished he had more years to give to the study of the book. Dubs says that in view of Confucius' generally agnostic attitude towards spirits, and his refusal to discourse upon the supernatural, a good deal of suspicion may be thrown upon this single passage as inconsistent with his general attitude. He suggests that it may have been inserted later to validate the inclusion of the work among the Classics. The point is that once the name of Confucius, as with Aristotle, was attached to any writing, an air of credulity, if not conviction, was laid down. If Dubs is right, Confucius could not have been the author of the ten sections or Ten Wings of it, as alleged by some. His name was merely used to strengthen a school of thought.

If, as others have maintained, the *I Ching* extends about 2,800 to 3,000 years back in time, its origins are too early to be linked with the name of Confucius. However, this theory does not preclude the possibility that the great philosopher made the additions imputed to him.

At any rate the Confucians did not really change or add anything to the book. Rather they interpreted it in accordance with their code of ethics.

Also having great influence on the development of the *I Ching* was the Taoist school of thought, which probably is responsible for its metaphysical and magical connotations.

According to the interpretation of the various commentaries, the entire universe is in a process of constant change. In order to achieve success in life, a wise man has to understand these processes, know the direction in which the universe is moving at the specific moment, and adapt his actions accordingly. Here is where the hexagrams enter in. They aid him by describing symbolically the steps in the process of change. Through divining to discover which hexagrams are descriptions of the present moment, one can determine the fitting course of action to adopt.

Each trigram is said to possess either *yin* or *yang*, the two being in perpetual conflict. The world, the moment, and the way of understanding is dependent on their interaction. The Five Elements, too, were worked into the interpretation of the hexagrams.

The Theriologic Principle

An important variant of the microcosmic theory is that since animals are a part of the universe it is legitimate to use them as standards of judgment for analyzing human beings. That is, to the extent that people have a resemblance to one animal or another they participate in the characteristics of the animal. This notion, which scholars in the Western world have termed "theriology," was stated well over two thousand years ago by Wang Hsü (王詡), also known as Kuei Ku-tzu (鬼谷子), in his *Hsiang Pien Wei Mang, No. II* (相辨微芒第二) when he said: "Man was originally without form, but assumed his shape from the universe; some adopted the form of birds and others took the shape of animals in myriad varieties" (*Shen Hsiang* I, 3b).

The theriologic principle is stretched to apply to animals of purely mythologic origin, as in the case of the phoenix, dragon, and unicorn. The phoenix, being associated with royalty as the symbol of the empress, signifies favourable things. But the bird is a figment of the imagination with various forms; at best it may have been suggested by the Argus pheasant (Burkhardt 1953: I, 137). Similarly, the dragon is another imperial emblem, representing the emperor and therefore likewise associated with desirable qualities. The dragon is conceived of in many ways but, as with the phoenix, the diviner could keep one of the stereotypes in mind when examining a client's features. The unicorn has the body of a deer, the hoof of a horse, the tail of an ox, and a single horn with a fleshy growth on it. It is full of gentleness and regarded as the king of all animals. Like the phoenix, it is a bringer of children (Couling 1917: 95).

The Principle of Harmony and the Mean

The Chinese were guided, too, by a principle of harmony, *ho* (和). To understand this it is necessary to trace out some philosophic concepts connected with the idea of *chung* (中), or centrality, which Confucius had used in the sense of conscientiousness to others.

The notion of *chung* was first formally elaborated upon in a book called the *Chung Yung* (中庸) (Doctrine of the Mean), which allegedly was written in part by Tzu Ssu, Confucius' grandson, but probably is the work of an unknown writer or writers who lived during the Ch'in or early Han dynasty.

There are many facets to the *Chung Yung*, but we can say that it refers, in the words of Hughes (1943: 1, n.1), to "a mean of truth between exaggerations of error," and takes the view that there is a true way for man, this being a middle way. Stated in another manner, *chung* means "just right," neither too little nor too much. It applies to experiencing emotions in due proportion, or even not experiencing any emotion at all. It applies in like way to the desires. To have no emotions of pleasure, anger, sorrow or joy is to be in a state of equilibrium.

Harmony, or *ho*, is achieved when a person satisfies all desires and emotions to the proper degree. It is the reconciling of difference into a harmonious unity. When it is achieved by the individual it results in good mental health, and when it is achieved by all the kinds of people constituting a society it results in peace and order. Harmony goes beyond the person and human society; it permeates the entire universe (Fung 1948: 173–74).

The man who has achieved the quality of realness, i.e., to have hit the mean without effort and to hold it without thinking of it, is said by the *Chung Yung* to have the ability to foreknow. When a country is about to perish, or when it is about to flourish, there are bound to be omens of evil fortune, revealed in the tortoise shell or the milfoil. The entirely real man has a likeness to the divine and can know when disasters or blessings are on the way (Hughes 1943: 130).

The body diviners took the concepts of *chung* and *ho* and applied them to their art. They said that features in harmony with one another by virtue of similarities in shape, size, and length are prognosticators of good. Features out of harmony with one another are indicators of things that are bad. If an individual possesses some features which ordinarily are considered to be unfavorable in themselves, he can offset this shortcoming if these features show harmony with certain others.

Take length, for example. Here we encounter the expression "five long and five short" (五長五短). When the head, face, arms, legs, and trunk are all long—or all short—with full bones and smooth flesh, good fortune will accompany a man always. Long legs and short arms, however, will lead to bankruptcy and a homeless life; but if both the arms and the legs are long, a man will enjoy a prosperous life (*Shen Hsiang* IV, 30b-32a).

Similarly, the principle of harmony is reflected in matters of size, as distinguished from length. The Chinese seem to have regarded smallness of body features as an unfavorable sign. But smallness, like shortness, can be offset by harmony among the five features, in this instance listed as head, eyes, stomach, ear, and mouth. If all these are small as well as straight and whole, a man will have a chance for success, but if only one or two are small and the rest big, he will suffer from poverty (*idem*).

In addition to these examples we may cite certain others. Thus, things that are in good harmony are: a thin man with leaking hands (holes between the fingers); a fat man with fat hands; a large man with large hands; a strong man with soft hands. In bad harmony are: a man who has large hands but short fingers; a man who has a small body but large hands. The former will always be blamed without cause, while the latter will be extravagant (*ibid*. VIII, 20ab).

Unfavorable features can be offset in another way, too, and that is by possessing good features which more or less neutralize them. Thus, good fortune will accompany one whose head may be too small yet has projecting bones at the side of the head; whose eyes are too small yet pretty and bright; whose belly is too small yet hangs downward; whose ears are too small yet are well shaped with clear outlines; or whose mouth is too small yet has lips that are straight (*ibid*. VIII, 20ab).

Conversely, features that are ordinarily favorable can be offset by those that are unfavorable. Here we encounter the expression, "six large" (六大), referring to the belief that it is good to have a large head, eyes, nose, mouth, ears, and stomach. But poverty will accompany him whose head is big yet lacks two projecting bones at the two sides of the forehead; whose eyes are big but dull; whose nose is big but flat at the bridge; whose mouth is big but has dropping corners; whose ears are large but without outlines; whose stomach is large but does not hang downward (*ibid*. IV, 30b-32b).

Ch'i and Li

We now come to two Neo-Confucian concepts that have been used in intuitive fashion by Chinese physiognomists and assigned high prestige by them in divining from the body. One is *ch'i* (氣), the other is *li* (理).

Ch'i is an intangible ethereal substance translated roughly as material-force, subtle matter, matter energy, or vital energy, and has been compared loosely with the Greek *pneuma*.

Li is usually translated as law or reason or rational principle. It is the cosmic principle of organization—the dynamic order and pattern in nature. These ideas had been mentioned at an early time by Confucius and Mencius, but were developed during the latter part of the Sung dynasty by Chu Hsi (朱熹, 1130-1200), the greatest of the Neo-Confucian philosophers.

Li, the rational principle, which is exhibited in every object in nature, in its cosmic operations impels the vital energy, *ch'i*, to generate movement and change. The two interact in mutual dependence, and the process results in the creation of matter. As a result, the two energy modes, *yang* and *yin*, as well as the Five Elements, are produced. When the metaphysical principle rides on the activating or physical principle (as a rider on a horse) and the pace is swift, the *yang* energy mode is generated; when the pace slows down, the *yin* energy mode is produced. After the two modes have been brought into being they give rise to the Five Elements.

What does this have to do with divination? The Confucians embraced the idea of fate and believed that their magical practices enabled fate to be known. They did not think that fate was entirely in the hands of supernatural agents; on the contrary, man could share in determining fate. They viewed the ethereal substance, *ch'i*, as a substance going into the making of not only Heaven but man as well. This permits the penetration between the Way of Heaven and the Way of Man. Man can share in determining his own fate through effort and cultivation (Yang 1961: 272-74).

Residual Principles

Numerous other principles and rationales have been used in Chinese physiognomics, and here again we encounter the emphasis on correlative thinking. Bodde (1939), who has looked into the frequency of the numerical categories resulting from the feeling for order and harmony, finds that five and nine are the most important. In glancing over the previous numerical categories and those mentioned below, it is at once apparent that five is indeed the most common; but there seems to be no reference to the number nine, although it must be conceded that this number undoubtedly has the importance which Bodde assigns to it if categorical thinking of other sorts is taken into consideration. On the other hand, Mayers' book, *The Chinese Reader's Manual* (1924), which lists 317 items distributed among various numerical categories, shows the number three to have the highest frequency, 68, and the number five to have the second highest frequency, 63, with the number six running third with 38, and the number nine ranking fourth with 31 items. However, Mayers' book was published originally in 1874 and is by no means complete; moreover, Bodde probably did not include items unconnected with harmony and order, as does Mayers. The incompleteness of Mayers' list is made evident when searching in his book for the numerical categories used by physiognomists. Most are lacking.

Let us now turn to those principles, all of them numerical, which have not already been discussed.

In incremental order, the residual principles begin with triads (the Yin-Yang dyad has already been discussed, and there remain no others). One of these triads is the Three Forces, *san t'sai* (三才) in nature: Heaven, earth, and man. These refer respectively to the forehead, nose, and chin. This triad of forces is inseparable. The Han philosophers maintained that order exists in all things, including both the natural world and society, and man plays a part in seeing that human activity remains in harmony with the divine and natural. This idea is expressed in the *Doctrine of the Mean*, where it is said of man: "Able to assist the transforming and nourishing powers of Heaven and Earth, he may with Heaven and Earth form a ternion" (Legge 1865–95: I, 416).

Another threefold division is one based on the Three Sections, *san t'ing* (三停). According to Giles (1912: 1159) these forces pertain to the forehead, nose, and chin in portraiture.

Fourfold categories are next. The Four Rivers or *ssu tu* (四瀆)—the Chiang or Yangtse (陽子), the Ho or Yellow (黃河), the River Huai (淮), and the River Chi (濟)—form the foundation for a division which derives its symbolism from natural features of the Chinese landscape. Their ultimate symbolism derives from the association of these rivers with four spirits who were great men in ancient times and were eventually apotheosized and designated as kings of various subsequent dynasties.

Something called Four Schools or *ssu hsueh t'ang* (四學堂) is used to designate four physiognomic features. These Schools are said to refer to civil service, prosperity, internal, and external, but it is not apparent as to what constitutes the logical basis for this classification.

The predilection for fives, already seen in the Five Elements, now asserts itself in physiognomics. There is a classification according to the Five Sense Organs, *wu kuan* (五官), these being: ears, eyes, mouth, nose, and tongue. Some authorities substitute eyebrows for tongue, other substitute heart. The Five Sense Organs, then, are not precisely the same as the "five senses" of Westerners.

The Logic of Interpretation

Five Planets, *wu hsing* (五星) form another method for explaining the features of the face. The planets in question are Mars, Saturn, Jupiter, Venus, and Mercury, their corresponding elements being fire, earth, wood, metal, and water, respectively. They have separate Yin-Yang values. Each planet is associated with a god, these being known as the Gods of the Five Planets. In turn, each god is associated with a color; red, yellow, green, white, and black. Each god has a name, a personality, and a jurisdiction, but there is no apparent effort to link the features and astrology with one's character or destiny.

One set of symbols follows the concept of the Five Sacred Mountains or *wu yüeh* (五嶽), these being five peaks located in the five different directions. They are Heng-shan (恒山), located in the north in Shansi; a different Heng-shan (衡山), located in the south in Hunan; T'ai-shan (泰山), located in the east in Shantung; Hua-shan (華山), located in the west in Shensi; and Sung-shan (嵩山), located in the center in Honan. According to tradition, they came into being when P'an Ku, the first man, died and his remains fell apart. His arms became two of the peaks, his head another, his two feet still another, and his body a fifth one. These mountains allegedly were worshipped as far back as four and a half thousand years ago. Associated with each is a god or spirit, but there is much disagreement in the lists identifying these spirits. At any rate, each spirit, and therefore each peak, has certain attributes assigned to it, and presumably this is what guides the physiognomist in his interpretations.

Sixfold categories are twice represented. A division is made according to the Six Treasuries, *liu fu* (六府) of nature: water, fire, metal, wood, earth, and grain. It is at once apparent that the Treasuries consist of the Five Elements plus grain.

Six Stars, *lu yüeh* (六曜) form the basis for another scheme to designate human features, but no astrological implications are present.

The number seven does not appear to be represented in classical Chinese physiognomics.

The number eight, we have seen, finds expression in the all-important trigrams, but this is not the only representative. Another classification consists of Eight Schools, *pa hsüeh t'ang* (八學堂) and is likewise used to designate features of the face. In some instances these eight refer to anatomical features designated in the above Four Schools, but in others they refer to additional features. The basis of this classification is not clear.

Ninefold, tenfold, and elevenfold classifications seem to be absent from classic Chinese physiognomics.

The number twelve, however, has a sole representative. A classification called Twelve Temples, *shih erh kung* (十二宮) forms the basis for designating certain features and parts of the face, but the reason for using the idea of a temple is not apparent as the referents are mostly assortments of concepts, qualities, people, and things.

Thirteen Parts, *shih san pu* (十三部) are used to designate thirteen horizontal divisions of the face. This is the most elaborate method of dividing any part of the body, for each division is in turn constituted of from nine to eleven smaller parts. The rationale for the selection of thirteen is not clear.

The "different years of a lifetime" constitutes an interesting approach to the reading of the face, for it involves a principle of chronology. According to this method, it is possible to tell at what age in a man's life certain conditions will prevail by examining the proper one of the ninety nine areas on the face.

While these, then, are some of the logical premises on which Chinese body divination is based, they are not always made explicit or followed in clear-cut fashion. In any given analysis there will often be a mixture of various points of departure. Of course, some premises are discarded altogether by the physiognomist, depending on the "school" to which he belongs. These points are well brought out in the chapter on physiognomy in that famous Chinese erotic social novel, *The Golden Lotus (Chin P'ing Mei)*, which portrays life around 1101–25 in the Southern Sung dynasty but was written towards the end of the Ming dynasty. The fortuneteller, a Taoist called Wu the Immortal, reads the physiognomy of the hero, Hsi-mên Ch'ing, and his wives—Moon Lady, Picture of Grace, Tower of Jade, Golden Lotus, Lady of the Vase, Beauty of the Snow—as well as his daughter, Orchid, and Moon Lady's maid, Plum Blossom. In answer to a question, Wu says that he has a slight acquaintance with thirteen schools of physiognomics and practices the method of Ma-i (Egerton 1939: II, 16). He proceeds to examine his subjects' brows, eyebrows, noses, lips, hands, moles, and various other features of the body, and includes color and the voice, as well as some astrology (II, 16–23).

In retrospect, Chinese physiognomics was the victim of the logical premises which have been reviewed in this chapter. It never broke out of the bounds imposed on it by the wider Sinitic view of the universe. Scholars who have sought to explain the failure of China to develop a true scientific method have given as one of the reasons the attempt to fit the universe into numerical categories. This was a fatal *cul de sac*. The Chinese, says Bodde (1939: 202), "failed to produce a true physical science, because, being based upon false, man-made analogies, they disregarded the use of the empirical method of direct observation of nature, and thus distorted and forced natural phenomena into an artificial pattern." In contrast, European physiognomy ultimately freed itself of its own restraining limitations and became the forerunner of the field of biotypology, or human constitution.

Chapter III

THE BODY AS A WHOLE

This chapter and the two that follow it depart from general principles, rationales, and symbolisms and confine themselves instead to a straightforward presentation of somatomantic signs and their meanings as they are envisioned by classical Chinese physiognomists. Although reference is made occasionally to the way in which a given approach or interpretation illustrates some methodological principles already discussed in the preceding pages, the principle itself is not the subject of analysis. This is even more true of matters of function, which will be considered separately in due course.

In some respects all that these three chapters offer is a digest of the 15th century *Shen Hsiang Ch'üan Pien*, the leading work on Chinese physiognomy. However, the digest is more than a simple translation; it is a reworking of the original book of thirteen volumes into a more systematic scheme. Omitted are detailed portions dealing with the physiognomy of women and children, the significance of color, and the influence of *ch'i*.

Although our descriptive portion is based on one book alone, it should be remembered that that book is the fountainhead of almost all subsequent works on physiognomy, and that it is itself largely the outgrowth of an earlier work attributed to Ma-i, or Mourning Clothes, as he was called. It is a compilation synthesizing all that had gone before it. To have brought other works on Chinese physiognomy into the picture would not only have been redundant but confusing as well. The *Shen Hsiang* is a scissors and paste enterprise which makes little effort to draw its materials together into a consistent whole. Its own contradictions are bewildering enough without adding to them the discrepancies of others.

This is not to say that it is not worthwhile to scrutinize other sources. For purposes not included here, it would be fascinating to make comparison of all known Chinese books on physiognomy, of which there are a vast number today, with the objective of recording trends in premises, methodology, and the interpretation of signs, as well as the tendency to work other forms of divination into the physiognomic approach. Some future investigator may wish to do so.

With this as a statement of intent, let us now proceed to the descriptive materials promised in the opening statement. It has been

The Body as a Whole

found convenient to consider them first as they apply to the body as a whole, and subsequently as they refer to the face and head, and then to the hands, feet, and trunk. This threefold division is, to be sure, somewhat arbitrary, yet it is not without merit because it has the virtue of systematization.

The body has often been used as a unitary organism to analyze character and foretell the future. One principle employed is the microcosmic, and in our discussion of that premise we gave an example of interpretation.

Another system divides the body into three sections called the *san-t'ing* (三停). The head is the upper section, the portion from shoulder to waist is the middle section, and the portion from waist to feet is the third section. If the three are in good proportion, whether all long or all short, the man will enjoy a blissful life. If they are not in good proportion, a long head would lead to a better fortune than a long waist, which in turn is preferred over long legs. Long legs or short head will likely lead to poverty or a wandering life, while a long head and short legs would probably lead to bliss (*Shen Hsiang* I, 36a).

More specific and detailed are the interpretations following the theriologic premise.

The Chinese have made comparison with fifty animals and birds, some of them imaginary, as follows (*Shen Hsiang* IX, 19a–35a):

phoenix	mandarin duck	dragon	mouse	cat
crane	magpie	unicorn	snake	roebuck
eagle	chicken	lion	horse	lobster
swallow	duck	tiger	sheep	leopard
pigeon	partridge	elephant	deer	donkey
goose	egret	rhinoceros	bear	fox
parrot	falcon	ape	fish	wolf
peacock	wild goose	monkey	pig	orangutan
small bird	crow	turtle	dog	rabbit
mynah	stork	cow	crab	camel

In general, men who have, for example, the morphology of a dragon, tiger, lion, cow, monkey, leopard, elephant, camel, crane, peacock, phoenix, mandarin duck, egret, or golden oriole are considered to be of higher quality and are entitled to wealth and honor. Those who, for example, have the form of a pig, dog, lamb, horse, deer, mouse, wolf, crow, or eagle are considered to be of low degree and may be subject to poverty and short life (*Shen Hsiang*, Introduction volume, 7a).

Following are seventeen selected examples of the various types of men based on the theriologic premise (*Shen Hsiang* IX, 19a–35a).

It will be noted that the forecasts tend to be favorable rather than unfavorable, even among types considered to be of low degree.

Phoenix. A man with a raised head, long eyes, high and narrow eyebrows, high and straight nose, tall and thin stature, will be intelligent, above normal, and able to see things far ahead. He will have good opportunity to obtain a good position.

Eagle. A man with a square head, round forehead, zigzag nose, mouth like a hook, red eyeballs, and prominent ears with small openings, is said to be like an eagle. He will probably like to kill and will be a good general, but he will not have a good ending.

Dragon. A man tall and large in stature, with high nose and erect ears, solemn demeanor, handsome bones, clear eyes and eyebrows, who is powerful, resourceful, and distinct from the crowd, is said to have the appearance of a dragon, which is an appropriate appearance for kings.

Lion. A man who has projecting bones on both the back of his head and on the forehead; a square forehead; a mass of moustache; disorderly eyebrows; square mouth; bent nose bridge; and big, round, clear eyes, is said to have the appearance of a lion. He would most likely be an introvert and easily win favor in the king's court.

Tiger. A man of tall and narrow stature; red, firm, round, and full face; two and a half inch eyes and eyebrows; large and red mouth, with square upper lips; short and round head, with high and square forehead; black and stiff hair and moustache; white teeth; long, red, and thick tongue; angry look; and a voice like thunder, is said to have the appearance of a tiger. He should be intelligent and ambitious, and easily attain a high position.

Elephant. A man who has a broad forehead, long eyebrows, small eyes, upward nose and lips, prominent teeth, long but shapeless ears, and a big and fleshy body, will probably be very dependable.

Monkey. A man who has a round head with projecting forehead, high cheek bones, red face, yellow ears, eminent nose, thin lips, round and deep eyes with angry glare; who is timid, undignified, unsteady, intelligent, and ingenious, will probably get an important position or even one to assist the king.

Turtle. A man with a round body, flat and full face, round back and shoulders, long neck and pointed head, round eyes, thick eyebrows, projecting nose, and long mouth; who is dignified and likes water and mountains, will enjoy long life like the turtle and will be wealthy.

Cow. A man with large stature and head, bright black eyes, moving jaw, bulky neck, and strong face, but a quiet and modest nature, will probably enjoy great wealth and bliss.

Mouse. A man with very small stature, small and round eyes, is said to be like a mouse. His small figure will be a limitation on his getting ahead. He will only get enough food and clothing.

Snake. A man with a long head, flat forehead, long eyes, big teeth, small ears, small and pointed nose, and pliable waist is said to be like a snake. He is apt to be cruel and pitiless and will hurt people when offended. He acts fast, so it will be hard to know what he is going to do next.

Horse. A man with a long face, big eyes, broad mouth, big teeth, long waist, and dignified bearing, will probably enjoy honor and all the good possibilities ahead of him.

Pig. A man who has a broad head with a flat forehead, long face, deep eyes, gathered mouth, pointed ears, a fat chin without any neck, and short legs, is said to be like a pig. He will probably be foolish and never have anything in reserve.

Dog. A man with a large head, pointed face, yellowish eyes, gathered mouth, and pointed ears, is said to be like a dog. If he gets a position he will be ever so faithful.

Donkey. A man with yellowish eyes, long face, long ears, and coarse voice, is said to be like a donkey, with a low and base nature. He is probably foolish and boasting, but if the ears are really long they should bring him honor and he will probably win favor in the king's court.

Wolf. A man with a square head, broad forehead, pointed chin, coarse eyebrows, big and round eyes, large mouth, close and pointed teeth, and ears close to the head, will be a suitable general. He will also enjoy long life.

Camel. A man with a round and long head, broad forehead, long neck, round back, high and coarse eyebrows, deep eyes, gathered mouth, coarse hair and bones, long limbs and loud voice, and who walks slowly, will be able to assume heavy responsibilities.

Another guiding principle used in the classification of body type, as we have noted, is one centering on the Five Elements. During the Tang dynasty Lü Tung-pin wrote, "To tell a person's future it is necessary to be able to discern which one of the Five Elements he represents" (*Shen Hsiang* I, 1a).

The broad physiognomic types described in terms of the Elements are fifteen in number, consisting of thee sets of five types each. The first set consists of five pure types, wherein a man has the unmixed form of one of the elements along with its corresponding virtues. These pure types, which are of course highly desirable ones, are described as follows in the *Shen Hsiang* (I, 6b–9b).

Metal. A man with a square, straight, and whitish appearance whose bones are not small and who is not fleshy is said to be like metal. As metal is strong and sturdy and can stand refinement, it represents righteousness. When a man is like metal and is righteous he will be firm and able to endure.

Wood. A man who is thin, tall, straight, greenish, and imposing, with sturdy bones, graceful eyes and eyebrows, is said to be like wood. Wood represents life and growth in the universe. It stands for benevolence. When a man possesses the appearance of wood and is benevolent, he will be, like the pines, always enjoying enough wealth and never fading.

Water. A man who has a round, heavy, and blackish appearance, with large eyes, thick eyebrows, hanging stomach, and erect shoulders, is said to have the form of water. When a man possesses the form of water and is endowed with wisdom, he will be like the rivers, embracing and directing scholarly knowledge with ease.

Fire. A man who appears pointed at the top, broad at the bottom, sharp, reddish, and dry, with little whiskers, is said to be like fire. Fire is used to cook and to refine metal. Its virtue is represented as propriety, power, and courage. When a man possesses the form of fire and is polite, majestic, and courageous, he will be able to adjust himself to any circumstance.

Earth. A man who is thick, straight, and heavy is said to be like earth. As earth cannot be easily moved, gives growth to all things on Earth, and is able to bear huge mountains and oceans, it

The Body as a Whole

represents the virtue of trustworthiness and sincerity. When a man has the appearance of earth and is trustworthy he will be creative, as well as able to bear heavy responsibilities without fail.

One seeks in vain here for process rather than merely fundamental matter. That is, the Elements are here treated more or less as elements rather than forces in process.

The matter is otherwise in the second set of types, which follow the "mutual production" principle outlined in Chapter II. This set consists of five types that are not pure as in the first set but are mixed in the sense that in addition to the presence of one element a man possesses another element capable of generating the first one in line with the principle of mutual production. This second element reinforces, as it were, the first one because it is capable of generating it. The person who has two elements in this kind of combination will inherit all the good qualities of these elements and become prosperous. The five types resulting from the possession of elements in this combination are described as follows in the *Shen Hsiang* (I, 1b):

Metal. When a man of metal has some qualities of earth, he will be successful in all his plans and will be happy and satisfied.

Wood. When a man of wood has some qualities of water he will enjoy honor and wealth, and will be above normal in scholarly undertakings.

Water. When a man of water has some qualities of metal he will win both wealth and fame. He will be wise in judgment and firm in the administration of plans.

Fire. When a man of fire has some qualities of wood, he will succeed early in life. He will get a high position around thirty years of age and will win world wide fame.

Earth. When a man of earth has some qualities of fire he will be successful in realizing the philosophy of life.

A third set of physiognomic types is derived from the principle of "mutual conquest," and, as one might suppose, is mixed and destroying. It is bad for a man to possess the qualities of those elements that would conquer each other, for be will lose the virtues and become handicapped in every undertaking. The prognostications that result from the possession of elements that destroy each other are described as follows in the *Shen Hsiang* (I, 1b):

Metal. When a man of metal has some qualities of wood [*sic*, for fire?], he will have some difficulties in youth but will rise above normal in later years.

Wood. When a man of wood has some qualities of metal, he will suffer through life.

Water. When a man of water has some qualities of earth, bankruptcy and sickness will be his lot through life.

Fire. When a man of fire has some qualities of water, death of wife and children, and poverty, will accompany him.

Earth. When a man of earth has some qualities of wood, he will be a failure in every undertaking. He will either die early or else suffer from solitude.

Chapter IV

THE FACE AND HEAD

When people cast a scrutinizing look at a person they are most likely to look first at his collective facial features and then to narrow this down to individual features, particularly the eyes, mouth, and nose. The head and its individual parts are so important in the somatomantic art that they form the basis of subtypes of physiognomy which maybe loosely termed, to use the jargon of Western body divination, "ophthalmoscopy," "metoposcopy," "nosology" (a barbarism of the hybrid kind), and "phrenology." The only other part of the body receiving as much attention is the hand, but it does not offer the same immediacy as the face. The hand does not thrust itself spontaneously upon the unsystematic observer; it is studied and interpreted in more arbitrary and less casual fashion.

Moles are here discussed in connection with the face, for while they may occur anywhere on the body the diviners of Sung and earlier times, perhaps for reasons of modesty, have left no descriptions or illustrations of body moles. This lacuna has only been filled in contemporary times, when we see the emergence of detailed mappings of body moles.

The Face As a Whole

Chinese physiognomists consider the face to be the most important constituent of the whole body and devote more attention to it than any other part. It is the reservoir of the hundreds of parts of the body and the center by which the five internal organs may be studied. Generally speaking, an oblong, full, straight, smooth, and shining face is considered to be of good quality; a crooked, gloomy, or pointed one is a sign of bad quality (*Shen Hsiang* IIII, 1b–2b).

More specific and systematic than this are the approaches to the whole face that are based on methods of breaking it down into components. These methods, whose premises have been described in Chapter II, are actually very numerous and have been reduced to a few for our purposes.

In the first method, illustrated by Figure 1, the face is divided into areas known as Treasuries, Forces, and Sections.

The location of the Six Treasuries may be seen in this figure. The two upper treasuries are formed by the bones that extend from the outer

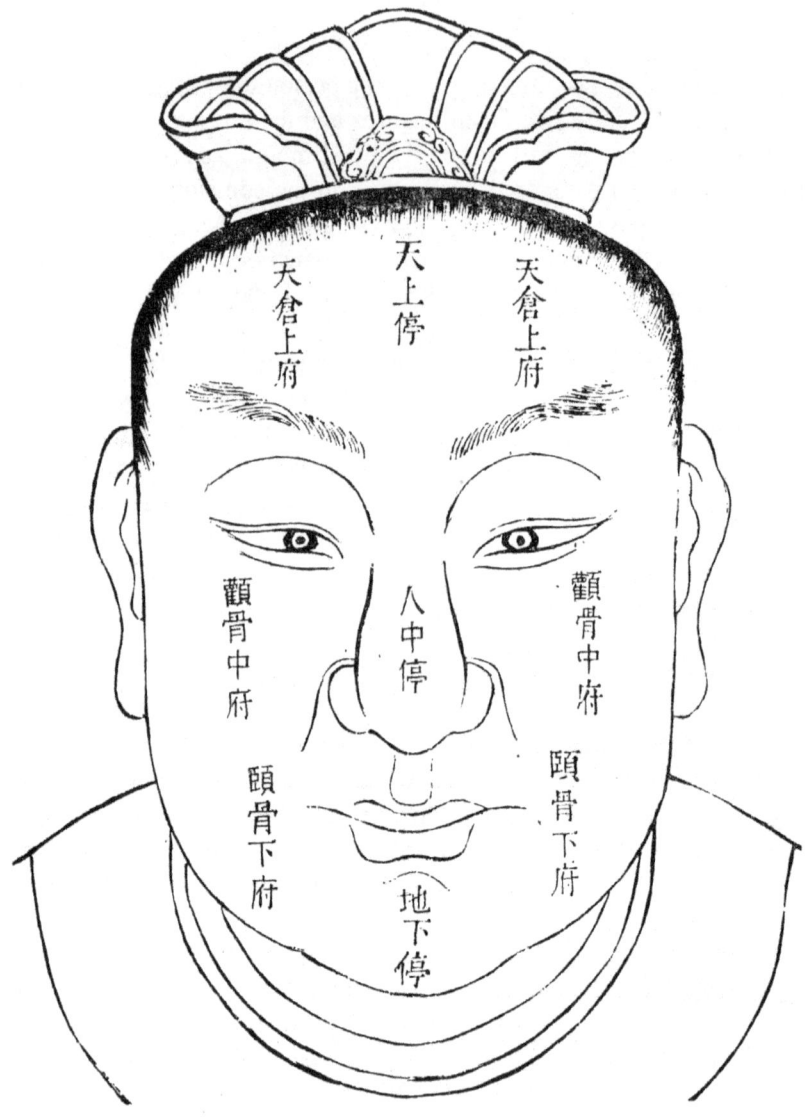

FIG. 1. The face explained in terms of Six Treasures, Three Forces and Three Sections. (From *Ku Chin*, 1728.)

corners of the forehead to the outer corners of the eyes. The middle treasuries are formed by the cheek bones that extend from the outer corners of the eyes to the lower tips of the ears. And the two lower treasuries contain the jaw that extends from the lower tip of the ears to the chin. If the bones of the upper treasuries project to form a broad forehead, while those of the middle treasuries are full and those of the lower form a square chin, the man should have all the possibilities to enjoy wealth (*ibid.* II, 21a).

The location of the Three Forces, *san ts'ai* (三才) representing sky, man, and earth, may also be seen in Figure 1 and is as follows: The sky is the forehead, man is the nose, and earth is the chin. A forehead round and smooth like the sky is a sign of honor. A nose that is straight and fat is a sign of long life. A chin that is broad and square like the earth is a sign of wealth (*ibid.* II, 21ab).

Completing the first method of reading the face are the Three Sections, located as follows in Figure 1: The upper section extends from the hairline to the middle of the eyebrows. The middle section extends from the middle of the eyebrows to the tip of the nose. The lower section extends from the tip of the nose to the chin. The principle of harmony is invoked in evaluating the sections. If all three are of equal length, a long upper section is preferred as it is a sign of prosperity. A long middle section means no chance of winning the king's favor. A long lower section is a sign of misfortune (*ibid.* II, 21ab). Another set of interpretations of the Three Sections does not make use of the harmony principle. A long, broad, and full upper section is a sign of honor. A fat, projecting, and straight middle section is a sign of long life. A full, thick, and straight lower section is a sign of wealth. In contrast to this one finds unfavorable characteristics of the sections. Thus, a pointed, narrow, or damaged upper section is a sign of disaster. A short, flat, or crooked middle section is a sign of bankruptcy at middle age, or of stupidity, or of lack of help from one's wife or brothers. A long, narrow, and pointed lower section is a sign of poverty and of suffering in old age (*ibid.* I, 36ab).

So much for the first method of reading the face.

In the second method, illustrated by Figure 2, the face is divided into areas known as the Four Schools and the Eight Schools, these having been discussed in Chapter II.

The Four Schools and their locations are as follows: The school of civil service, *kuan hsüeh t'ang* (官學堂), is represented by the eyes. The school of prosperity, *lu hsüeh t'ang* (祿學堂), is represented by the

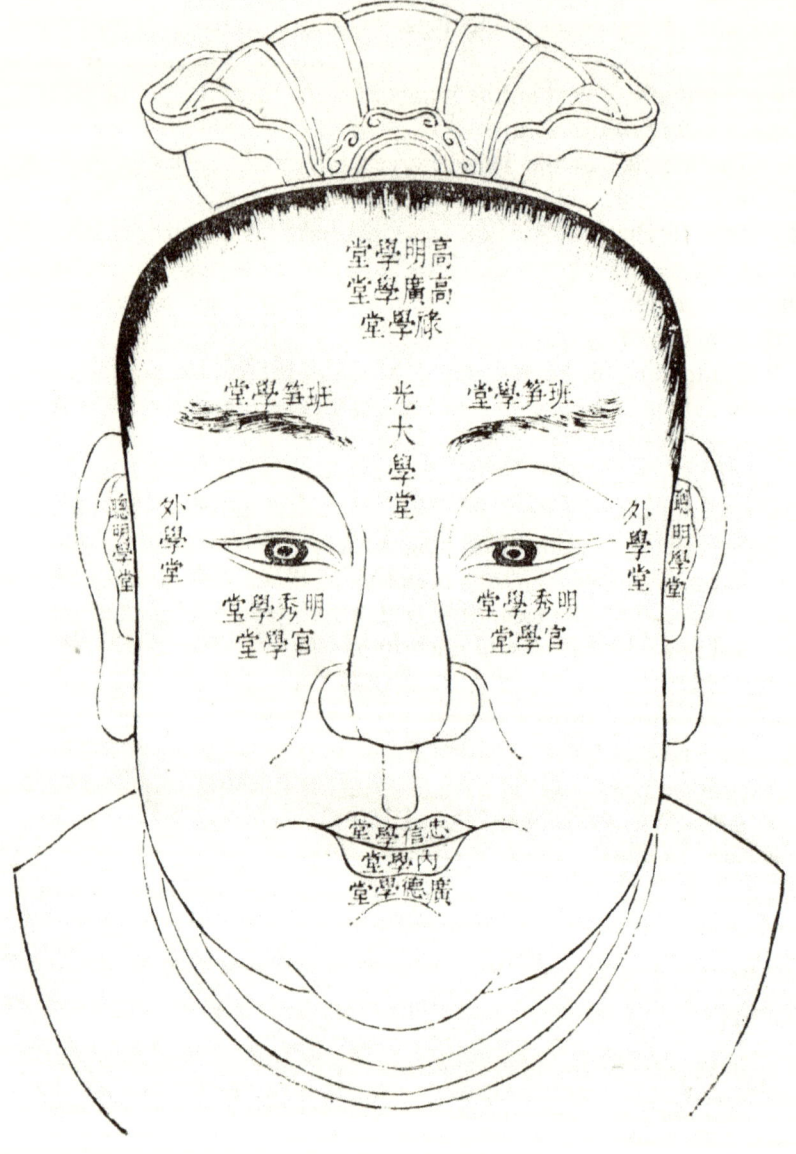

FIG. 2 The face explained in terms of Four Schools and Eight Schools. (From *Ku Chin*, 1728.)

The Face and Head

forehead. The internal school, *nei hsüeh t'ang* (內學堂) is represented by the two upper front teeth. The external school, *wai hsüeh t'ang* (外學堂), is represented by the parts in front of the ears. Long and graceful eyes are favorable. A broad and high forehead is favorable. If the two upper front teeth are straight and close set they are supposed to represent filial piety, loyalty, reverence, and sincerity (*Shen Hsiang* I, 34b).

The names and locations of the Eight Schools, also indicated in Figure 2, are as follows: The school of distinct heights, *kao ming hsüeh tang* (高明學堂) is represented by the head. The school of broad heights, *kao kuang hsüeh t'ang* (高廣學堂) is represented by the forehead. The school of brilliancy, *kuang ta hsüeh t'ang* (光大學堂) is represented by the part between the eyebrows. The school of distinct grace, *ming hsiu hsüeh t'ang* (明秀學堂) is represented by the eyes. The school of intelligence, *ts'ung ming hsüeh t'ang* (聰明學堂) is represented by the ears. The school of loyalty and sincerity, *chung hsin hüeh t'ang* (忠信學堂) is represented by the teeth. The school of great virtue, *kuang te hsüeh t'ang* (廣德學堂) is represented by the tongue. The school of bamboo shoots, *pan sun hsüeh t'ang* (班笋學堂) is represented by the eyebrows. With reference to these features, the following are all favorable: a round head with curious projecting bones; a square and projecting head; a smooth and bright part between the eyebrows, without scars or defects; bright eyes with more black than white; red, white, or yellow ears with well defined outlines; even, white, and closely knit teeth; a tongue that is red and long enough to touch the tip of the nose; and long and graceful eyebrows (*ibid.* I, 35ab).

So much, too, for the second method.

In the third method, illustrated by Figure 3, the face is explained in terms of the Five Planets, Six Stars, Five Sacred Mountains, and Four Great Rivers.

The names and locations of the planets are as follows: Mars, *huo hsing* (火星) represents the south, so it stands for the forehead. Saturn, *t'u hsing* (土星) represents the middle, so it stands for the nose. Jupiter, *mu hsing* (木星) represents the east, so it stands for the right ear. Venus, *chin hsing* (金星) represents the west, so it stands for the left ear. Mercury, *shui hsing* (水星) represents the north, so it stands for the mouth. A square forehead will bring honor. A thick nose forecasts long life. When the ears face towards the face, they are signs of bliss. The mouth is favorable if it is red (*Shen Hsiang* II, 16b–17a).

The names and locations of the Six Stars, also indicated in Figure 3, are as follows: The star *tsu ch'i* (紫炁) stands for the part between

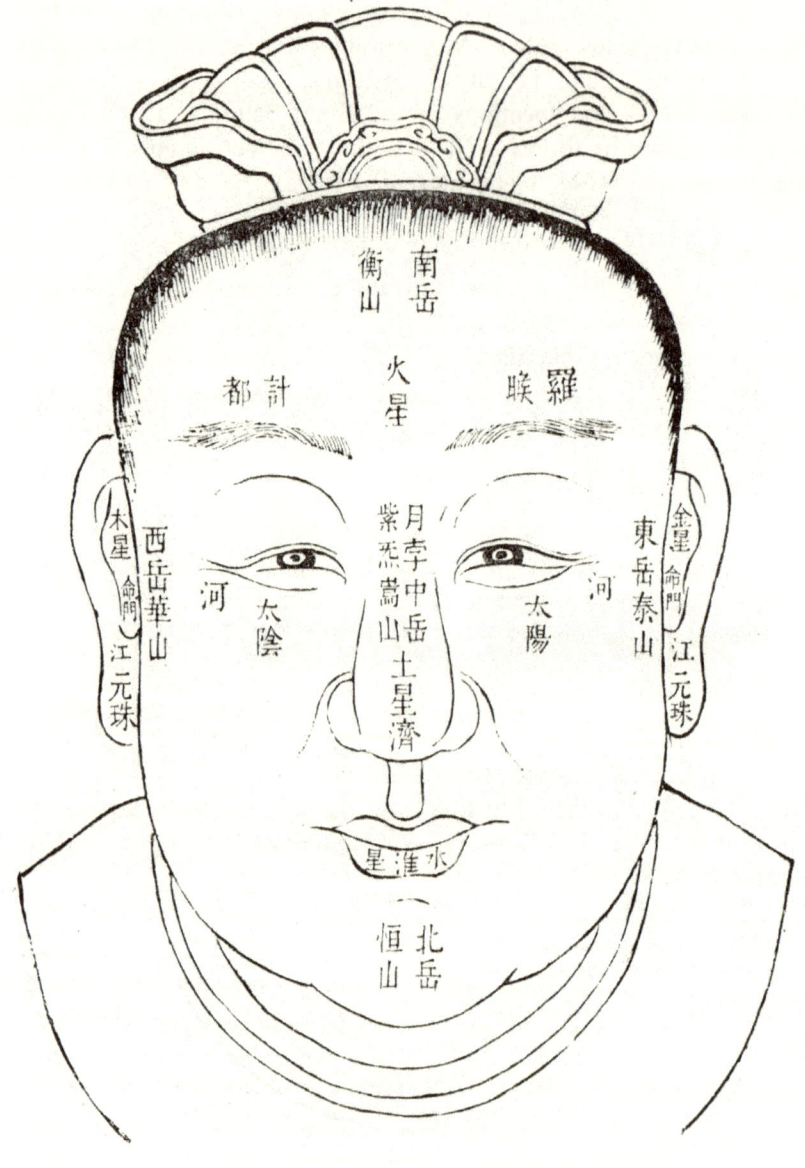

FIG. 3 The face explained in terms of Five Planets, Six Stars, Five Mountains and Four Rivers. (From *Ku Chin*, 1728.)

the eyebrows. The star *lo hou* (羅睺) stands for the left eyebrow. The star *chi tu* (計都) stands for the right eyebrow. The star *yüeh po* (月孛) stands for the bridge of the nose. The moon *t'ai yin* (太陰) stands for the right eye. The sun *t'ai Yang* (太陽) stands for the left eye. It is good if the part between the eyebrows is round. Long and even eyebrows are favorable. It is good if the bridge of the nose is straight. Dark and bright eyes are favorable (*ibid.* II, 16b–20a).

The names and locations of the Five Sacred Mountains, again illustrated in Figure 3, are as follows: *Heng shan* (衡山) is in the south and is used to represent the forehead. Another *Heng shan* (恒山) is in the north and is used to represent the chin. *Sung shan* (嵩山) is in the middle and is used to represent the nose. *T'ai shan* (泰山) is in the east and is used to represent the right cheek bone. *Hua shan* (華山) is in the west and is used to represent the left cheek bone. The five sacred mountains should stand out in good proportion and should be well balanced. Of the five, the middle one is the most important. It should be straight and well projected. All of the five mountains should be in position to face one another. If the nose is flat, there is lack of balance. If the forehead is flat it means bankruptcy. If the chin is flat it means poverty and old age. Low cheek bones signify lack of power (*ibid.* II, 15a).

The names and locations of the Four Great Rivers, also indicated in Figure 3, are as follows: *Chiang* (江) or Yangtze, representing the ears; *Ho* (河) or Yellow, representing the eyes; the river *Huai* (淮), representing the mouth; and the river *Chi* (濟), representing the nose. The ears should have holes that are big and tight in order to be favorable. Deep eyes mean long life, bright eyes mean intelligence, small but long eyes mean honor, short or round eyes mean short life, and gloomy eyes mean a difficult life (*ibid.* II, 15ab).

So much for the third method.

In the fourth method, illustrated by Figure 4, the face is explained in terms of the Twelve Temples and Five Senses or Sense Organs.

The names, locations, and significances of the temples, indicated in Figure 4, are according to the *Shen Hsiang* (I, 23b–32a) as follows: The destiny temple, *ming-kung* (命宮), is located between the two eyebrows. When shiny and smooth it means long life, but when full of lines it is a sign of bankruptcy and a difficult life. The wealth temple, *ch'ai-po* (財帛) is located on the nose. When it stands up straight like a tube, or hangs like a gall bladder, or is projected and full, it means wealth, but when it is like an eagle's beak, or if the nostrils

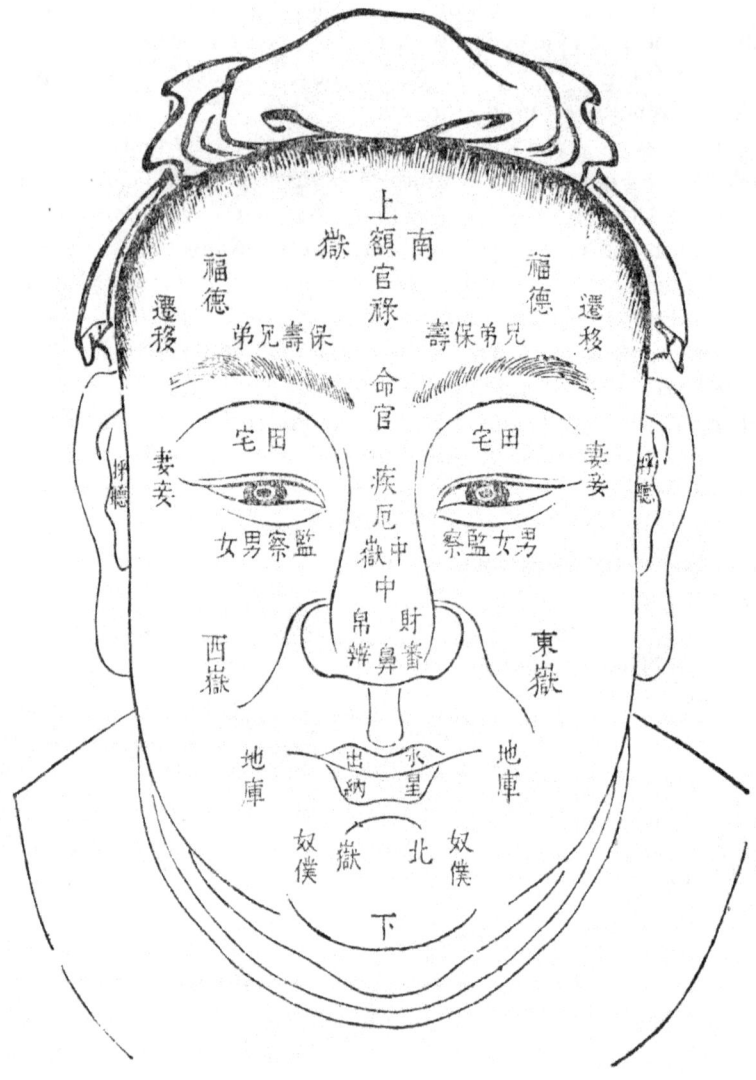

FIG. 4 The face explained in terms of Twelve Temples and Five Senses. (From *Ku Chin*, 1728.)

The Face and Head

turn upward, it means poverty. The brothers temple, *hsiung-ti* (兄弟) is located within the two eyebrows. If the eyebrows are longer than the eyes, it signifies three or four brothers; if the two eyebrows are not the same, one will have to adopt another mother; if the eyebrows meet or are yellowish or thin, they signify death in a foreign land. The property temple, *tien-chai* (田宅) is located in the eyes. If the eyes are reddish or dry they forecast bankruptcy and poverty, but if they are dark and bright, wealth will follow. The children temple, *nan-ni* (男女) is located below the eyes. If smooth and even, they signify bliss, wealth, and glory for the children, but if they are sunken, with lines or moles, the children may not enjoy long life. The servants temple, *nu-pu* (奴僕) is located between the corners of the mouth and the chin. If full it signifies many servants. The wife temple, *ch'i-chei* (妻妾) is located at the two outer corners of the eyes. If the wife temples are shiny, smooth, full, and without lines, they signify a virtuous, wealthy, and long lived life; if they are dark and sunken with lines, the wife may not live long. The sickness temple, *chi-erh* (疾厄) is located on the bridge of the nose. If full and projected it signifies health, peace, and long life, while if it is sunken or crooked, with lines, it means constant sickness and a toilsome life. The travel temple, *ch'ien-i* (遷移) is located at each of the two outer corners of the eyebrows. If they are full, smooth, and shiny, they signify pleasant long trips, but if they are sunk or dark with moles they signify misfortune on trips. The position temple, *kung-lu* (官祿) is located on the lower part of the forehead. If bright, projected, and without moles, it signifies a long term honorable position. The bliss and virtue temple, *fu-teh* (福德) is located between each of the two outer corners of the forehead and the lower parts of the cheeks. If full, round, and shiny, they signify much bliss. The appearance temple, *hsiang-mau* (相貌) includes the whole facial feature. The Three Sections, the Five Sacred Mountains, and everything else concerning the face will have to be taken into consideration.

The Five Senses or Sense Organs, *wu kuan* (五官) are also indicated in Figure 4 as part of the fourth method of reading the face. These are the eyes, eyebrows, nose, mouth, and ears. Their meanings will not be considered at this point but rather in separate detailed sections devoted to them in subsequent pages.

So much for the fourth method.

In the fifth method, illustrated by Figure 5, the face is explained in terms of the Thirteen Parts. Each part is a horizontal band extending all the way across the face from one lateral border to the other. The

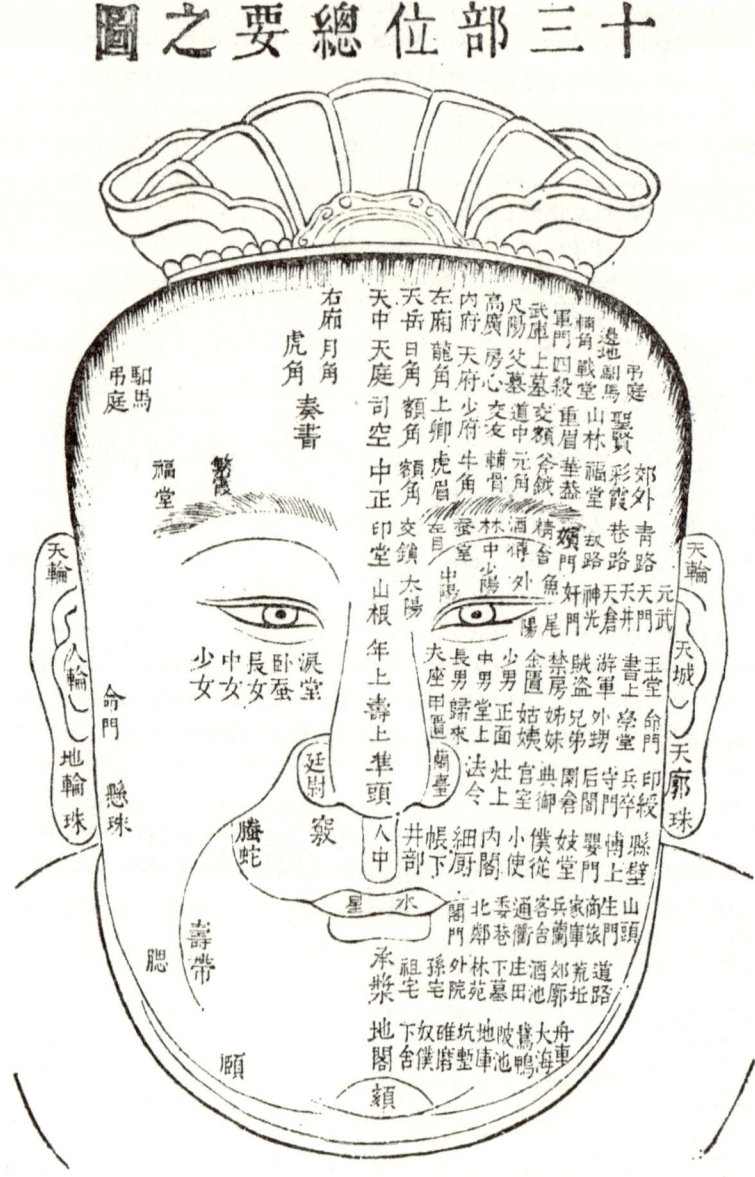

FIG. 5 The face explained in terms of Thirteen Parts. (From *Ku Chin*, 1728.)

first such division or band is at the hairline, the second is below it, and so on down to the chin. Each of the thirteen parts contains nine to eleven subparts, all indicated by individual names. In the figure these names begin at the midline and extend successively in a double row of characters towards the lateral extremity.

Since the total number of these subparts exceeds 100 it would be impractical to give any more than a sampling of their names and significances. The following selected examples will demonstrate the nature of the interpretations made by this method: In the first part, the first subpart is called *t'ien chung* (天中) and signifies wealth, honor, and high government position; the third subpart is called *tso hsiang* (左廂) and stands for position; the seventh subpart is called *wu k'u* (武庫) and stands for military success. In the second part, the second subpart on the right side is called *jih chiao* (日角) and stands for father's health; the counterpart on the left side is called *yüeh chiao* (月角) and stands for mother's health. In the third part, the ninth subpart is called *shan lin* (山林) and stands for an office in the country [rather than in the city]. In the fourth part, the fourth subpart is called *niu chiao* (牛角) and stands for royal attendant. In the fifth part, the first subpart is called *yin t'ang* (印堂) and stands for high office. In the sixth part, the eleventh subpart is called *t'ien men* (天門) and stands for good relationships with friends, sisters, and brothers. In the eight part, the eleventh subpart is called *ming men* (命門) and stands for long life. In the ninth part, the third subpart is called *fa ling* (法令) and stands for office at court. In the tenth part, the eleventh subpart is called *hsien pi* (縣壁) and stands for position of many servants. In the twelfth part, the first subpart is called *ch'eng chiang* (承漿) and stands for wealth. In the thirteenth part, the first subpart is called *ti ke* (地閣) and stands for the possession of great mansions (*Shen Hsiang* I, 18b).

The general rule regarding the subparts is that when they are protruding they signify some good fortune, while if they are sunken they portray some misfortune.

We come now to the sixth and final method of explaining the face and its features, and for this Figure 6 may be consulted. This is done in terms of each year of a lifetime, the number of years indicated being from one to ninety nine. The location of the various ages tends to group in clusters, but despite this there is considerable scattering in different portions of the facial features.

The general location of each group of years, as seen in Figure 6, is as follows: Age 1–7: represented on the left ear, from top to bottom. Age 8–14: represented on the right ear, from top to bottom. Ages 15–

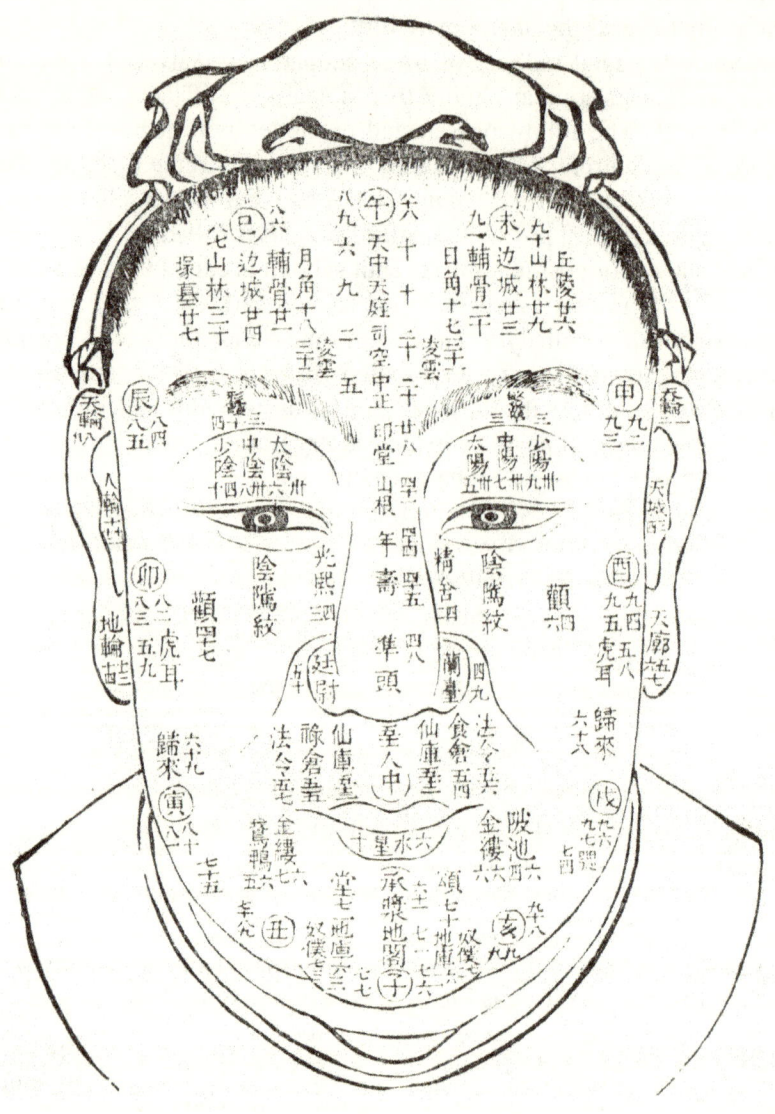

FIG. 6   The face explained in terms of the different ages of a lifetime. (From *Ku Chin*, 1728.)

50: the years move from the middle of the forehead to the sides of the forehead, along the nose and eyes and cheeks, down to the tip of the nose. Ages 51–60: the years move from the upper lip to the sides of the upper lip and the parts in front of the lower tip of the ears. Ages 61–76: the years move from the mouth to the parts of the chin and jaw. Ages 77–99: the years start to move around the face along the outer circle of the face, starting from the right jaw, moving upwards to the forehead and then downwards along the left side, until it reaches the left jaw at the age of 99. If any of the parts of the face are well formed a man will enjoy good fortune at the respective ages, but if any part is sunken he will suffer at that age. For instance, if the left ear is well formed one will enjoy seven years of happy infancy. If the tip of the nose is big and fat, he will enjoy wealth at the age of 49 or 50, but if his chin is pointed he will suffer from poverty between 61 and 70 years of age (*Shen Hsiang* I, 21a–22b).

For the reader who may have noticed that in Figure 6 certain characters are circled, an explanation is forthcoming. They are group headings, equivalent to our "A," "B," "C," etc.

The Lines of the Face

The Chinese have paid some attention to the lines of the face. Good lines on the forehead, representing good fortune, are represented as follows:

- Three lines on the forehead like a moon lying on its back are called lying moon lines (偃月紋). They represent high government position.

- If there is one straight line added to the lying moon line (above) it is called suspended rhinoceros line (縣犀紋). The man will take a military position.

- 王 character lines are a sign of a marquis.

- A straight line from the forehead to the middle of the eyebrow is called a sky pillar line (天柱紋). Such lines are signs of high government position.

⟪ Two lines between the eyebrows that run straight up to the forehead are called crane feet lines (鶴足紋). They are signs of a governor.

井 mark is a sign of government position.

十 character is a sign of wealth and prosperity.

⊕ mark is a sign of wealth and honor.

山 character is a sign of opportunity in court.

女 character is a sign of glory, honor, and prosperity.

The bad lines are fewer in number. In general, disorderly lines on the forehead are a sign of poverty and disaster. The bad lines, which, like the good ones, often take the form of a character, may be illustrated by a few examples, as follows:

≋ Three zigzag horizontal lines on the forehead are signs that his father will die early.

∼ One horizontal crooked line on the forehead is called crawling snake line (蛇行紋). It is a sign that the man will die while travelling.

⫶⫶⫶ character is a sign of sadness, trouble, or possibly punishment.

≡ Three horizontal lines on the forehead of a woman are signs of misfortune to the husband or son (*Ku Chin* v. 2987, sec. 642, p. 4).

Figure 7 depicts some unfavorable lines throughout the face. In the center of the forehead are lines of solitude. Flanking them on one side are lines that indicate "destroy younger brother" and on the opposite side are lines that indicate "elder brother will meet death away from home."

In one eyelid is a line indicating "mother will die from sickness," while in the other is a line saying "father will die a cruel death."

The lines below one eye indicate "destroy daughters," while those below the other eye say "destroy sons."

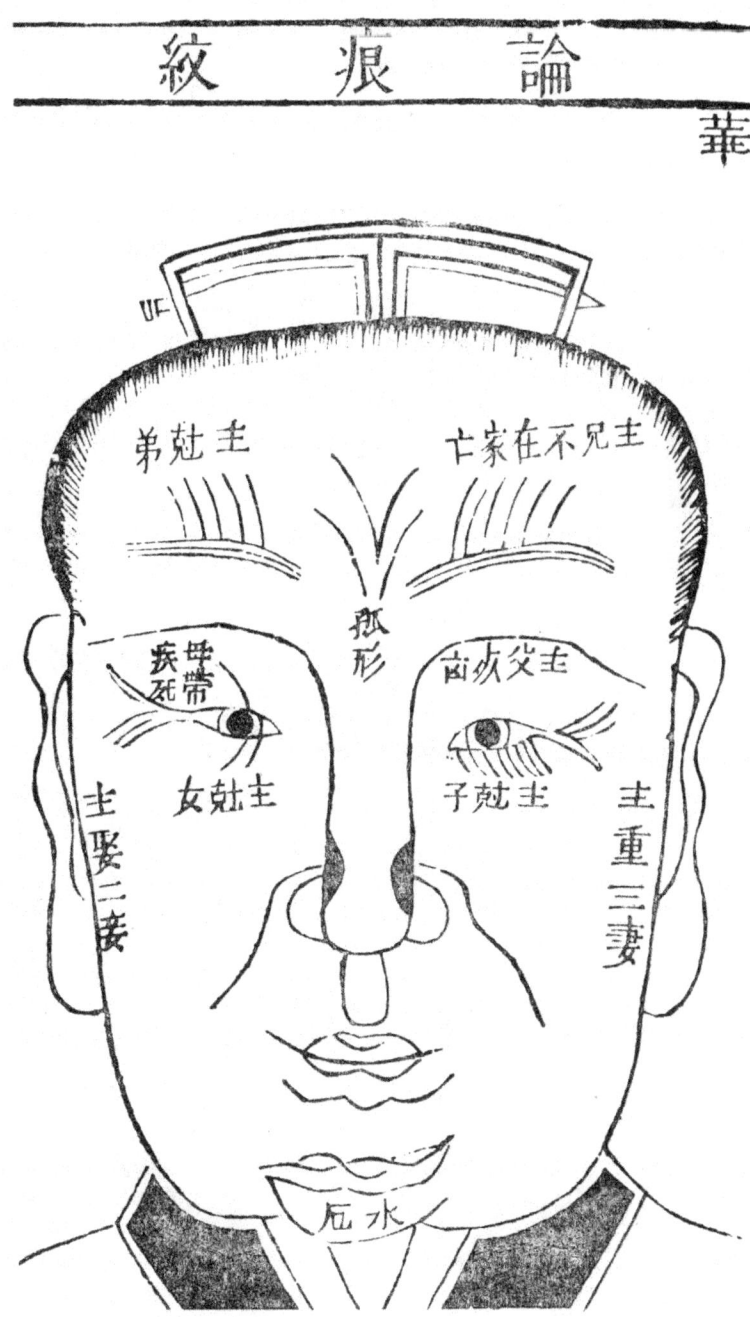

FIG. 7 Lines of the face (a). (From *Shen Hsiang*, 1793.)

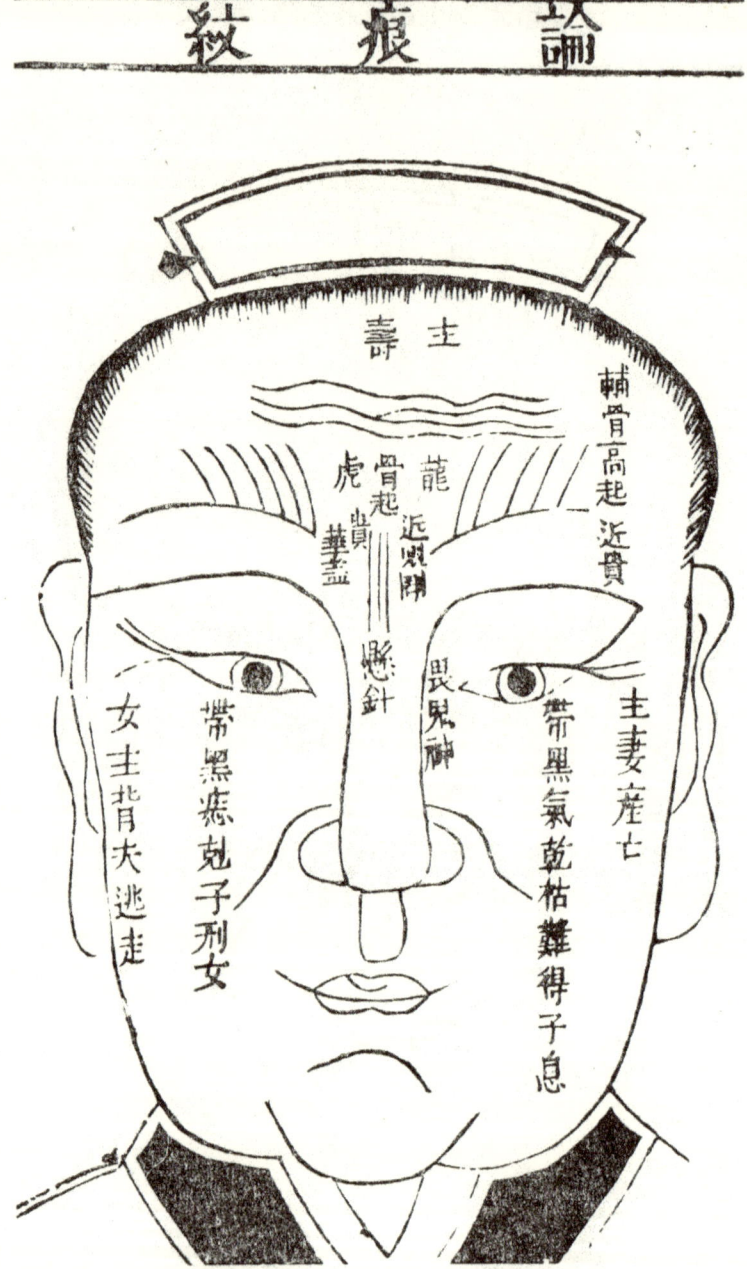

FIG. 8 Lines of the face (b). (From *Shen Hsiang*, 1793.)

The Face and Head

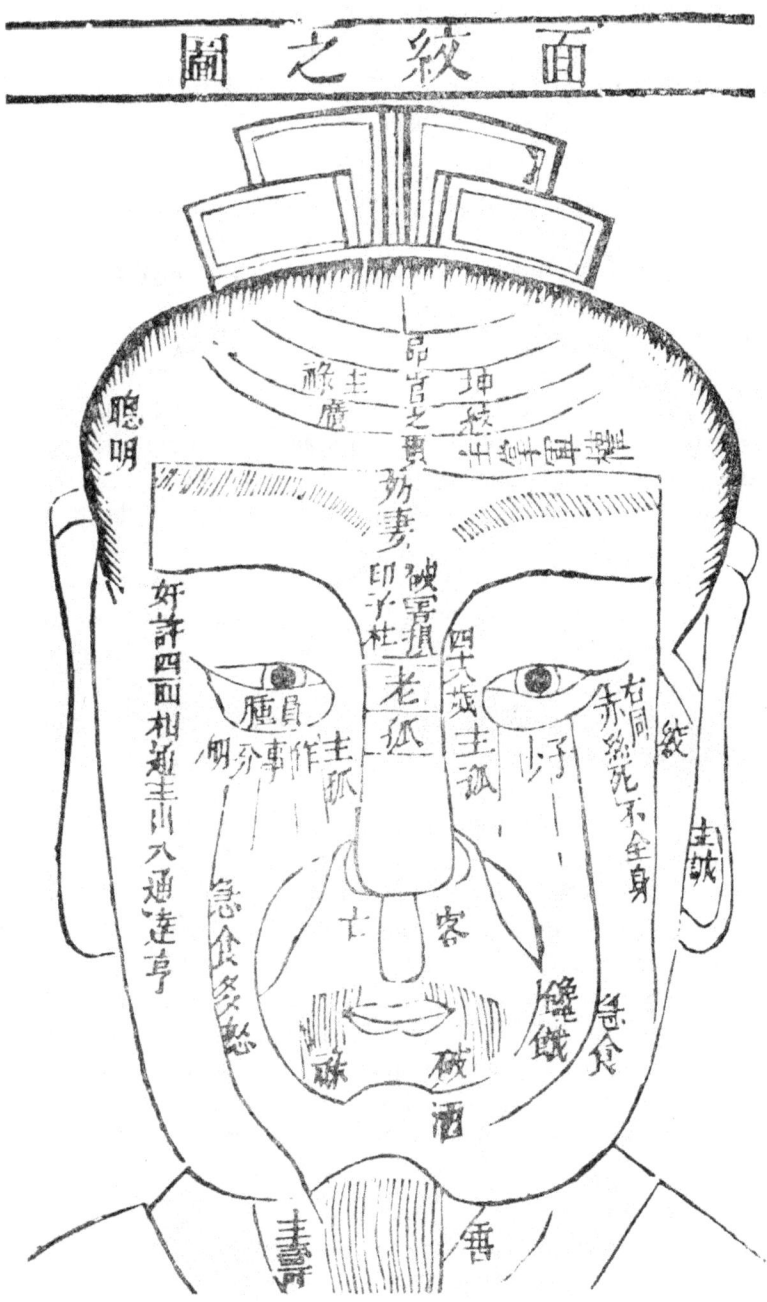

FIG. 9 Lines of the face (c). (From *Shen Hsiang*, 1793.)

The lines in the chin indicate "water peril."

Figure 8 depicts some other lines in the face: in the forehead, "long life"; at the corner of the left eye, "death of a wife"; at the corner of the right eye, "wife deserts husband," between the eyebrows, "hanging needles," indicating robustness and nobility.

Figure 9 depicts both favorable and unfavorable lines, such as "honor of high government position," "high government salary," "lines of military power," "lines of solitude," and "lines of hunger."

The Eyes

The eyes are considered to be the single most important feature of man's physiognomy. They show not only a man's future but also his very nature, character, and inner feelings. The fortune-teller in the *Golden Lotus* pays suitable attention to the eyes. He informs the hero that one of his eyes is male and the other female, a sign that he is wealthy and alert of mind (Egerton 1939: II, 19). He tells Plum Blossom that unfortunately her left eye is rather large and that this means she lost her father in her childhood, and that her right eye is small, which shows that her mother died when she was one year old (*ibid*. II, 23).

In general, the eyes are considered to be the sun and the moon of the whole body. The left eye represents the father and the right eye the mother (*Shen Hsiang* III, 10b–11a).

Long, deep bright, and spirited eyes signify great honor. Dark and black eyes signify intelligence. Narrow, deep, and long eyes signify long life. Short and small eyes signify stupidity. Eyes with fallen corners signify divorce. More white than black in the eyes signifies life toil (*ibid*. III, 10b).

According to Chang Chung-yuan, round and projecting eyes signify early death or disaster (*ibid*. II, 7b), and large, straight, and clear eyes signify great talent (*ibid*. II, 7a). According to an even earlier writer, Hsü Fu, red eyeballs signify evil (*ibid*. II, 6b). Chang Hsing-chien says that triangular eyes signify cruelty (*ibid*. II, 7b).

These sporadic comments about the interpretation of the eyes give way to a more systematic analysis based on the theriological principle. Like the general morphology of man, the eyes have the forms of animals and birds. Using this approach the Chinese recognize at least thirty-nine kinds of eyes, in addition to some that are labelled Yin-Yang, peach blossom, and drunken. They include among others the following, each of which is described and illustrated in the *Shen Hsiang* (III, 13a–17b):

The Face and Head

Dragon. Large clear eyes with long waves and spirit. They symbolize wealth, honor, and talent.

Phoenix. Graceful and clear eyes with long waves. They symbolize intelligence, wisdom, success, and fame.

Monkey. Spirited black iris with waves in tiers. They symbolize wealth, honor, and an appetite for fruit.

Turtle. Eyes with round iris and fine wavy lines. They symbolize long life, health, bliss, and plenty of food and clothing.

Elephant. Narrow eyes with long graceful wavy lines. They symbolize kindness, wealth, and honor.

Magpie. Eyes with long graceful lines over them. They symbolize reliability, loyalty, and goodness.

Lion. Large, wild, and powerful. They symbolize glory, bliss, health, and longevity if one is kind.

Tiger. Large eyes with golden iris. Tough, steady character, without worries. They symbolize wealth and loss of children.

Cow. Large eyes with round iris. They symbolize long life, bliss, and wealth.

Phoenix, lying. Eyes that are horizontal and straight, mild and graceful. They symbolize a kind nature, liberal mind, wealth, and honor.

Crane. Graceful and spirited, clear eyes. They symbolize ambition and that one may be able to enjoy the honor and wealth of a prime minister.

Goat. Eyes with light black and yellowish iris, dim and unclear pupils. They symbolize lifelong poverty.

Fish. Eyes that are spiritless and listless like water. They symbolize early death.

Horse. Spiritless eyes with broad eyelids shaped like triangles and with tears. They symbolize a toilsome life.

Snake. Eyes with round reddish iris and red veins. They symbolize treachery and cruelty.

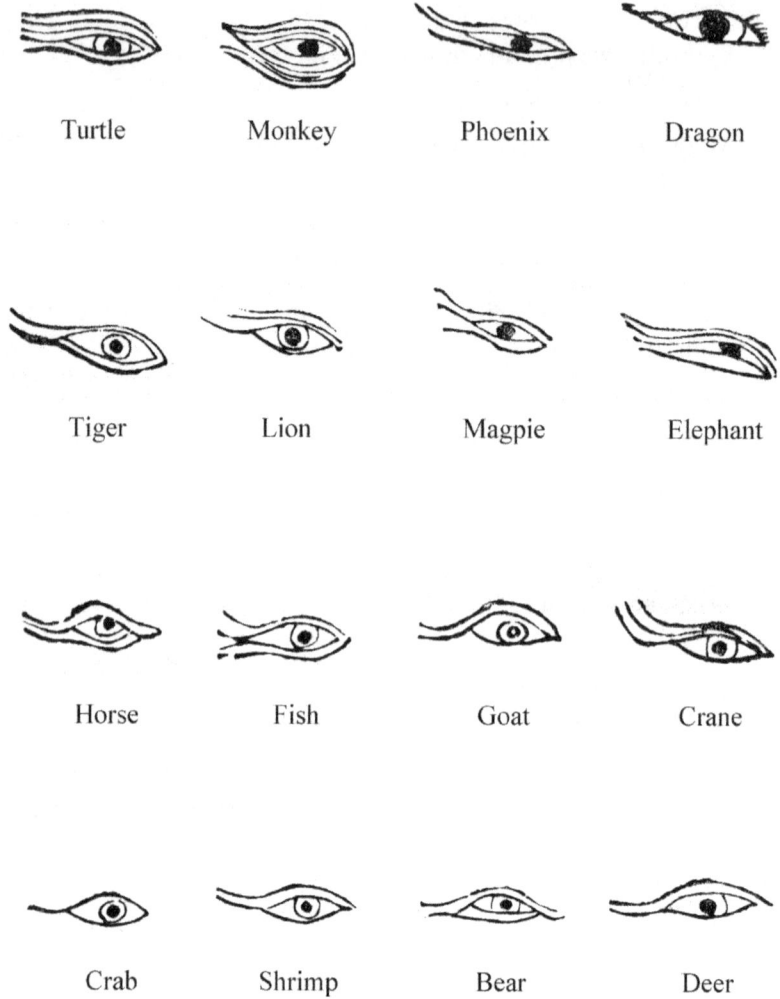

FIG. 10 Types of eyes (selected). (Adapted from *Ku Chin*, 1728.)

The Face and Head

Deer. Eyes that are black and with long wavy lines. They symbolize determination. Life in the woods and away from civilization would be most suitable.

Bear. Eyes that are round and show foolishness, uselessness, courage, and strength.

Shrimp. Eyes that are outwardly calm but worrisome beneath. They symbolize bravery. Although honored in his later years, he will not live long.

Crab. Eyes that are spiritless and foolish looking. They signify a love of pleasure but a solitary and independent old age.

Swallow. The eyes are deep, with clear-cut white and black. They signify truthfulness, intelligence, and diligence. One will never get rich but will have enough food and clothing.

Partridge. The eyes are reddish yellow. A man with the eyes of a partridge will never become rich.

Cat. The eyes are brownish. They indicate that one is mild, tame, good natured, very capable, and likes good food, but he will always depend on some man of repute to help him.

In addition to these there are the following, not described above: the rhinoceros, wolf, mouse, pig, dog, peacock, egret, eagle, chicken, goose, wild goose, luan bird (鸞鳥), mandarin duck, and sparrow.

Figure 10 illustrates some of the types of eyes that have been described above.

The Eyebrows

Detailed attention is paid to the eyebrows, which are not interpreted according to any single scheme. While there is a minor reliance on theriology, for the most part the meanings of the eyebrows seem to be extracted from all sorts of principles.

Fine, sleek, and long eyebrows symbolize intelligence, whereas short, coarse, thick, upside down or disorderly eyebrows indicate foolishness and cruelty. When the eyebrows are longer than the eye they signify long life, wealth, and honor, but when they are shorter they signify lack of wealth. When the eyebrows are close down to the eyes, or when the two meet at the ends, they mean poverty. When the outer corners of the eyebrows point toward the forehead they

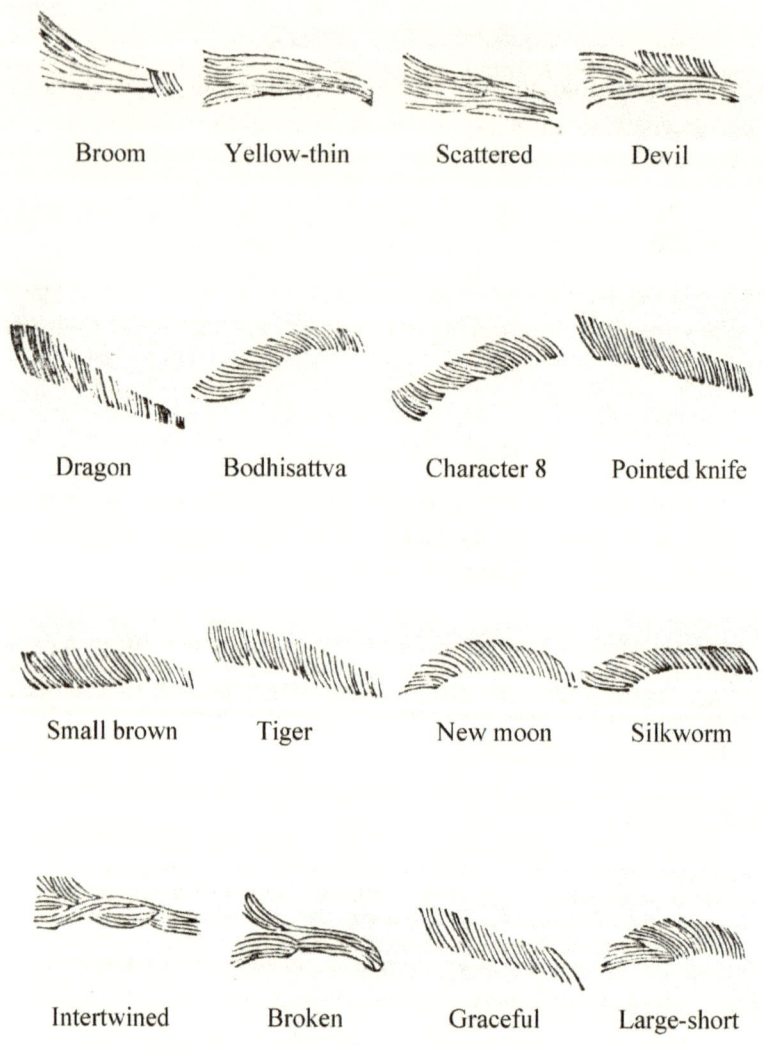

FIG. 11 Types of eyebrows (selected). (Adapted from *Ku Chin*, 1728.)

The Face and Head

signify determination and courage, but when the two corners fall downward they mean weakness. Projecting bones at the eyebrows signify evil. Black dots in the eyebrows mean intelligence, honor, and virtue. High eyebrows forecast power and wealth. White hairs in the eyebrows signify long life. Vertical lines over the eyebrows signify wealth and honor, but horizontal lines indicate poverty. Defective or thin eyebrows signify treachery and trickery (*Shen Hsiang* III, 5a–6b).

It is said that Hsü Fu stated (in 206 BCE) that eyebrows that curve gracefully like the new moon indicate intelligence, and forecast wealth, honor, and fame (*ibid.* III, 5b).

Chang Hsing-chien of the Chin dynasty wrote in his *Ta T'ung Fu* that when the hairs of the eyebrows stand up it means that the man will be impatient and cruel and will like to fight and kill (*ibid.* III, 6a).

In addition to the general types of interpretations, of which the above are a sample, the Chinese have made a systematic classification of eyebrows into types, as follows (*ibid.* III, 7b–10a) (Figure 11):

Devil's eyebrows. Coarse and close to the eyes. They are a sign of an unkind heart, hypocrisy, and a dangerous nature. It would be difficult for a man with such eyebrows to earn a living.

Scattered eyebrows. Wealth comes and goes. A man will neither suffer from want nor have enough to save.

Yellow, thin, scattered, and short eyebrows. Wealth of early years is only a display. One will never be able to keep a good position very long. His later years will be in confusion and he will die in a foreign land.

Broom shaped eyebrows. A man will have jealous brothers, and he will not be as wealthy in his old age as when he was young.

Eyebrows shaped like a pointed knife. Coarse eyebrows with this shape are signs of a dangerous heart. One will be cruel and hypocritical but will be punished with death.

Eyebrows shaped like the character 八. Eyebrows that are thin at the beginning and scattered at the ends indicate that the man will be a widower in his old age. He will have sufficient money to live on but he will not have a son by blood.

Bodhisattva eyebrows. Makes people sad because he will have a late marriage and a late son. In his older years he will be able to have a son only by a concubine because his legal wife will not be able to bear him a son.

Dragon eyebrows. Beautifully curved and thin at the ends. These are the eyebrows of a genius whose brothers will all enjoy high offices in court and whose parents will enjoy long life and honor.

Willow leaf eyebrows. Coarse but orderly. A man with these eyebrows will win faithful friends, prosperity, and fame, but will have little relationship with brothers or sisters.

Sword eyebrows. Beautiful and long. A man with these eyebrows will have enough intelligence to become the king's advisor and will enjoy honor in spite of poverty. His children will enjoy prosperity and health.

Lion eyebrows. Thick and high at the two outer ends. These eyebrows are signs of prosperity, honor, glory, and wealth in the latter part of life, or old age.

Eyebrows that are orderly at the beginning but thin at the end. These are signs that the early years will be ordinary but the middle and later years will flourish in fame and wealth.

Light and orderly eyebrows. Beautifully curved and thin at the ends. Such eyebrows will enable one to win a position in the king's court, the love of brothers, and the loyalty of friends.

Short and beautiful eyebrows. Such eyebrows forecast long life, loyalty, filial piety, and benevolence.

Spiral eyebrows. These are signs of power and therefore are good for military men.

Eyebrows shaped like the character 一. Orderly and even from head to tail. These are eyebrows of men who start their success at youth and enjoy long life with their wives.

Silkworm eyebrows. Beautifully curved. Men with these eyebrows are usually clever, pleasing, plausible, and obliging. One will become an outstanding person but one's brothers will not be friendly with him.

New moon eyebrows. Beautifully long eyebrows that touch the temples. These forecast success at the king's court, with wealth and honor.

Tiger eyebrows. They are thick and symbolize power. They are signs of courage, capability, long life, and honor without wealth.

Small brown eyebrows. Thick, but the hair is not coarse. It comes down to the temple but the end is not dry. The brothers will not be very brotherly; they will be separated. Close relatives may get in difficulty with the law.

Large short eyebrows. Short, pretty, and orderly, with yellowish ends and standing hair at the heads of the eyebrows. One will possess wealth but it is difficult for him to save money. He will have handsome sons, an amiable wife, and many brothers.

Graceful eyebrows. Longer than the eyes and beautifully curved. They symbolize intelligence, success, and love of brothers and friends.

Broken eyebrows. Yellowish and not orderly. A man with these eyebrows will have no brothers. Even if he had some they would die before he. His mother will pass away before his father.

Intertwined eyebrows. These symbolize great evil, imprisonment, bankruptcy, and separation.

Wu the Immortal pays some attention to the eyes in reading the fortunes of the several characters in *The Golden Lotus*. He communicates to the hero that each of his eyebrows has a fork, a sign that all through his life pleasure will mean much to him, but that below them are three wrinkles, which mean that in middle age he will suffer a great loss (Egerton 1939: II, 19). He tells Golden Lotus that her eyebrows are arched, but does not say what this signifies (*ibid.* II, 21). Plum Blossom's hair is fine, he says, but her eyebrows are thick, a sign of hot temper (*ibid.* II, 23).

The Nose

In general, the nose symbolizes the earth. It is like a mountain and therefore should be high, fat, and thick.

According to Hsü Fu, when a nose hangs like a gall bladder with a fat round tip, is high and big, and has a straight bridge up the middle of the eyebrows, it is a sign of wealth and position. A nose which turns upward is a sign of solitude. A flat nose is a sign of misfortune. A short and small nose is a sign of poverty. If the nose is like an eagle's beak, the man would probably be a leech and would be treacherous, envious, hypocritical, and covetous. According to Chang Hsing-chien, a nose with a straight, large, and fat bridge, a round tip full at each side, is a sign of a large family and much house property. Upward nostrils are also signs of poverty. If there are disorderly lines on the nose it means the man will have to work hard throughout life (*Shen Hsiang* II, 8b–11a).

In addition to these general types of interpretation, of which only a sampling has been given, the Chinese have made a systematic classification of the nose into types, based mostly but not entirely on the theriologic principle. The types are as follows (*ibid.* II, 20b–23a) (Figure 12):

Dragon nose. A full and straight tip, with high and straight bridge. Signifies high government position.

Tiger nose. A round tip, small at each side of the tip, high and straight bridge, with inconspicuous nostrils. Symbolizes great wealth, honor, and fame.

Mongol goat nose. A large and full tip, full on each side of the tip, too; a high bridge but not bony. Symbolizes great honor and wealth.

Lion nose. The bridge is slightly low but the tip and the sides of the tip are all large and full. Symbolizes that wealth comes and goes.

Nose like a suspended gall bladder. The tip of the nose is straight but the sides of the tip are small; the bridge is high and straight. Symbolizes glory, wealth, and honor.

Rhinoceros nose. The nose projects straight toward the forehead, with a full bridge that is neither too fleshy nor too bony. Symbolizes high government position.

Cow nose. A large bridge but neither too high nor too low, with clear cut lines at each side of the tip. Symbolizes wealth and harmony in the family.

Tube-like nose. The top of the bridge is a little low but the lower part of the bridge is full and has a straight tip. Symbolizes wealth, honor, and a nice family at middle age.

Garlic nose. A small and narrow bridge, but both the tip and the sides of the tip are full. Symbolizes unfriendly brothers, but the person will be prosperous at middle and old age.

The Face and Head

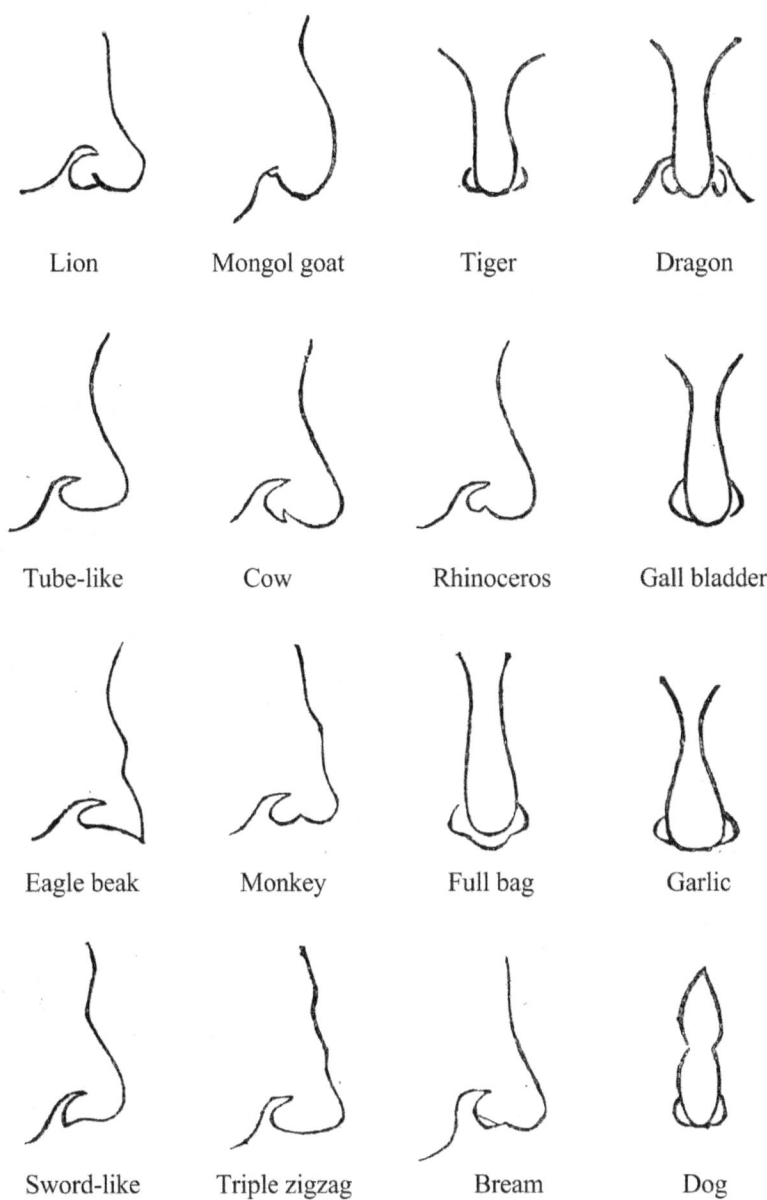

FIG. 12 Types of noses (selected). (Adapted from *Ku Chin*, 1728.)

Full bag nose. The sides of the tip are small but the whole nose is full like a bag. Symbolizes great wealth, fame, and high position.

Monkey nose. The bridge is large and flat and the tip is full and red, with clear cut sides and inconspicuous nostrils. Symbolizes wealth and treachery.

Eaglebeak nose. The bridge is ridged, the tip is pointed and shaped like the beak of an eagle, and the sides of the tip are short and small. Symbolizes treachery, trickery, and cruelty.

Dog nose. The bridge is bony and the tip and the sides of the tip look sort of hollow. Symbolizes loyalty but one is apt to steal when poor.

Bream nose. The lower part of the bridge is high like the back of the fish, the top part of the bridge is narrow and small, and the tip slants downward. Symbolizes no immediate relatives and not enough food and clothing.

Triple zigzag nose. A nose with a zigzag bridge is a sign of tears and extermination.

Sword-like nose. A ridged bridge like the back of a sword, and a bony tip with practically closed nostrils. Symbolizes a toilsome and solitary life.

Indented nose. A low and small bridge, but the tip and the sides of the tip are full. Symbolizes normal length of life but a great deal of sickness.

Nose like a solitary peak. Low cheek bones but a precipitous, large, bony nose with conspicuous nostrils. A man with such a nose can never accumulate any wealth. He is suitable to be a monk.

Ridged nose. A bony, ridged, and small bridge. Symbolizes poverty and solitude.

Nose with conspicuous nostrils. A high nose with large and long nostrils. Symbolizes poverty, trouble, and a toilsome life.

Musk deer noses. A small nose, with pointed tip, conspicuous nostrils, tight flesh. Although he works very hard it is difficult for his descendants to keep what he passes on. He finds work difficult to complete without repetition.

Orangutan nose. A high bridged nose. Symbolizes a liberal and broad mind, and a virtuous and heroic nature.

Deer nose. A full, straight nose with a round tip. Symbolizes a broad mind, kindness, loyalty, bliss, and wealth.

Ape nose. Small nostrils. Symbolizes a violent and nervous nature, hot temper, much grief, and a fondness for flowers and fruit.

The Mouth

In general, a large, broad, and oblong mouth is considered a sign of good fortune, while a pointed mouth like that of a monkey, goat, magpie, or tied up bag is considered to be a sign of misfortune (*Shen Hsiang* II, 12ab).

In addition to these general types of interpretation, the Chinese have made a systematic classification of the mouth into sixteen types (Figure 13), based mostly on the theriologic principle. These are as follows (*ibid.* III, 30b–32a):

Mouth shaped like the character 四 (*four*). When the mouth is large and broad, and oblong like the character 四, with even lips and the two corners turning slightly upward, the man is likely to be intelligent and talented and will enjoy wealth and honor.

Square Mouth. A square mouth with red, even, lustrous lips which can cover the teeth when smiling will bring wealth, honor, and glory.

Lying moon mouth. A mouth with upturned corners is a sign of wealth.

Bow-like mouth. A mouth which turns up like a bow and has thick, red lips is a sign of talent. One will enjoy wealth and honor throughout life.

Cow mouth. The lips are thick and red. Such a mouth is a sign of intelligence, honor, wealth, position, health, and bliss.

Dragon mouth. The corners are clear cut, the lips are full and even. A dragon mouth is a sign of power. It is very scarce and belongs only to the imperial class.

Tiger mouth. It is large and broad and symbolizes wealth and happiness.

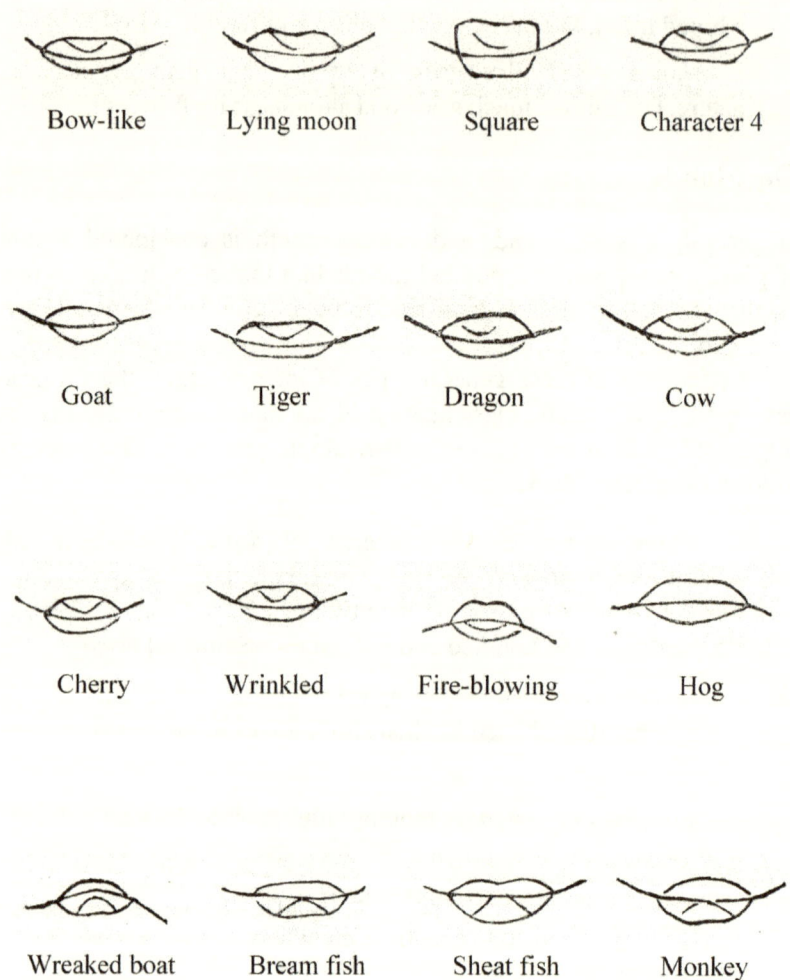

FIG. 13 Types of mouths. (Adapted from *Ku Chin*, 1728.)

Goat mouth. It is long and pointed, and symbolizes poverty and evil.

Hog mouth. The upper lip is long, coarse, and sleek, while the lower one is pointed, small, and wet. It is a sign of treachery, and the man will probably be persecuted by others.

Mouth shaped as if it were blowing fire. It is pointed and is a sign of poverty and early death.

Wrinkled mouth. A mouth with wrinkles on the lips. It is a sign of a solitary, long life. One will enjoy happiness in his early life but will suffer from failure in later life.

Cherry mouth. A large mouth with red lips. It is a sign of unusual intelligence.

Monkey mouth. Long lips with a deep raphe on the upper lip. One will never need food and clothing but will enjoy glory, bliss, long life, and health.

Sheat (fish) mouth. A broad mouth with corners pointed downward and with thin lips. It is a sign of poverty and sudden death.

Bream (fish) mouth. A small mouth. It means poverty. Clothing and food will never be abundant. Bad breath, dried up appearance. Bankruptcy and bad fortune.

Wrecked boat mouth. The corners of the mouth hang downward like a wrecked boat, and the lips are dark. It is a sign of poverty.

The Lips, Raphe, Teeth, and Tongue

For purposes of organization we have combined the lips, raphe, teeth, and tongue under one section heading. These features are discussed relatively little by Chinese physiognomists. In a way, the lips could be included as part of the mouth, but here we have preferred to describe them as separate entitles.

If the lips cannot cover the teeth it is a sign of solitude and poverty. If the lips are red it is a sign of wealth and honor. If there are lines on the upper and lower lips they are signs of generosity, virtue, and mildness (*Shen Hsiang* II, 12b–13a).

If the lips are blue or shrunken it is a sign of early death, and if they are black it is a sign of cruel death (*ibid*. III, 33a).

If both the lips are thick it is a sign of loyalty, wealth, and bliss. If the lips are thin and weak it is sign of poverty. If the lips are not straight, or if the corners hang downward, it is likewise a sign of poverty. If the lips fit each other it is a sign of uprightness. If the upper lip is longer it means the father will die first, while if the lower lip is longer the mother will die first. If the two lips do not fit or if they are pointed or if the corners hang downward it is a sign of poverty. If the upper lip is thin it is a sign of trickery, but if the lower lip is thin it forecasts poverty (*ibid.* III, 32b).

The raphe of the upper lip, according to Hsü Fu, should be long, deep, broad, and straight. In the raphe, length is a sign of long life, shortness is a sign of early death. Breadth is a sign of wealth, narrowness is a sign of poverty. Straightness is a sign of loyalty, crookedness is a sign of disloyalty. If the raphe is narrow at the top but wide at the bottom it is sign of many children; but if it is wide at the top and narrow at the bottom it is a sign of few children. If it is narrow at both the top and bottom but wide in the middle it means the children are not healthy. If the raphe is not deep it means many obstacles (*ibid.* III, 24a).

Teeth, according to Hsü Fu, that are large and long, white and strong, straight and closely set, are considered to be more favorable. Strong and closely set teeth are signs of long life. If the teeth are white as jade they are signs of success, while if they are white as silver it means an average occupation. Teeth like pomegranates mean bliss and wealth. Teeth like a sword mean long life. When teeth are wide on top and pointed at the bottom the man is likely to be carnivorous, while if they are pointed at the top and wide at the bottom he is likely to be vegetarian. Zigzag, projecting, thin teeth with a crevice, or short and missing teeth, are signs of poverty and stupidity. Yellowish teeth are signs of obstacles, while black teeth are signs of early death (*ibid.* III, 34ab).

Princes and earls, according to Hsü Fu, have 38 teeth, while ministers have 36, court officials have 34, and average people have 30 to 32. (Modern dentists might be interested in this mention of supernumerary teeth!) It is a sign of poverty to have 28 teeth (*ibid.* III, 34b).

A tongue that is long and broad is the tongue of a minister. A broad and thin tongue is a sign of dishonesty. When the tongue is so long as to be able to reach the nose it is a sign of nobility. Lines on the tongue are signs of high position. Small and pointed tongues are signs of poverty. A tongue with black spots is a sign of hypocrisy. A man with a short and big tongue is usually stupid and lazy. If the tongue is too big the man will probably suffer from hunger (*ibid.* III, 35a–36a).

The Moustache, Beard, and Head Hair

Hair on the lower lip means wealth, bliss, and long life. Hair on the chin means high position. If there is hair on the upper lip without any on the lower, the man will enjoy wealth, bliss, and long life, but if there is some on the lower part and none on top he will suffer from poverty. The best would be that he has some on both the upper lip and chin (*Shen Hsiang* III, 36a).

The hair of the head, when fine, lustrous, black, and shining, symbolizes honor. Yellow, red, and dry hair are signs of low degree. Stiff and coarse hair belongs to strong headed and solitary men. A mass of hair predicts poverty. If the hair line on the forehead is high and exposes a high forehead, it is a sign of wealth, honor, fame, and long life. But if the hair line at the back of the head is high, it indicates a mean nature. A low hair line on the forehead usually means stupidity and short-livedness (*ibid.* III, 3a).

The Ears

Speaking in general, the ears are considered to be good when they are fat, firm, upright, long, roundly curved, close to the head, large, wide in opening, red or white in color, sleek, and with a piece of flesh at the end and long hairs in the ears. They are considered of bad quality when they are thin, coarse, dry, dark, leaning forward, or turning outward (*Shin Hsiang* III, 25a).

According to Kuo Lin-tsung, when the ears are higher than the eyebrows they are signs of intelligence, talent, wealth, and honor. If the ears are red and sleek it is a sign of peaceful life, but if they are bluish and black they forecast a wandering life and death in a foreign land (*ibid.* II, 2b).

According to Chang Hsing-chien, if the ears are whiter than the face it means the man is generous and faithful and will win wide fame (*ibid.* II, 3a).

According to Hsü Fu, when the ears are as high as *jih chiao* (日角, see p. 49 above) it is a sign of unusual intelligence, long life, and health. When the ears are so close to the head that they cannot be seen clearly from the front it is a sign of wealth and honor (*ibid.* II, 2b).

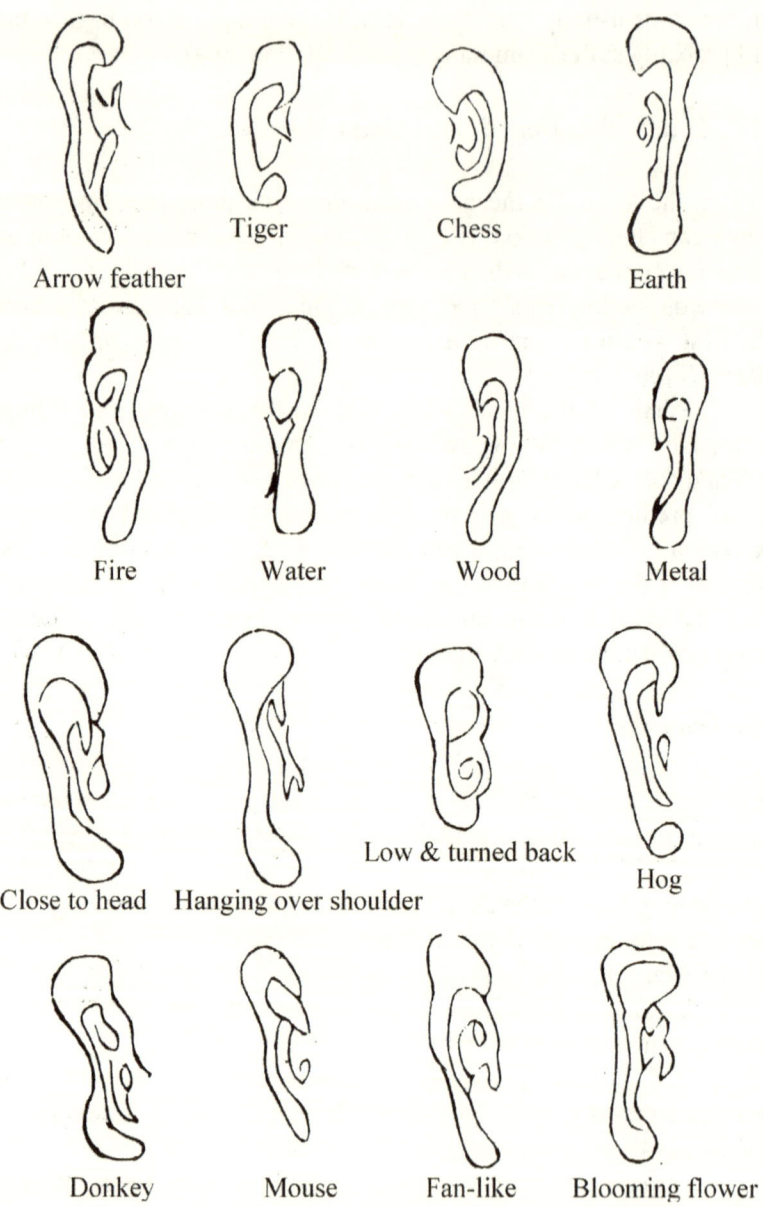

FIG. 14 Types of ears. (Adapted from *Ku Chin*, 1728.)

When the ears are thin or the openings small they are signs of poverty and early death. If the ears have a firm outside outline it means fortune, even though the inside is formless. But if the outside is formless it is a sign of misfortune, even though the inside has a clear cut form (*ibid*. II, 3b).

In addition to the general type of interpretation above, the Chinese have made a systematic classification of the ears into sixteen types that are based mostly on theriology and the Five Elements. The types (Figure 14) are as follows (*ibid*. III, 26b–28a):

Earth ears. Firm, large, flat, shining, and red. They are signs of wealth, honor, and many relatives. Even when old, one will be able to serve society like a youth.

Chess ears. Round and well shaped. A man with these ears will have to start life empty handed but he will be successful in his undertakings and will become very wealthy at middle age.

Tiger ears. Small, crooked, but close to the head, so they cannot be seen clearly from the front. A man with these ears will be adventurous and enjoy honor and dignity.

Arrow feather ears. The ears are over an inch higher than the eyebrows, but thin and hairy at the lower part. Although the man inherits millions in wealth, he will be bankrupted and will have to seek a living hither and thither.

Meal ears. The ears are and inch higher than the eyebrows, round at the top, but small and white at the bottom, with a piece of thick flesh at the ends. They are signs of wealth and honor, but solitude at old age.

Wood ears. The lower part of the ears turn outward. This is a sign of poverty and no close relatives.

Water ears. The ears are round and higher than the eyes. They are also close to the head, with a piece of fat flesh at the ends. They are red, firm, and sleek. These are signs of great wealth and honor.

Fire ears. The ears are higher than the eyebrows, but the lower parts turn outward. Even though the ends consist of pieces of fat flesh like beads, the man will suffer from solitude at old age.

Hog ears. The ears are fat and round on top, but the lower parts are slanting. Even though the man possesses wealth he will suffer from many misfortunes in the latter part of his life.

Low and turned back. The ears are short, unround at the top, and with the lower parts turning outward. These are signs of poverty, orphanhood, bankruptcy, and friendlessness in the latter part of life.

Hanging over shoulder. The ears are fat, long, and sleek, with clear outlines. The upper parts are higher than the eyebrows; the lower parts contain pieces of fat flesh at the ends and hang over the shoulders. These are signs of the highest honor.

Close to head ears. The ears are higher than the eyebrows, close to the head, firm, and well shaped. These are signs of fame and happiness for generations to come.

Blooming flower ears. The ears are thin and unround like a blooming flower. Although one may possess millions in wealth, he will be bankrupted and suffer from poverty in old age.

Fan-like ears. The ears lean forward like fans. This is a sign of bliss in childhood, failure in middle age, and poverty in old age.

Mouse ears. The ears are higher than the eyes but they are pointed at the lower parts. These are signs of a stealing and stubborn nature. One will suffer misfortune in old age.

Donkey ears. The ears are fat and well shaped, but floppy and thin at the ends. These are signs of poverty and misfortune in old age.

The Moles of the Face

The Chinese pay a good deal of attention to the study of the moles of the face. They call divination from moles, *mien tsu* (面痣). Contrasted with the protuberance on the occipital bone, moles are usually a sign of bad luck. This is seen in the old Chinese proverb, "The head has no bad bones, the face has no good moles" (*Shen Hsiang* X, 11a).

The moles are best explained by referring to them in the accompanying drawings.

In Figure 15, moles of good and bad luck are indicated. The twelve moles stretching across the forehead from left to right indicate the following: great wealth, short life, tremendous wealth, very fortunate, public affairs, obstacle to father, auspicious, cruel nature, good government position, great wealth, die in a foreign land, unsuitable for monastic life or to live in the mountains.

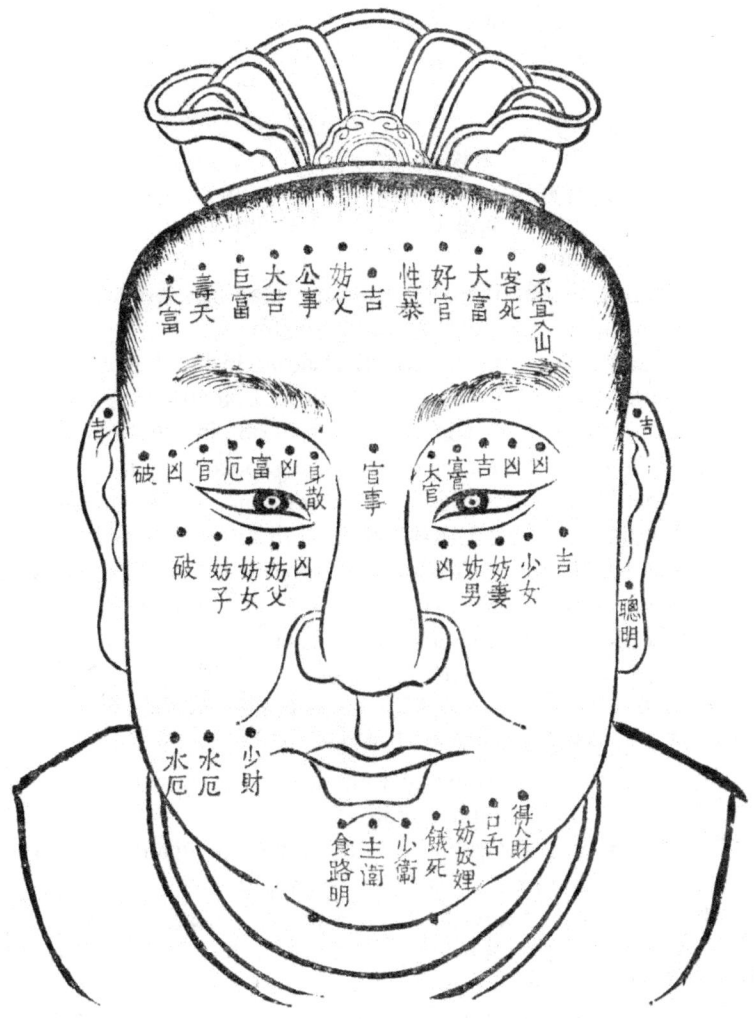

FIG. 15 Moles of the face (a). Moles are generally unfavourable indicators. (From *Ku Chin*, 1728.)

The seven moles above the eye on the left in the figure, reading from left to right, mean: bankruptcy, disastrous, government position, distress, wealth, disastrous, departure (?).

The moles above the eye on the right in the figure are five in number, and reading from left to right they indicate: great official; suitable to take government employment; fortunate; disastrous; disastrous.

The five moles under the eye on the left, reading from left to right, indicate: bankruptcy; impediment to son; impediment to daughter; impediment to father; disastrous.

The five moles under the eye on the right, reading from left to right, mean: disastrous; impediment to son; impediment to wife; few daughters; fortunate.

The moles at the side of the mouth, reading from left to right, mean: water distress; fire distress; little wealth.

The seven moles under the mouth, reading from left to right, mean: the way for a living is clear; like wine; little protection; die of hunger; unfortunate for the slaves; quarrelsome; will obtain wealth.

Other moles shown in this figure have good signs. The mole at the top of the ear shown at the left means fortunate, and so does the one at the top of the other ear. The mole between the eyebrows is a sign of government employment. The mole at the lower part of the ear at the right is a sign of intelligence.

In Figure 16, another set of interpretations of the moles of the face is made, in this instance for males only. The five moles on the forehead mean: impediment to parents; good government position; high government position; die from war; unfortunate when travelling.

The six moles above the eye at the left indicate: lose money; bad; water distress; fortunate; unfortunate; honorable.

The five moles above the eye on the right mean: great honor; government position; water distress; lose wealth.

The five moles below the eye on the left mean: licentious; few daughters; much occasion to weep; father will die early; wife will die early.

The five moles below the eye on the right mean: self; son will die early; no children; few sons; treacherous.

The three moles shown to the left of the mouth mean: die in a foreign land; while the single mole to the right of the mouth denotes: obtain great wealth.

The four moles shown below the mouth indicate, respectively: intelligent; like wine; fortunate; virtuous.

The Face and Head

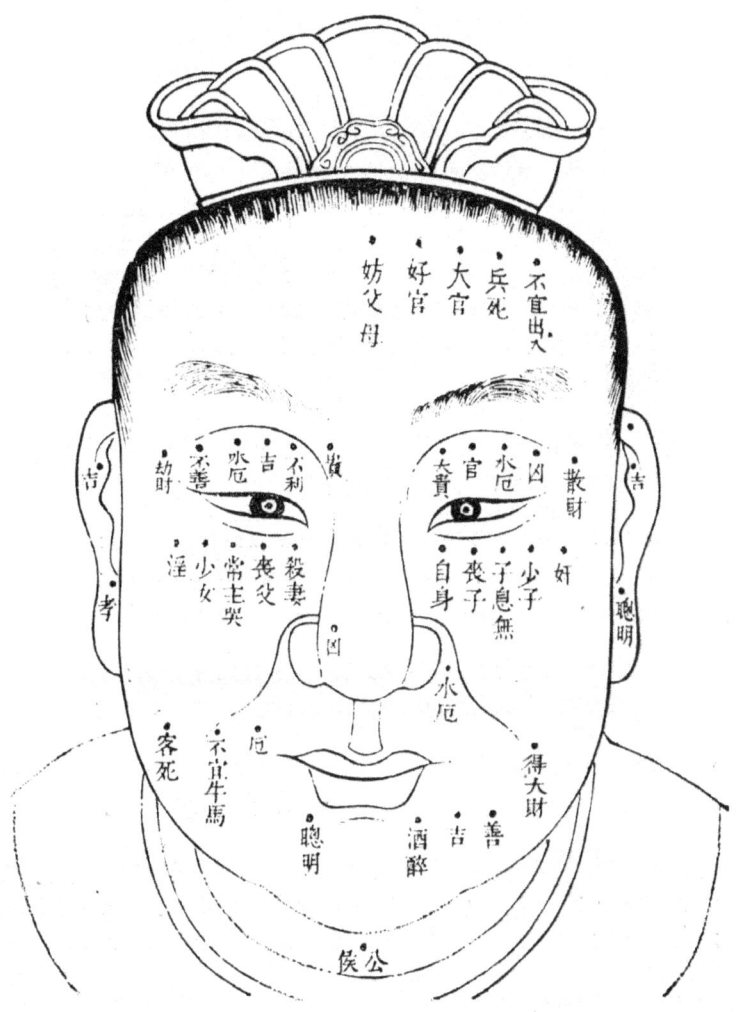

FIG. 16 Moles of the face (b). (From *Ku Chin*, 1728.)

Six other moles are shown, with those at the upper part of each ear being a sign of good fortune. The mole at the lower part of the ear at the left is a sign of filial piety, while that at the lower part of the other ear is a sign of intelligence. The mole shown on the lower left part of the nose is a sign of disaster. The mole shown to the right of the wing of the nose is a sign of water distress, and the mole under the chin is a sign of a position similar to that of a marquis.

In Figure 17 the moles are given for the female face. They are interpreted differently than those on a man's and have a more lugubrious character. The ten moles across the forehead, reading from left to right, signify: a member of the nobility for her husband; she will have nine husbands; harm to parents; as a girl will be a slave; will marry again; harm to relatives; impediment to husband; will die in a foreign land; injurious to husband; distress at childbirth.

The four moles over the eyes shown at the left mean: fortunate; divorce; fortunate for husband; in prison.

The five moles over the eye at the right mean: fortunate in raising silkworms; fortunate for sons; honorable husband (or will make husband honorable); impediment to husband; long life.

The five moles under the eye to the left mean: thief (or will be robbed); always fortunate; treacherous, few sons; fire distress.

The four moles under the other eye mean: disastrous; impediment to sons; will weep for husband; licentious.

On each side of the mouth there are various moles. In the upper row there are three to the left, meaning: she will commit suicide; jealous; water distress. In the upper row to the right, these are three more, meaning: will kill sons; quarrelsome: impediment to husband. The two lower ones to the left mean: water distress; bad health and hard life. The single one to the right of the mouth means: impediment to slaves.

Other moles are interpreted in the following way. That between the eyebrows means: impediment to husband. That at the root of the nose means: distress. That at the raphe means: will have twins. That below the mouth means: little property. That at the bottom of the chin means: kill husband. That on the ear at the left means: wisdom. That on the lateral side of the cheek bone means: respect husband.

The moles of the women in *The Golden Lotus* are mostly unfavorable in nature. Thus, Wu the Immortal tells the Moon Lady that she has some inauspicious points, among them being a mole in her *Lei T'ang*, indicating that if she were not so frequently ill she would

The Face and Head

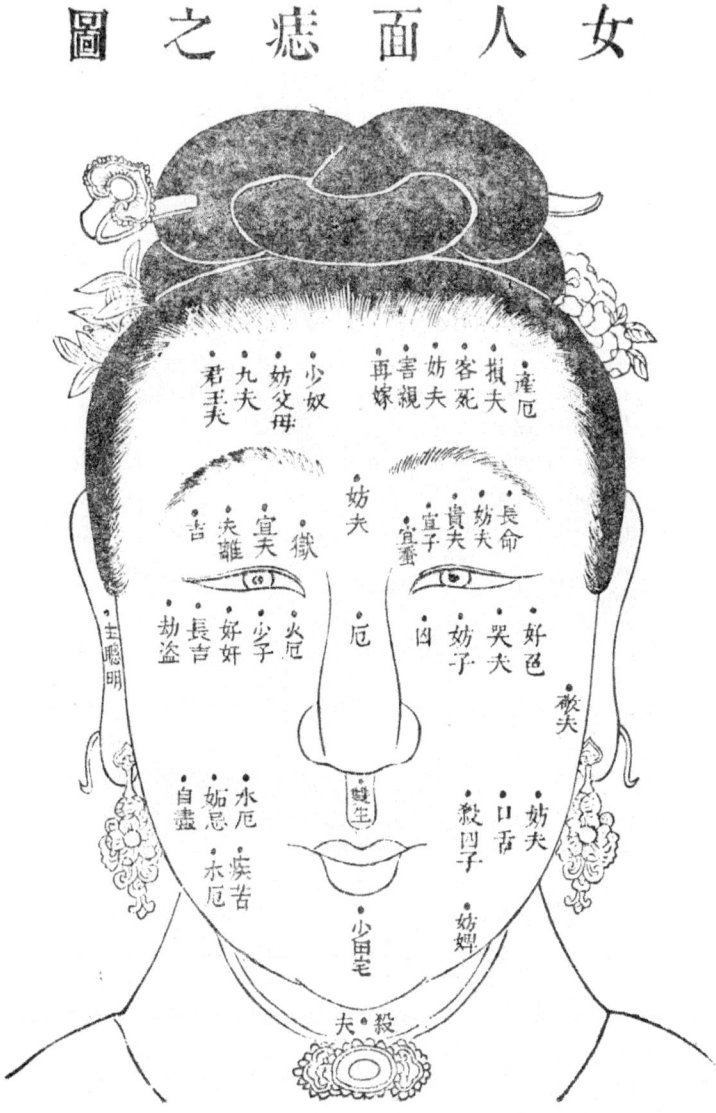

FIG. 17 Moles of the face (female). (From *Ku Chin*, 1728.)

most certainly destroy her husband (Edgerton 1939: II, 20). He tells Golden Lotus that the moles upon her face mean she will be the end of her husbands (*ibid.* II, 21). And he informs Plum Blossom that the mole beneath the left corner of her mouth is the sign of a quarrelsome disposition, but that the mole on her right cheek indicates that her husband will love and respect her as long as she lives (*ibid.* II, 23).

The Occipital Bone

The Chinese interest in the occipital bone seems to be unique, although it has been referred to in a loose way as "phrenology." Perhaps it may better be described—to coin a term—as occipitomancy.

Actually, the interest is not really in the bone *per se* but in the protuberances to be found on it. These bumps are called "pillow bones." Even though these refer to bones in the plural, there is of course only one bone there, unless one wants to include the occasional Wurmian bones or Inca bone. The Chinese evidently had nothing of this sort in mind. It is the bumps themselves, sometimes referred to as pillows, which have relevancy for destiny and character. Figure 18 illustrates some of the pillows.

In general, when the pillow bones are protuberant they mean wealth and honor, while if their locales are hollow or flat it is a sign of poverty and low breeding. Good bones must, however, be accompanied by other good features, too.

Getting down to the specific we find that there are thirty-five differently shaped pillows at the back of the head, each with its own name. The types are described and interpreted as follows (*Shen Hsiang* X, 9a–10b).

> *San ts'ai* (三才) *pillow*. Three round bones. They are signs of a minister.
>
> *Five mountain pillow*. Bones projecting from the four corners and one from the middle. They are signs of a marquis.
>
> *Double dragon pillow*. Two bones pointed. They are signs of a general.
>
> *Cart wheel pillow*. High all around but hollow in the middle. They are signs of a lord.
>
> *Continuous light pillow*. Three rising parallel bones. They are signs of high government pay if the bones are small, but if they are large they are signs of a prime minister.

The Face and Head

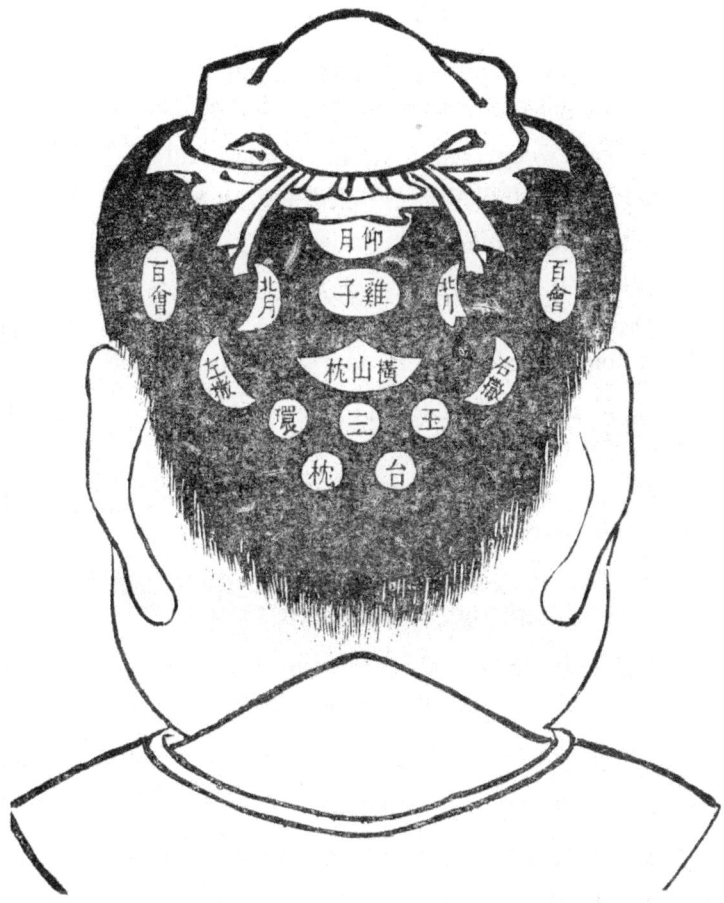

FIG. 18 The pillow bones. In reality, these refer to topographical features of the occipital bone. There is no connection with phrenology. (From *Ku Chin*, 1728.)

Lying moon pillow. One bone curving upward. It is a sign of a government official.

Upside down moon pillows. One bone curving downward. It is the sign of a government official.

Back to back pillow. Two bones, one upward and one downward. They are signs of a defence corps.

Three star pillow. One bone on top and two at the bottom. They are signs of an office of a government institution.

Erected square pillow. Bones rising at all of the four sides. They are signs of high government pay.

Round moon pillow. One round projecting bone. It is the sign of an office in the court.

Dropping dew pillow. One bone square at the top but round at the bottom. It is a sign of a minor government office.

Jade goblet pillow. Round at top and bottom and shaped like a dish. It is the sign of a cabinet minister.

Back to back moon pillow. (The source gives no description and no illustration).

一 *(one) character pillow.* This is a sign of honesty, sincerity, and strong mindedness.

Spiral pillow. It is a sign that there will be honor throughout three generations—the grandfather, the father, and the son.

Left long pillow.
Left cast pillow. } All three of these are signs of a long life.
Right cast pillow.

Three frontier pillow. These are signs that there will be several honors in one family.

Continuous pillow. These are signs of honor and long life but an unstable nature.

Chicken egg pillow. This indicates a hot temper and a conceited nature.

Horizontal mountain pillow. It is a sign of honesty and strong mindedness.

Suspended pin pillow. (The source gives no description and no illustration).

Hanging pin pillow. A sign of long life.

Wine goblet pillow. A sign that one will come in contact with some honorable man and will receive a government pension.

上 *(above) character pillow.* A sign of high ambition, great courage, and a long life.

Waist pillow. A sign of small honor and no definite good fortune—sometimes it will be good and sometimes bad.

Bead-like pillow. A sign that one will come in contact with some man of honor but hardly possess anything himself.

丁 *(adult male) character pillow.* This is a sign of a generous nature. One will come in contact with some honorable men.

山 *(mountain) character pillow.* Three straight bones on top with one horizontal bone beneath. They are signs of intelligence, wealth, and long life.

Layer jade pillow. One round bone on top and one square bone at the bottom. They are signs of wealth and glory.

Elephant tooth or ivory pillow. One projected bone with pointed top. It is a sign of military power.

Suspended needle pillow. A projecting bone with four corners. It is a sign of military office.

One sun pillow. One horizontal bone. It is a sign of great wealth and very long life.

Chapter V

THE HANDS, FEET, AND TRUNK

We now consider the remaining portions of the body.

The study of the hands receives considerable attention from the Chinese; the study of the soles of the feet is much less important but is nevertheless present; and the study of the trunk of the body is brief and uninspired.

The Hand

In *The Golden Lotus*, the Taoist fortune-teller does not pay much attention to the hands in reading the physiognomy of the several members of the hero's household, and in any event makes no reference to either the lines or the mounts. Of the hero he merely says: "Your hands is so fine and soft and firm, you are certainly destined by fortune for the enjoyment of wealth and happiness" (II, 19). Later he asks the Moon Lady to show him her hands, and he tells her that they are like dried ginger, a sign that she is well capable of controlling those under her charge (II, 20). He does not examine the hands of the other women. This lack of interest in the hands may be attributed perhaps to literary license; it certainly does not correspond to the historical facts.

Palmistry appears to be very old in China, but how old cannot be determined, for the earliest references to it are unreliable. For instance, it has been said that certain lines in the hands of the Emperor Shun formed the character "to praise," yet the Emperor is said to have lived 2317–2208 BCE. a time that places him in the mythological golden age when the government of the world was perfect.

In divining from the hand, the Chinese do not use astrology, as do their Western counterparts. Their method is "natural" rather than starlinked.

They use the left hand to make their diagnoses, except that the right is used for women. Where there is doubt or ambiguity, both hands are used.

Before looking into the comments made by the Sung books, some general comments made by Arlington (1927–28), who does not cite his sources, may be considered. Some of these refer to relationships and proportions; others consider softness, shape, and color. Thus, a tall man with small hands will suffer poverty; but conversely a small man with large hands will become wealthy. When long feet are combined with small hands, this is a sign of nobility. Again, long hands signify that the owner is honorable. The lines on the hand should be like embroidery, the hands soft as cotton. The inside of the hands should be as red as cinnabar, with a sheen like water and warm as fire. The back of the hand should resemble the curved back of a prostrate tortoise. The center of the palm should be deep (depressed) so that an egg could be contained in it. The skin on the hands should be slack, the sinews thick but hidden beneath the flesh. All of the above signs in the hands indicate a rich and noble person (1927: 175).

Getting down to the palm proper, we are told that a soft square palm indicates wealth, and if long and thick it signifies nobility. A hard palm signifies a fool and toil-worn person. A short and thin palm indicates a poor and common man. A concave palm with the "mounts" surrounding it very high represents wealth and high advancement in official life. A flat palm with "mounts" surrounding it indicates a fool who will lose much (Arlington 1927: 175).

Color, too, must be considered. The color of the skin on the palm should be red mottled, the palm glossy; this indicates a noble and wealthy person. If the color is blue and white, dry and thin, or the color of dust, it signifies failure in everything and a common fellow. It is very important that the color of the skin on the inside of the hand be the same as that on the back of the hand, which is a sign of wealth and nobility; but if the reverse, it is a sign of poverty (Arlington 1928: 228–29).

The Five Element principle is used by some physiognomists. The palm of a Metallic-natured man should be square; of a Wooden-natured man should be round; of a Fire-natured man should be thick and heavy. A man's hands should correspond to his physiognomy, and particularly with the Five Elements (Arlington 1927: 229).

Figure 19 shows, in addition to some lines indicative of wealth and nobility, the three bumps or mounts at the roots of the fingers. They are referred to as *san ch'i* (三奇) or Three Essentials and occur in the areas of the three trigrams known as Sun, Li, and K'un. They correspond to the bumps known among Europeans as Jupiter, Saturn, and Mercury. The thicker the mount, the more favorable the indication. Their significance is as follows:

> *Bemp at root of index finger*, called *teh-fung* (德峯). This represents wealth and governs the first twenty-five years of a person's lifetime.
>
> *Bump in the middle*, called *lu-fung* (祿峯). This represents position and governs the second twenty-five years of a person's lifetime.

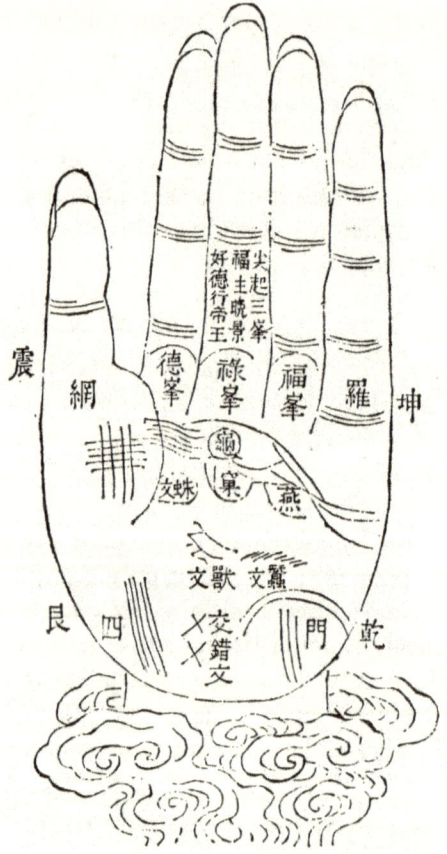

Fig. 19 Palm lines indicative of wealth and nobility. (From *Ku Chin*, 1728.)

Bump at root of fourth finger, called *fu-fung* (福峯). This represents bliss and governs the third twenty-five years of a person's lifetime.

One's fortune will be highest in that period of life associated with the bump which is the most prominent of the three (*Shen Hsiang* VIII, 23b).

There are three main lines in the palm (not especially depicted in any of the accompanying figures.) They are equated with Three Forces or *san-ts'ai* (三才). The location and significance of these lines are as follows: The sky line (天) is the top line in the palm and represents the sky. It is a sign of honor. The length and depth of the line determines whether or not a man will enjoy honor. The man line (人) is the middle line and represents man. It is a sign of wealth. The length and depth of the line determines whether the man will be wealthy or poor. The earth line (地) is the lower line and represents earth. It is the sign of life. The length and depth of the line determines whether the man will be able to enjoy long life. In general, it is better to have clear, deep, and generous lines on the palm, rather than few, unclear ones (*ibid.* VIII, 14ab, 23b–24a.)

The Eight Diagrams (cf. Table 4) are used to map out the palm into eight areas, and to these is added a ninth, the *ming-t'ang* located in the center of the palm. The interpretations of these positions, which are arranged clockwise in Figure 20 and are intermingled with the Twelve Temples, are as follows (*ibid.* VIII, 20b–22a):

Ch'ien (乾). If this position is thick, a man's descendants will enjoy honor.

K'an (坎). If this position is thick, a man will enjoy honor and fortune.

Ken (艮). If there are many lines in this position, a man will have very few brothers and he will lead a solitary life.

Chen (震). If this position is thin, a man's wife will die early.

Sun (巽). If this position is thick and high, a man will enjoy prosperity and be good natured.

Li (離). If this position is high and thick, a man will enjoy high position.

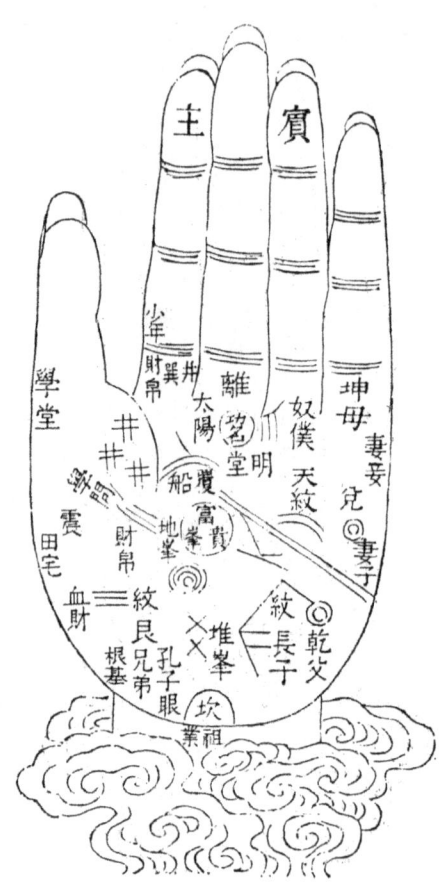

FIG. 20 The eight diagrams in the palm. (From *Ku Chin*, 1728.)

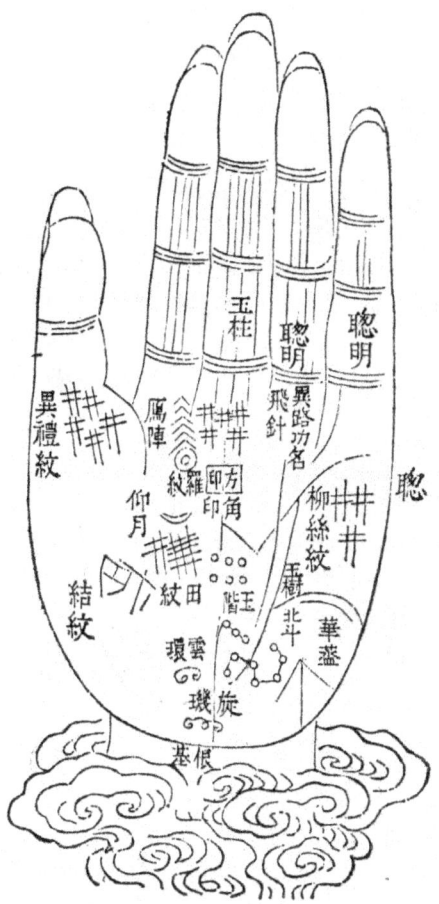

FIG. 21 Some favourable lines in the palm. (From *Ku Chin*, 1728.)

K'un (坤). If the lines in this position are deep and disorderly, it would be unfortunate for the children.

Tui (兌). If this position is high a man will enjoy many servants, and he will be kind and mild, while if it is thin it would be unfortunate for his servants.

Ming-t'ang (明堂). If there are square shaped lines in this position a man will enjoy honor, while if this position is dark it would be most unfortunate.

Parenthetically, it is interesting to consult Arlington's (1928: 229–232) more detailed exposition on the subject. He gives a fuller Chinese analysis but at no time cites his Chinese sources, which appear to be more recent than anything in the Sung dynasty's classical writings. As a Western practitioner of palmistry he derides the Chinese emphasis on lines instead of form and size. This is because he himself is not the conventional kind of Western palmist but is of the kind linked with chirognomy, a modern version of chiromancy which had a brief vogue beginning in 1843 with the writings of a Frenchman named D'Arpentigny.

Figure 21 indicates some favorable lines.

Various lines, other than the three main lines of the palm and those already discussed, have importance for divination.

Lines of the following shapes are signs of good fortune (*Shen Hsiang* III, 15b–17b):

- *Tied fish.*
- *Fish net.*
- *Stone steps.*
- *Golden well.*
- *Flying needle.*
- *Wild geese column.*
- *Lying moon.*
- *Cloud.*
- *Southern star.*
- *Dipper.*
- *Animal.*
- *Turtle.*
- *Money.*

The Hands, Feet, and Trunk

Lines shaped like any of the following seals are signs of good fortune (*ibid.* VIII, 15b–19a):

- ⊠   *Cross line seal.*
- ⌂   *Elephant seal.*
- △   *Triangle seal.*
- 手   *Hand shaped seal.*
- 女   *Female character seal.*

Lines shaped like any of the following are likewise signs of good fortune (*ibid.* VIII, 15b–19a):

三, 쓰, 女, 志, 井, 凡, 壬,
手, 可, 头, 化, 武, 友, 虎.

Contrasted to the above lines are lines indicative of great misfortune (*ibid.* VIII, 15b–19a). They are as follows:

- ◐,⊕,ᷗ   *Cut head.*
- 匕   *Lying corpse.*
- 刀   *Knife character.*
- 丁   *丁 character.*
- 开   *Lock.*
- メ   *Demon.*
- ⌒   *Wrecked ship.*
- 土   *Earth character.*
- 火   *Fire character.*
- 巛   *Death.*
- 乃   *乃 character.*
- 血   *Envious wife.*
- ◎   *Coiled.*
- ◇   *Coffin.*

Various lines, most of which are not included in the lists above, have good or bad significance in terms of their particular locations on the palms. Some of these lines include the Eight Trigram positions. These lines and their interpretation are as follows (*ibid.* VIII, 15b–19a):

##### ##	These lines in the Li position promise the highest government office.
▫	These lines in the palm promise positions equal to earls or dukes.
xxx xxx	These lines on the fingers indicate a happy and easy life.
人, ≷	These lines at K'an position indicate wealth and honor.
丰	These lines in the middle of the palm indicate a man will hang himself.
##, ###	The lines in the K'an or Chen position indicate tremendous wealth.
|	This straight line, from the K'an to Li position, indicates great prosperity.

Stone step lines in the palm indicate success in civil service examinations, while chess lines in the Ken position indicate a worrying nature. Eye lines on the thumb are called teacher's lines and indicate intelligence; eye lines in the K'un position are called Buddha eye lines and indicate solitude; eye line in the palm are called Tao eye lines and indicate cleverness. Triangular eye lines in the K'an position are called mouse eye lines and indicate a stealing nature. Flower willow eye lines in the K'un position are called eyes of tears; on the second finger they are called blue eye lines and indicate honor; in the Sun position they are called string eye lines and indicate wealth through dishonesty.

A systematic presentation of all the types of lines of the palm appears in the *Shen Hsiang*. They number seventy-two. A digest of the descriptions of these kinds of lines is here given as abstracted from that work (VIII, 4a–12b). The illustrations of these lines are shown in Figures 22–29, these pictures having been taken from the *Ku Chin* (vol. 2986, sec. 640, pp.4a–15b) rather than the *Shen Hsiang* because of their greater clarity than the originals from which they were copied. Two features of these lines may be pointed out in advance: they obviously pertain to an elite class and they are overwhelmingly optimistic. To these observations there may be added another: many of these lines are figments of the imagination; like many other physiognomic features described by the Chinese they simply do not occur as natural markings.

Four season lines. (Actually these are areas rather than lines.) If spring is bluish, summer pinkish, autumn whitish, and winter darkish, they are signs of good fortune. If spring is whitish,

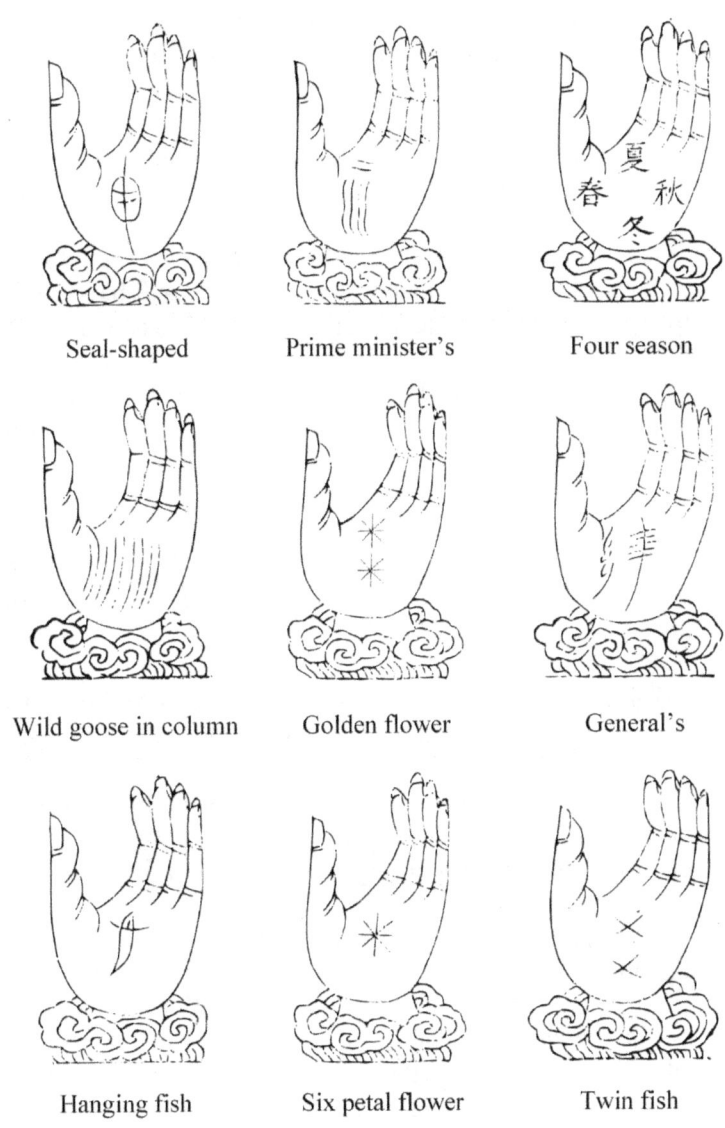

FIG. 22 Types of palm lines. (Adapted from *Ku Chin,* 1728.)

summer darkish, autumn pinkish, and winter yellowish, they are signs of misfortune.

Prime minister's lines. These lines are signs of generosity, honesty, sincerity, and scholarly nature. Men with these lines will easily win favor from the king.

Seal shaped lines. These lines are signs of future fame, wealth, honor, and high civil service position.

General's lines. These lines indicate success in the civil service examination. One will win a military position, will be successful in foreign wars and in defending the borders of his country.

Golden flower lines. These are signs of wealth and honor. If they appear in a man's hand, he will become a high official, while if they appear in a woman's hand she will marry some member of the royal family.

Wild geese in column lines. These are signs of success and fame. One will have the opportunity of becoming the prime minister.

Twin fish lines. These are signs of scholarly success. If the lines are red and smooth, one will surely obtain very high position.

Six petal flower lines. These are signs of future bliss and of possible government service with attendants. He will become more prosperous in court during the latter part of his life.

Hanging fish lines. Immediate success. He will enjoy wealth and honor at youth.

Four straight lines. These are signs of fame and a prosperous middle age. It would be better still if the palm is red, smooth, and glossy. He would easily obtain a high government position.

Personal royal interview lines. These indicate intelligence. He will have the opportunity to be promoted to government service in middle age.

The Hands, Feet, and Trunk

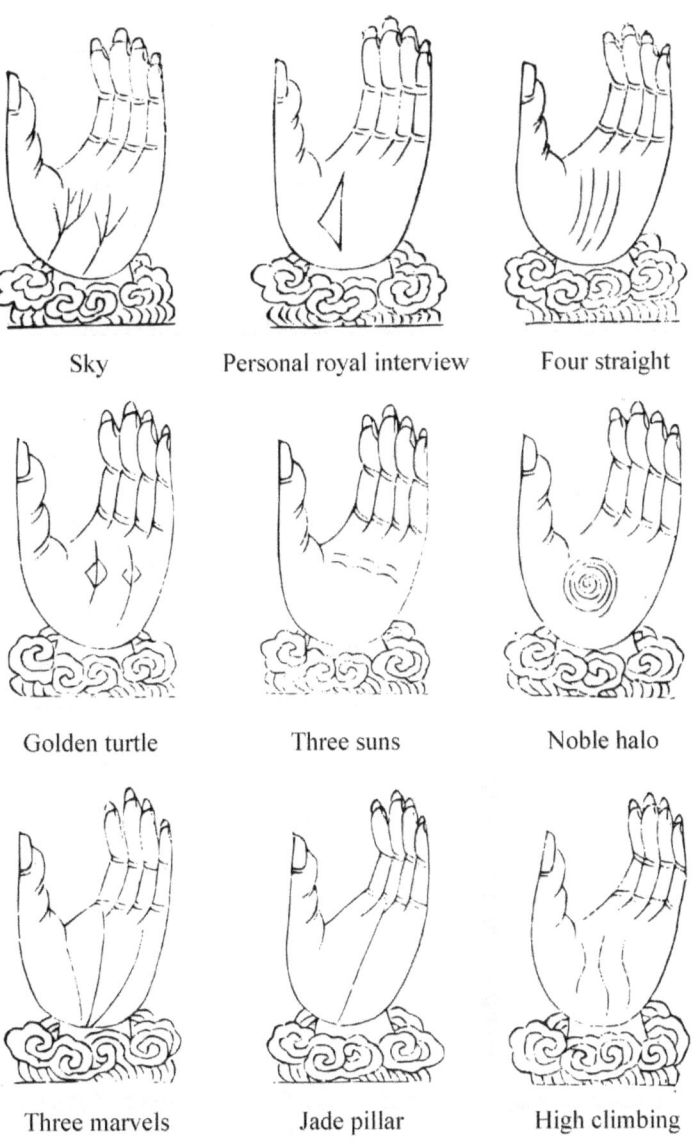

FIG. 23 Types of palm lines (continued). (Adapted from *Ku Chin,* 1728.)

Sky lines. These are signs of scholarly success. As an official he will be able to traverse the world; as an ordinary citizen he will enjoy plenty of wealth.

Noble halo lines. If these lines are round like rings, the man will surely become a lord of some sort. If the lines have the shape of money, he will be the possessor of much wealth.

Three suns lines. These are indications of early success in obtaining the highest scholarly rank in the civil service examination. He will also win world wide fame.

Golden turtle lines. These are signs of long life and wealth. He will live to be over a hundred years old.

High climbing lines. These are lines of peerless courage. If the hand is red and glossy, he will enjoy wealth and honor throughout life.

Jade pillar lines. This is a sign of courage and intelligence. If the palm is bright it forecasts that he will obtain some high office in his middle age.

Three marvels lines. These three lines come out from one source. They are signs of high position equal to that of a prime minister.

Columns of pen lines. Achievement in the highest scholarship, at least ten years of gratification in civil service position, and endless bliss throughout a long life.

Self establishment lines. These are signs of future glory and honor. He will eventually become a prime minister.

Jade well lines. One water-well shaped line indicates bliss and virtue. He will be honorable and will be able to work in the king's court. Two and three wells are even better.

Three peaks lines. When the three bumps are high and round like dates, glossy, red and smooth, they are signs of plenty of jade, gold, and good land property.

The Hands, Feet, and Trunk

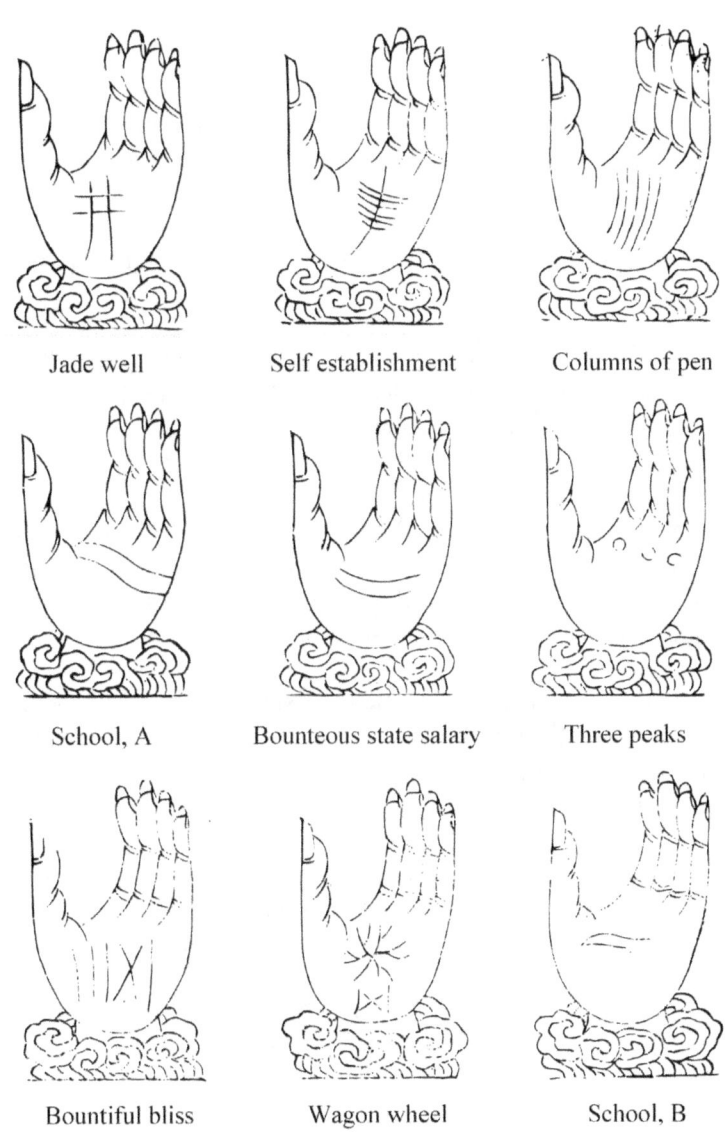

FIG. 24 Types of palm lines (continued). (Adapted from *Ku Chin*, 1728.)

Bounteous state salary lines. These are signs of plenty of wealth and widespread fame.

School lines, A. These are signs of a skillful hand. He will enjoy honor and bliss.

School lines, B. These are lines of scholarship. He will be chosen as one of the best among those who take the civil service examination, and he will win wide fame.

Wagon wheel lines. These are signs of the imperial court to which he will be related.

Bountiful bliss lines. These are signs of generosity and compassion. He will encounter very little misfortune in life. He will be generous and compassionate to the poor and will enjoy long life and wealth.

Unusual lines. Unusual lines need unusual deeds. His fame is only appreciated by men of honorable origin. If he becomes a monk he will win an unusual name, but if he undertakes an ordinary career he will be in lack of a large sum of money.

Little honor lines. These are signs of a small office in government. Even if he does not get an office he will earn enough money for savings. It the hand is red, smooth, and soft, he will hold power even as a monk.

Heavenly rapture lines. This is the line of bliss. All through his life he will enjoy bliss, glory, prosperity, happiness, and peace, and everything will proceed in accordance with virtue.

River character (川) *lines.* These lines on all the fingers indicate long life for all members of the family. His sons will live as long as metals will last and his daughters as long as Wang Mu-hsien (王母仙) the fairy.

Laurel prize lines. Successful candidate for Han Lin honors (the highest scholarly degree).

The Hands, Feet, and Trunk

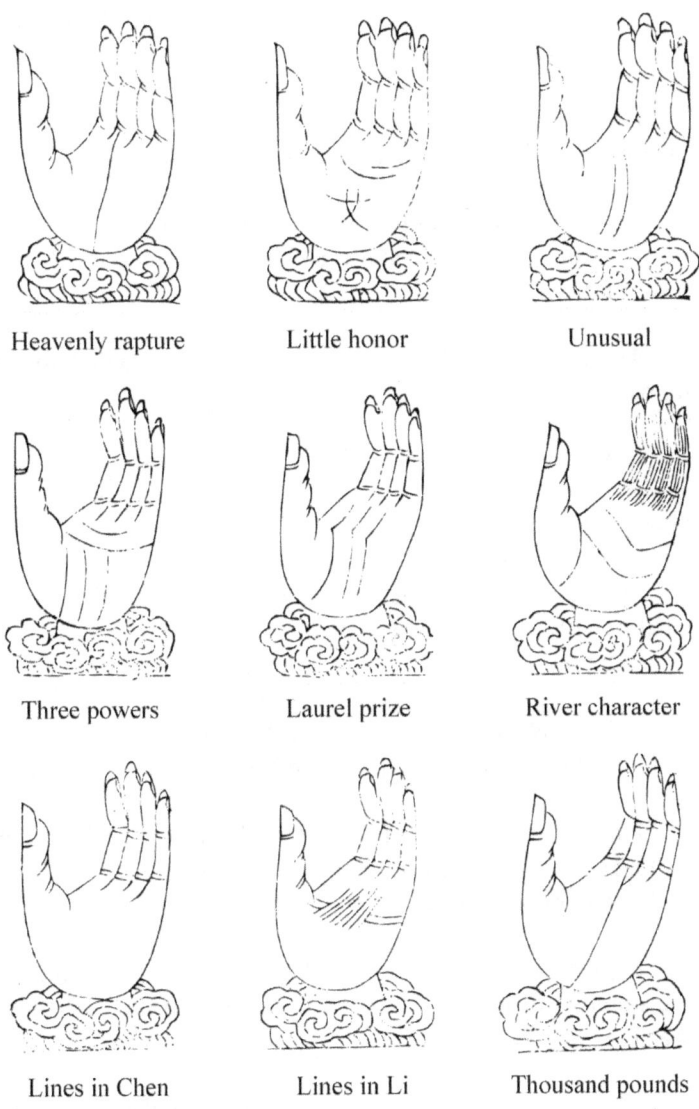

FIG. 25 Types of palm lines (continued). (Adapted from *Ku Chin*, 1728.)

Three powers (Heaven, earth, man) lines. These are lines of fairly good fortune.

Thousand pounds (of gold) lines. A man with these lines will have plenty of wealth and honor before him.

Lines in Li ("Fire" 離*) position.* When lines in Li are crossed by other lines it is a sign that he will toil for life.

Lies in Chen ("Thunder" 震*) position.* When the lines in Chen position can hardly be seen it is a sign that the man will have very few children.

Milky Way lines. These lines indicate that his wife will die and he will have to marry again.

Covering of a bier lines. These lines will be signs of remission of sins or the protection from evil if the man should devote himself to good deeds.

Distinctive lines. The fish shaped lines are the sign of a wealthy wife, and the well shaped lines are signs that the son will obtain a high position.

Private virtue lines. These are lines of personal virtue and wisdom. No evil in his heart, for he loves kindness and prayers.

Lines of wisdom. A man with these lines will have widespread fame. He is considerate in his behavior and kind in his heart. No evil will come to him.

Light of the mountain lines. These are signs of quietude. They are suitable for monks, but if they appear in ordinary hands they are signs of solitude.

Mountain dwelling lines. These are signs that the man likes quietude and enjoys living in the mountains, but at the same time he likes pleasure, too. He will regret in his old age his ungratified lusts.

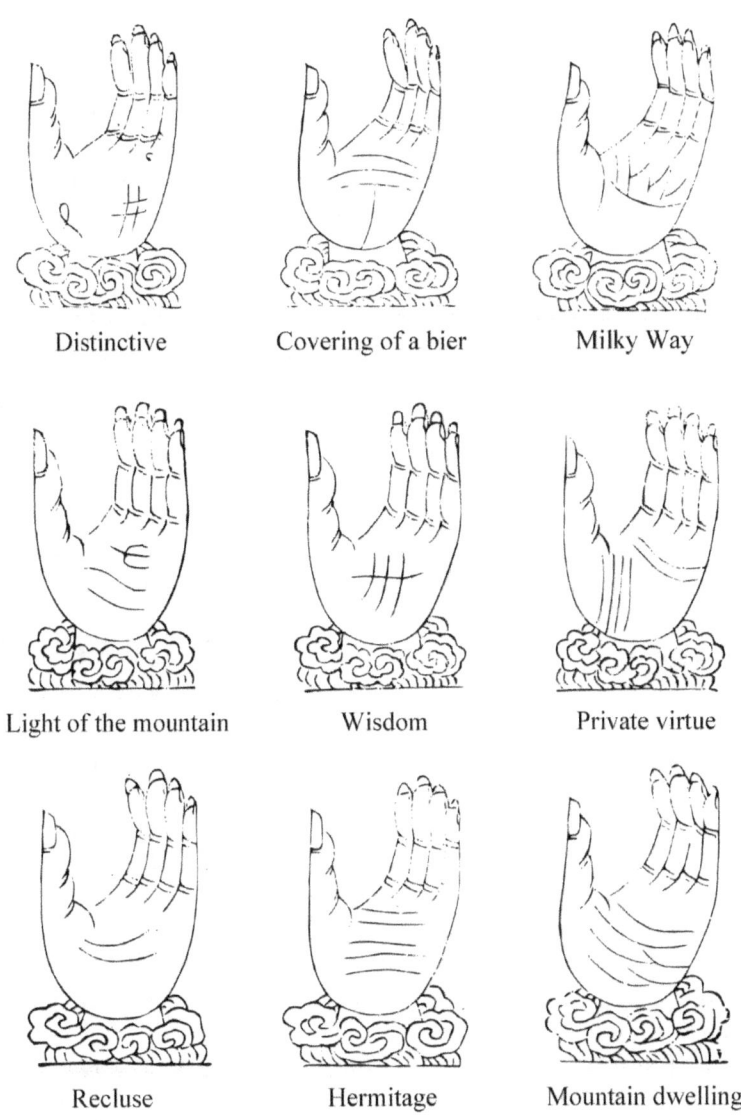

FIG. 26 Types of palm lines (continued). (Adapted from *Ku Chin*, 1728.)

Hermitage lines. There are signs of a compassionate and kind nature. He loves quietude. He will be aware of the true meaning of life and become a monk in his old age.

Recluse lines. There are signs of a quiet nature. He loves quietude and will always be afraid of disturbances and noise.

Lines of lust. These lines are like disorderly grass. They show that the man will always be infatuated with women, even at the age of ninety.

Disorderly Flower lines. A man with these lines will be fond of luxury. He will always be entangled with other women and will have no concern for his own wife.

Sexual lines. A man with these lines will be extremely sexual. He will suffer from pain in old age.

Flower and wine lines. A man with these lines will spend his life among girls and wine. He will always be enticed by young girls and can never save any money.

Peach blossom lines, A. A man with these lines will be luxurious and will love women and wine. His life will be entirely spoiled by his loose life and he will have no family even in middle age.

Flower and willow lines. A man with these lines never worries over anything. All he is concerned with is to seek pleasure with women and seldom rises early in the morning.

Mandarin ducks lines. A man with these lines is licentious. The love of women and wine never ceases; it continues even in old age.

Flowery hairpins lines. Secret association with women.

Peach blossom lines, B. Sentimental with women. Bad places are his home. He thinks of women even in his dreams.

Stolen flower lines. These are not good lines. They mean that the man is never satisfied with his own wife but is always attracted by somebody else's wife.

The Hands, Feet, and Trunk

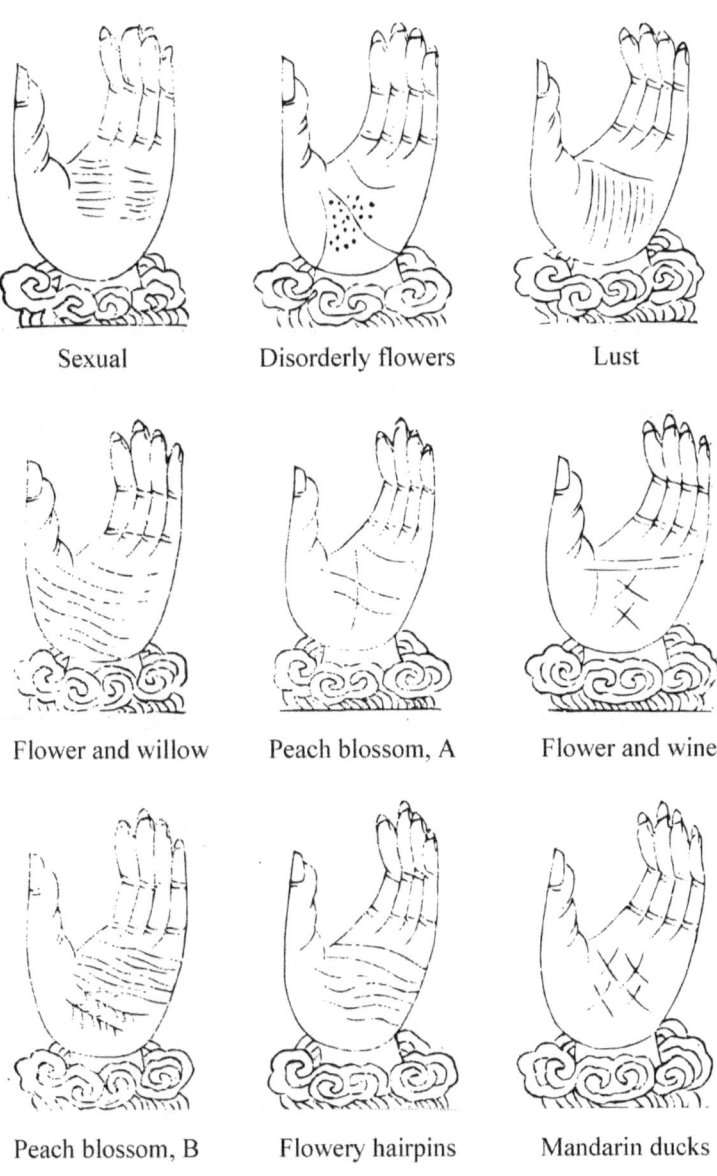

FIG. 27 Types of palm lines (continued). (Adapted from *Ku Chin*, 1728.)

Fish lines. These fish lines appear at the wife's position. They mean that the wife will be honorable and virtuous.

Canopy lines. These are signs of a wealthy wife and the promise of sons. (A covering over the line represents the wife.)

Facing the sky lines. The wife's line rising toward heaven is a sign that the wife is attracted by her husband's father and a bad relationship will follow.

Slave lines. If the slave lines face toward the wife line, there will be a bad relationship between the wife and the slave.

Branch lines. Branch lines at the wife position are signs of a tricky wife.

Wife and concubine lines. The wife may be interested in some other man.

One layer line. If there is only one line at the wife's position, it means that the man will have neither wife nor brothers. But if there are three or four lines he will surely have descendants.

Destroy father lines. These are signs that his father will die early and he will have no one to support him during childhood.

Destroy mother lines. These are signs that his mother will die early unless he is adopted by some other parents.

Adoption lines. No support in childhood. He will either have to follow his mother at her second marriage or be adopted by someone else.

Covetousness lines. These are signs that the man tends to be a sponger.

Feminine lines. These lines show that the man will always receive wealth from some woman.

Lost god or lost spirit lines. These are signs of bankruptcy. He will not only affect the welfare of his relatives but also his own life.

The Hands, Feet, and Trunk

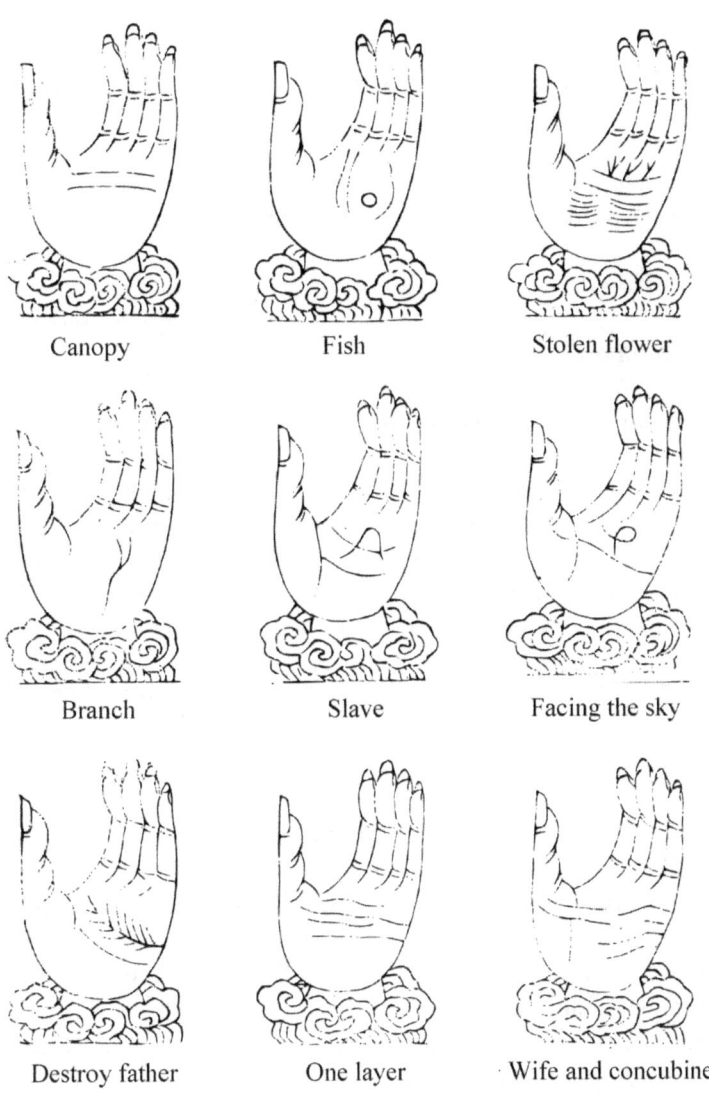

FIG. 28 Types of palm lines (continued). (Adapted from *Ku Chin*, 1728.)

Baleful invading lines. The lines are disorderly and invade each other. He will have much success but will also encounter much failure. He will have to be very cautious in order to get satisfaction.

Three baleful lines. These lines are baleful to the wife. He must be very cautious else he become a widower.

Red sparrow lines. These lines indicate trouble throughout life. The crossed lines are not too bad; the two uncrossed lines are worse.

Wine and food lines. He will always get himself invited to feasts.

The Fingernails

Divination from the fingernails has not received much attention from the Chinese.

The fingernails are said to be related to the muscles, liver, and gall bladder. If they are large and hard, a man will be ambitious and daring. If they are short and soft, he will be timid and cowardly. Strong nails are a sign of strong mindedness and eagerness to get things done. Soft nails indicate laziness. A person with such nails will learn a good deal but accomplish very little. He starts a project very easily but never finishes it. He is irresolute, stupid, and resourceful (*Shen Hsiang* VIII, 26ab).

The Foot

Divination from the foot, or pedomancy, as it has been called by Westerners, has been developed to a unique degree by the Chinese, who refer to it as *hsiang tsu* (相足). In some ways it resembles palmistry, for it uses the form of the foot and the lines on the sole in a way comparable to the use made of the form of the hand and the lines of the palm. Chinese pedomancy does not have an astrological basis; instead, like Chinese palmistry, it falls into the category of natural physiognomy.

According to Chinese theory the feet symbolize the earth, so that although they occupy a low position their usefulness is supreme. The function of the feet is to carry the weight of the body and to move it about. By this usefulness should the value of the feet be judged (*Shen Hsiang* VIII, 27a–28b).

When the feet are square and broad, straight and long, oily, smooth, and soft, they signify wealth and honor. When they are narrow and thin,

The Hands, Feet, and Trunk

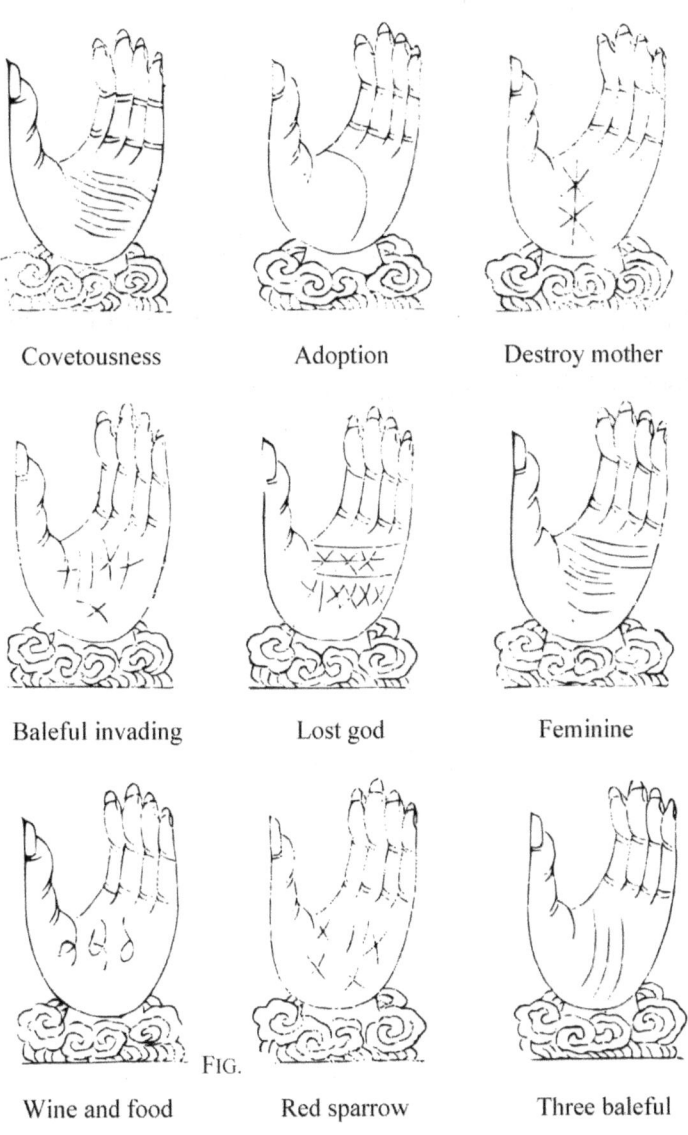

FIG. 29 Types of palm lines (continued). (Adapted from *Ku Chin*, 1728.)

sideways and short, coarse and hard, they signify poverty and low grade. Thin feet with long toes mean no sons or descendants. If the feet grow sideways, even though they are thick they still indicate poverty. If a man has distinctive heels or good arches, his bliss will be carried down to his descendants. But when the feet are flat like boards they signify poverty and simplicity. When the arch is so formed that it can cover a turtle, it forecasts wealth and honor, dukes and lords. Long toes mean virtue and fidelity; even toes are sign of chivalry. If the middle toe is long it means that one will die in a foreign land. Feet four inches thick are signs of tremendous wealth and high government position. If the feet are both thick and square they signify tremendous wealth. When three toes are in a straight line they signify power. In general, men of honor have small but thick feet, while the lowly have big and thin ones (*ibid.* VIII, 27a–28b).

As for the soles of the feet, dark and purplish soles are signs of high government position. Moles on the soles mean high government position; but if the feet are thin, even though they have moles they are

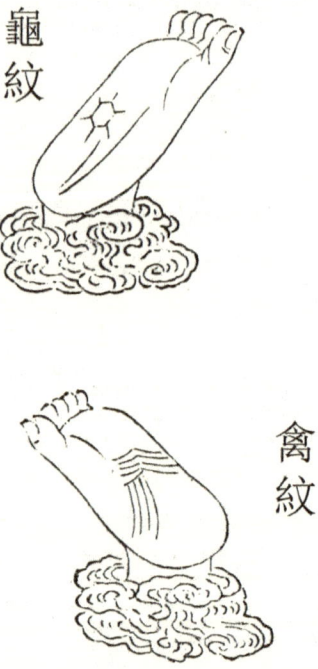

FIG. 30 Pedomancy: two types of foot lines. (Adapted from *Ku Chin*, 1728.)

of low grade (*ibid.* VIII, 27a–28b). Black moles indicate virtue, wealth, and honor (*ibid.* VIII, 29a–30a).

Lines on the sole like a turtle indicate 2,000 piculs of rice, as well as lifelong fame; lines like birds of a cross indicate a prime minister (see Figure 30). Lines like embroidery indicate a million dollars government pay. Lines like scissors indicate ownership of millions of wealth. Lines like the shape of a man indicate an honorable government position which is superior over thousands of other positions. Three lines like a whip indicate bliss and wealth. Blow (to strike) lines indicate wealth and honor. Coil lines on the two little toes indicate a peculiar nature. No lines on any toes indicates breakage and dispersion. Any lines on the soles indicate prosperous descendants (*ibid.* VIII, 29a–30a). If there are no lines on the soles the feet are of low grade, and this is a sign of poverty (*ibid.* VIII, 27a–28b).

It is good to have much hair on the feet but it must be of a certain quality. Fine and soft hair are signs of honor and high government pay, while coarse hair signifies poverty and low grade (*ibid.* VIII, 29a–30a).

The Neck

In general, the neck is considered to be a good one if it is fat, round, strong, and straight. But if it is weak, thin, small, or long, it is considered to be bad. A round or fat neck like those of a tiger or swallow is a sign of bliss and wealth. If the neck leans forward it is a sign of mildness and goodness, while if it leans backward it is a sign of cruelty. A straight neck is a sign of uprighteousness and bliss. A thin and long neck like that of a snake or crane is a sign of poverty (*ibid.* III, 36b–37a).

The Chest

The chest is the reservoir of blood and breath. If it is flat, broad, and square it promises position and glory, but if it is crooked, projecting, or hollow, the man will have to labor all through life for his living (*ibid.* IV, 3a).

The Belly

The belly is the furnace of the body by which all important nourishment is refined. If it is round, long, thick skinned, and hanging downward, it is a sign of wealth and long life. The belly is like the earth, which holds all the elements of the world. If the belly hangs downward, it will better be able to hold all the wealth of the body. According to Hsü Fu, "A small downward belly signifies great wealth and honor. A belly like a little bird is where poverty comes" (*ibid.* IV, 2b).

The Navel

The navel is the representative of the intestine. If it is deep, broad, and pointing upward, it signifies bliss and intelligence, and vice versa (*ibid.* IV, 6a).

The Waist

The waist is the mountain on which the stomach leans. It therefore should be straight and strong. A straight, thick, and long waist signifies wealth and position. A good back without a good waist means success in youth. A good waist without a good back means no success until middle age (*ibid.* IV, 1b–2a).

The Back

A broad and full back foretells much bliss and little misfortune, and vice versa. A back with projecting bones like that of a turtle means wealth. A fat thick back means poverty and solitude. A square and long back means bliss and intelligence, and vice versa. A round and thick back is a sign of great honor (*ibid.* IV, lab).

At this point in our study the purely Chinese portion ends, to be followed immediately by an extended comparative analysis using materials from Mesopotamia, ancient Greece, the Arabic world, Europe, and other places where physiognomics played some role in the cultural life of the people. Not only will matters of history be clarified but so will questions of function. It is only by extensive comparison that the Chinese situation can be given some elucidation, although regrettably the coverage of other civilizations cannot be as thorough as one would desire. This is due only in part to failure to delve extensively into such sources as those from India, Iran, Turkestan, Tibet, and Mongolia. The lamentable truth is that information from many of these places is scant and sometimes very unreliable.

Chapter VI

GENETIC CONNECTIONS

Is there some sort of historical connection between Chinese body divination and that of the West (Europe)? This question is a reasonable one to ask, for the parallels between the two are often striking, yet the answer is one that is not easily forthcoming.

It is necessary to go far back into the past in order to explore the possibility of genetic relationships, for while somatomancy does not manifest itself in writing in China until the middle of the Chou dynasty, as a form of divination it suggests that it is merely one aspect of the wider phenomenon of mantic activity, and of course we know that the latter is present at the dawn of Chinese history.

Oracle bones made from mammalian scapulae and the shells of turtles have inscribed on them the earliest discovered Chinese writing. Prior to the exhumation in Honan in 1899 of some bones mixed with turtle shells, and especially before the excavations made at Anyang beginning in 1928, bones inscribed with a kind of writing often had been discovered in Chinese apothecary shops, where they were considered to be dragon bones and were used for their alleged medicinal value. After the discovery of similar bones at the former Shang capital it was not only verified that the commercially sold bones were ancient but that the inscriptions on them were authentic.

The importance of divination, at least for royalty, is easy to see. For instance, in 1936 there was discovered a full pit with 17,096 specimens of inscribed bone and turtle shell, mostly the latter. Nearly 300 complete turtle shells, dating back to the Wu Ting period (1324–1255 BCE) were found, with a few pieces probably even earlier than this (Tsien 1962: 21). The shells probably came from the south, as they did not occur in their natural state north of the Yangtse, and were presented as tribute to the Shang court by many vassal states and individuals. The most common bone used for divination was not the shell, however, but the scapula of the ox, providing as it does a smooth and wide surface; but also used occasionally were the shoulder blades of water buffaloes, deer, sheep, pigs, and horse. Bones and shells were used for more than one examination.

Not only did the discoveries at Anyang establish the antiquity of divination in China, it also showed its importance, for almost all the inscriptions handed down to us are oracular. Moreover, the inquiries were those made by the royal house, and even though a disproportionate number of them were concerned with hunting, the kingly interest in them attests to the great prestige that the shells and bones enjoyed.

The Sources of Sinitic Civilization

The question to be resolved, however, is not the antiquity of manticism in China but rather the source of Chinese physiognomics. It is impossible to divorce this problem from the broader question of the sources of Sinitic civilization, and so it will be imperative to explore this matter in the light of recent research. Cultural borrowing, however, is always a two-way street and we should be prepared for the possibility that China was as much a donor as a recipient.

Perhaps characteristic of the many prevailing views regarding Western influences in early China are those of Fairservis, who conjectures that about 5000–3000 BCE agriculture was introduced from western Asia (1959: 139). During the period 2000–1600 BCE (pre-Shang) there was, he says, a movement of Western Asian civilizing traits into the Chinese culture sphere: large villages and towns, city states, the divine monarch, human sacrifice, slavery, the idea of writing, improved agricultural methods, carts, scapulimancy, elaboration of the agricultural pantheon, counting, elaborate burial customs, and early bronze manufacture. But, he adds, this stage is thus far indeterminate (*ibid.* 140).

Archaeologists have been even more intrigued over the significance of the next period, the Shang.

The excavations at Anyang proved the existence of the hitherto unauthenticated Shang dynasty, and showed that this was a bronze age civilization. But it did not tell us how the Shang culture developed into what it was when it flourished in the Yellow River area. The fact that the scripts are 1,700 to 1,800 years later than the earliest Sumerian writings does not necessarily prove that Chinese writing began that much later and might therefore have received its inspiration by diffusion from the valley of the Tigris and Euphrates. The Shang writing is highly complicated, with more than 2,000 characters, and is totally unlike the cuneiform scripts in both form and structure. It must have had a long developmental period prior to its first discovered manifestations. Besides, North China in the middle of the second millennium BCE was the only place bordering on the Pacific east of the Ural Mountains and the Indian peninsula that was literate. Li Chi (1957: 17), the discoverer of Anyang, has pointed out these realities, without denying the importance of diffusion in the birth of all great civilizations. "Even the most earnest diffusionist must prove his thesis by gathering evidence in the intervening region between Mesopotamia and the northeastern China plain before any convincing argument can be made to support the idea of complete borrowing" (*idem*).

The antecedents of the Shang culture, then, are difficult to ascertain. Li does point out certain resemblances between the West and Shang. These are limited to a few specific traits, such as a monster decorative pattern with two intertwining bodies, found not only in China but a thousand years earlier in the Middle and Near East; a tiger motif which seems to be a degenerated version of the famous Hero and Beast motif which originated in Mesopotamia and was then transmitted to Egypt, and later immortalized in Mycenaean times by the famous Lion Gate; and, best of all, a distinctive pottery jar cover in the shape of a flower pot with a phallic shaped handle standing upright in the center inside the pot, this being found not only in China but Jamdet Nasr and Mohenjo-daro as well (Li Chi 1957: 28–29).

The real foundation of Shang culture may indeed be in the Near East, for evidences of contact are not lacking, but how strong and influential the West may have been is another matter to be determined by more archaeological research. Perhaps one good illustration of the need to go slow is to be found in the fact that oracular bones, without inscriptions, date back in China to the Neolithic, the Lungshan people being known to have practiced a primitive form of scapulimancy in the lower Huangho, using ox and deer shoulder blades (Cheng 1959: 90).

A writer who has pleaded with great authority for the acceptance of a Lungshanoid origin for the Shang civilization, Chang Kwang-chih (1963: 135–42), says: "The fact the Lungshanoid culture was the forerunner of the Shang civilization is certain" (p. 141). He has marshalled numerous archaeological evidences in support of his claim for continuity between the Neolithic of North China and the Bronze Age. They outnumber and perhaps outweigh the discontinuities.

Much of the argument in favor of the Shang as an intrusion from the West has been based on the apparently sudden appearance of a bronze culture in the lower Yellow River area. Fairservis (1959: 84) thinks that probably it was merely the idea and perhaps some of the techniques of simple bronze manufacture that reached China, possibly from prehistoric Iran or Turkestan, and that the characteristic Chinese forms were derived from wooden prototypes. But Chang (1963: 140-

41) insists that newer research renders likely the possibility that the new bronze technology was independently invented. He lists five cogent reasons for his position, but space precludes repeating them here.

That contact with the lands to the west after the Shang period had already begun, is evidenced in certain bronze weapons and axes peculiar to the Karasuk culture found in Minusinsk in southern Siberia. The Karasuk culture, dated approximately at about 1200–800 BCE, manifests the bag-shaped axe or adze known as the socketed axe, and this was adopted in the earlier Bronze Age of the Shang dynasty. So was the spearhead, with its elegant leaf-shaped blade and tubular socket, on which are set two ring-lugs to help the hafting. Most striking of all are a number of knives excavated at Anyang; their finish and ornament fall out of the context of the Shang bronze tradition and are closer to the more naturalistic art of southern Siberia. Watson (1961: 85–87) feels that these artifacts are significant, and in the instance of the knives, at least, show evidence of a direct contact of the Chinese and the inhabitants of Minusinsk.

Even more striking are the resemblanaces in the forms of artifacts from Europe and China reported by O. Janse and others, and summarized by Needham (1954–: I, 159–63). These artifacts go back to a time even prior to the Shang dynasty and continue well into the Chou. Many of them belong to the European Hallstatt culture (900–500 BCE). Without going into the detailed correspondences we can say that they occur in specific forms of bronze and iron swords, stone hammer-hatchets, cruciform tubes and buttons, the reversed spiral motif of the Yangshao painted pottery, triple-finned arrow heads, zoomorphic pot handles, zoomorphic gold ornaments, scabbard furnishings, chalices, bronze lance points, torques or neck rings, ceremonial adzes, harness buttons, and bronze socketed celts. The areas concerned are the Hallstatt region, south Russia, and China. Ideas and techniques appear simultaneously at opposite ends of the Old World. Using V. Gordon Childe as his authority, Needham says that "The view now generally accepted is that there was continuity of type from the Severn to the Huang-Ho, but that the point of origin was somewhere in between" (p. 161).

Parallels between the ancient East and regions in the west also exist in literature, folklore, and art. Some of these will be briefly described. One is the "uniped," a divine being with a mermaid tail depicted in both Gaul and China. Another is a crane dance which seems to be part of a culture pattern of sacrificial and funerary ritual extending from the Aegean through the Fertile Crescent to China and southeast Asia. Also, from ancient Europe to China there apparently was a kind of ritualistic ploughing. Parallel bull rites and spring rites occurred in ancient Crete and Egypt as well as China. In the field of folk tales many stories and motifs are held in common, with the movement generally conceded to be from China to Europe. Striking mythological and folkloristic parallels also exist between Persian and Chinese narratives, particularly certain epics. In the realm of art, the one outstanding example of a widely dispersed motif is that of the "flying gallop," a position which in point of fact is never taken by horses. This imaginary posture goes back to about 1000 BCE in Mycenaean, Minoan, and Phoenician art and diffused east to Sassanid Persia, Bactria, and China from the second century of the Christian era onwards. Numerous other parallels in art have been established, and so have exchanges in matters of clothing (Needham 1954–: 163–68).

Overland and maritime trade routes from the Mediterranean to China, India, and southeastern Asia are so well documented as to prove beyond cavil that intercourse between West and East is indeed ancient. As far back as more than 2000 BCE the Indus Valley civilizations of Harappa and Mohenjo-daro were in touch with the Sumerian cities of Iraq, although here we do not know the routes taken by travelers.

Aristeas of Proconnesus and later on Herodotus have left us accounts of central Asian tribes and possibly even of the Chinese (their identification as Hyperboreans is not conclusive). In the time of Herodotus (5th century BCE) a trade route existed from the Sea of Azov to Lop Nor, the lake in southeastern Sinkiang. It began at the mouth of the Don and from there extended to the Volga somewhere near modern Kamyshin, then to the vicinity of modern Orenburg on the Ural River, next across the plain of Kazakhstan to near modern Semipalatinsk on the Irtysh River, then to the area around the Zayzan Nor with the main mass of the Altai just to the northeast, and finally to Lop Nor in western China (Hudson 1931: 32–37).

Alexander the Great, as we know, crossed Bactria and Sogdiana in 329 BCE and then turned south into northern India. The Greeks ruled Bactria and Sogdiana for two centuries after the death of Alexander. But an exploratory move came also from China in the east. During the 2nd century BCE a Chinese ambassador who had started out to enlist the aid of the Yüeh-chih, an ancient Indo-European people, against the Huns, reached Bactria and Sogdiana. He knew of the existence of trade routes between Szechuan and India by way of Yunnan and Burma or Assam. He brought back information about Parthia, Seleucid Media and Syria, possibly Egypt, and Babylonia. His mission initiated the development of the silk trade (Hudson 1931: 53–67).

By sea, Greek travelers began to reach Persia in 416 BCE and India in 302 BCE. Movements also went the other way. The records of Greek and Indian contacts are ample, testifying to the good measure of exchange of religious, philosophical, medical, botanical, technological, and artistic elements. Graeco-Roman ships were reaching Indian ports from the 1st century CE to the middle of the 3rd, and eventually some reached what may have been either Honoi or Kwangtung. Chinese long distance navigation began when the Graeco-Egyptian phase of development ended and reached full flower in the 13th century. The Chinese sailed to Penang, Ceylon, Iraq, and Aden. Arab ships began to travel to China and in CE 758 burned and looted Canton. The Arabs set up colonies in various cities of Kwangtung, and enterprising traders extended their voyages even to Korea and Japan. The Chinese replaced Arab navigation in Pacific waters after the end of the 12th century (Hirth and Rockhill 1911: 1–39; Needham 1954–: I, 176–80).

A remarkable account of overseas countries was collected early in the 13th century by Chau Ju-kua, a descendant of the Sung emperor Tai-tsung, and published as a book, *Chu Fan Chih* (Records of Barbarous Peoples). As a superintendent of customs at the port of Ch'üan-chou in Fukien, Chau came into contact with Chinese and foreign traders. While some of his sources are secondary, he relied on direct oral information to describe over half the many places he deals with. These include Ceylon, Malabar, the Somali coast, Egypt, and Sicily. The *Chu Fan Chih*, which has been tranlated by Hirth and Rockhill (1911), is so specific and detailed as to cause us to realize the extent of intercourse there was between China and the outside maritime world.

To return to land, by about 106 BCE the trans-Asian silk trade was well established. Silk was transported along routes that diverged in several places and offered various alternatives. Hudson (1931) provides us with considerable information about the Old Silk Road of classical times. One section of the route went as far west as the Pamirs, another went from the Pamirs to the Merv oasis (Antiocha Margiana) in the Kara-Kum desert, a third from Merv to Seleuceia in modern Iraq, and a fourth from there to the Roman frontier. Though wars and barbarian invasions occasionally interfered with the silk route, and it suffered a great decline in the 11th and 12th centuries, it attained tremendous importance under the Mongols and was a safe and open road over which many merchants traveled. Of it, the Swedish geographer-explorer Sven Hedin, who traversed a 930 mile stretch of the road in 1934–53, has said that it "is the longest, and from a cultural historical standpoint the most significant connecting link between peoples and continents that has ever existed on earth" (Hedin 1938: 228).

The exchange between India and China became marked with the beginning of the great period of Buddhist interchange during the 4th century. Many Chinese, especially, journeyed to India to learn more about the religion founded by Gautama, and these pilgrims left many accounts of their travels, as well as of Buddhist rituals and practices. They continue into the latter part of the 10th century, although the peak of the Chinese-Indian period was reached in the 7th century. Religious and theological notions of course flowed north, but there is some evidence too of an exchange of art, music, mathematics, and scientific ideas, mostly from north to south in this instance.

This lengthy digression into matters of trade, travel, and cultural exchange has been made only in order to emphasize that China was in contact with the rest of the Old World for a considerable length of time starting over four millennia ago. It is not intended to show that China owes its heritage to the West or any other regions of the Eurasian continent. This view is a far cry from the imaginative and impassioned insistence of Terrien de Lacouperie (1894) that, based on what he perceived to be Sino-Elamitic parallels, Chinese civilization originated as the result of an invasion from southwest Asia. It would be equally erroneous, as some have insisted, to think of China's development as being autonomous.

In retrospect, whatever it may have been that moved back and forth from China to the rest of Asia and Europe, there is nothing that can be specifically identified as body divination. All that we have really demonstrated is that channels of communication were ample and old and that much else did diffuse.

If archaeology and documentary sources can shed no direct light on the problem of genetic connections, another approach must be pursued, and this is the comparison of the varying physiognomic traditions themselves. An analysis of the internal aspects of somatomancy ought to be able to disclose enough in the way of resemblances and differences to justify taking some sort of stand on the question of historical relationships. And so, it is to this method that we shall now turn.

Concepts Common to China and the West

In seeking to discover the sources of Chinese and Western body divination it is not very fruitful to compare the extent to which morphological features have been examined in common. Each of the two somatomantic traditions is a full one and has left almost no external part of the body free of exploration. There is nothing remarkable about this, for any determined effort to divine from the body will eventually end up with a full coverage, even though some features will receive much more attention the others, e.g., the eyes as compared with the raphe, or the nose compared with the thorax.

The conceptual or theoretical side of body divination is another matter. Here there is greater chance for unevenness of interest and uniqueness of concept than is the case with physical traits. Any sharing of a common rationale, especially one that is specialized rather than general, should alert us to the possibility of borrowing or development from a common source. And so, it is with basic premises rather than morphology that we shall deal.

The first set of concepts to be examined are those found in China as well as the West. They are five in number: (1) destiny, (2) the macrocosm-microcosm, (3) the doctrine of signatures, (4) harmony and the mean, and (5) theriology.

Destiny

The idea of destiny, while found in Chinese, Arabic, European, and Old World physiognomics, does not have much diagnostic value because it is an idea common to all systems of divination, except where they attempt to read character, or discover the identity of a culprit in a crime, or locate things that are lost or concealed. It would be almost impossible to think of the mantic arts apart from the idea that a state or an end is predetermined. The word "fate" is probably less desirable than destiny because while both mean about the same thing the former has the added implication that an outcome is not only inevitable but usually adverse. However, we may use the two words interchangeably.

Physiognomists must perforce deal with the question of fatalism, determination, and libertarianism. Fatalism maintains that every event is pre-ordained, causes or no causes, and that one cannot act as he wills. Fatalism is thus said to be blind. In China, the Mohists denounced this belief over two millennia ago (Wieger 1927: 210). In Europe fatalism was regarded, by those who opposed it, as a world view whose logical issue has to be pessimism, for fatalism assumes an external power which decrees inexorably every event that ever occurs. The ancient Greeks, as the tragedies of Aeschylus, Sophocles, and Euripedes show, entertained the idea of fatalism. The gods brought on man's disasters, although it is not clear what their motives might be. A parallel concept was that there were three goddesses who controlled the lives of men, one of whom spun the web of life, another who measured its length, and a third who cut it. The Romans had three similar Fates. Germanic myths describe three Norns who spun and wove the web of life. The Chinese did not always anthropomorphize fate, but usually did. For instance, both Confucius and Mencius, especially the latter, regarded Heaven as "a personified predeterminer," showing that "in spite of their this-worldly and rationalistic orientation to many human problems, they never fully abandoned the supernatural anthropomorphic notion of Heaven as the governor of man's fate" (Yang 1961: 249). One commentator on this question drives home his point by reproducing the figures in an ancient bronze in which Heaven is depicted as a person of anthropomorphic shape (Wieger 1927: 49). The tendency for influential philosphers to personalize Heaven brings the Sinitic view closer to the European.

Determinism is linked with the concept of fate but is perhaps softer than fatalism in that it sees relations determined not by an external directing will but within a relation of cause and effect. Determinism says that one can act as one wills, but that one's will is determined in such a way by the interaction of a complex of antecedent causes that one cannot help but choose the right course. It assumes the dependence of all things, including the wills of individuals, upon sequences of cause and effect. Divination may be regarded as an effort to ascertain, in the face of human lack of omniscience, what the sequences will be.

This leads to the problem of free will, for without it physiognomy or any other kind of divination would have no other purpose than to satisfy curiosity regarding future events. It would defeat the main purpose of the mantic arts if no allowance were to be made for human intervention, even though it might be limited in scope. The client who is concerned by something in the future would like to know how to deal with it on the basis of the information which the physiognomist provides for him. He can do so through proper calculation and adjustment. It is therefore not surprising to find that in both China and the West there has been some room for free will, or libertarianism, as it is sometimes called, in which the source of determinism is the self.

Thus, the Chinese attitude toward life was not entirely subordinated to the idea of fate as controlled by supernatural agents. "While relying on the concept of fate to steel themselves in the face of momentous crises or to help them resolve conflict in life situations, the Confucians reserved for man an important role in the shaping of fate" (Yang 1961: 272). Man must exert the utmost of his abilities and must plan things;

however, it is up to fate to decide if this will result in success or failure. It was the Confucian dogma of man as a member of the trinity of the universe, giving him a high position in the cosmic order, which gave rise to the concept that man can share in determining fate through effort and cultivation. The Confucians called this "establishing fate" (*ibid.* 273–74). This is not exactly analogous to the idea of free will because it does not relinquish the role of fate; but it comes close. As we shall see, Western thinkers too made compromises between the idea of fate and free will.

Most Westerners struggling with the doctrine of fate were motivated by a desire to reconcile astrology with religious beliefs. This is a theme that recurs throughout the centuries, although fate and free will could and did appear in the speculations of men not drawn into the controversy through astrology or any other form of divination.

One of the early writers to interest us is Philo Judaeus (c. 20 BCE–CE c. 50), the Alexandrian Jewish philospher whose writings were the first to attempt to reconcile Hellenic philosophy with Biblical religion and to serve as a transition from them to Christian thought. He criticized the Chaldean genethlialogists for their position that fate and necessity are gods. He denied that stars are independent gods or that they are first causes.

Apuleius (fl. 2nd century) declared in his *Apology*, in which he attempted to defend himself against a charge of magic, that belief in fate and magic are in disagreement because if all is governed by fate there is no place left for the force of spells and incantations (Thorndike 1923–58: I, 240). This Platonic philosopher was an initiate into many religious cults and mysteries and had more than a passing interest in the problems under consideration.

The early Christian philosopher, Bardesanes (154?–222?), who some suspect was tainted with Gnosticism, asked in his treatise, *The Hymn of the Soul*, why God did not make men so that they could not sin, and replied that moral freedom for good or evil is a greater gift of God than compulsory morality. Because man enjoys individual freedom of action he is equal to the angels. In his treatise he considers how far man is controlled by fate, by which he means the power of the seven planets in accordance with the doctrine of astrologers. He takes a middle position between those who attack astrology as a lying invention and those who hold that the human will is free and man's unavoidable evils are due to chance or to divine punishment—but not the stars. The fate exerted by the force in the stars does not rule everything, for it is established by the one God who imposed motion upon the stars and elements. This fate is limited both by nature and human free will. But the regular course of nature is often upset by the stars. However, fate in its turn may be counteracted by the exercise of free will (*ibid*. I, 375–76).

The Neo-Plationist philosopher, Plotinus (c. 204–70) of Egypt, who had a strong interest in the stars, criticized the genethliac aspects of astrology; but he acknowledged that each part of the heavens has an effect on terrestrial objects. Nevertheless, he objected to attributing the crimes of men to the will of the stars, or every human act to a starry decision. The force produced by the constellations is not the only one in the universe, which on the contrary is filled with countless different powers. The sequence of events may be varied by chance circumstances, including the dispositions of individual souls. The soul is free of the stars unless it comes under their control by slipping and being stained by the body. Men can look to their inner souls and try to liberate themselves from the sensible world. "Thus Plotinus arrives at practically what was to be the usual Christian position in the middle ages regarding the influence of the stars, maintaining the freedom of the human will and yet allowing a large field to astrological prediction" (*ibid*. I, 306).

Another Neo-Platonist, Porphyry (233–c. 304), who studied philosophy under Plotinus, continues in somewhat the same vein, contending that men who reduce religion to astrology submit everything to fate and assign no freedom to the human soul (*ibid*. I, 315).

By way of final example, the problem of fate and free will, providence and predestination, occupied the attention of Boethius (c. 475–525), the great Roman philosopher and statesman. While imprisoned he wrote a great work, *The Consolation of Philosophy*, which was destined to have much influence on medieval thought. In it he asserted that Providence or the divine mind is the source of all generation, change, and movement, with fate being the regular arrangement inherent in movable objects by which Providence is realized. One way in which fate is exercised is through the celestial motion of the stars, which "constrains human fortunes in an indissoluble chain of causes, which, since it starts from the decree of an immovable Providence, must needs itself also be immutable." But Boethius was not a believer in complete fatalism, saying that there are some things which are under divine providence but not subject to fate. The human will is free to choose its course; divine providence does not impose fatal necessity on the human will. Boethius came to have persisting influence, and during the middle ages his ideas were used by Christians who were disturbed by the Church's antagonism towards genethliacs (*ibid.* I, 619–22).

There is no need to elaborate further on the preccupation with fate and free will that was manifested by Western philosophers, theologians, astrologers, and other diviners. Perhaps, however, the names of a few other men may serve to stress the importance of the problem. These are Origen, Firmicus, Augustine, John of Salisbury, Thomas Aquinas, and the unknown author of the *Speculum Astronomiae*.

Chinese and Western views regarding destiny, then, are fairly similar and are the *sine qua non* of the divinatory arts, whatever form they may take. Because man has an inclination to have hope, he will not ordinarily resign himself to the prospect of unswerving fate and will develop some ameliorating factor, such as free will, to enable him to change things in his favor. A good deal of rationalization of course always enters into these philosophies but this seems unavoidable, unless one is willing to look upon this world as transient and less desirable than that of the afterlife. World rejection of course is characteristic of Indian Buddhism, Taoism, early Judaism, Christianity, and Islam, and there is some indication that where it is strong it tends to discourage divination, but not enough to suppress it entirely.

An inevitable consequence of the belief in fate is the effort by man to ascertain it. Both Sinitic and Western philosophic traditions provided explicitly for man's ability to "know fate," to use the expression employed often by the Chinese. Writing about the religious aspects of Confucianism, one author says: "With belief in the supernatural Heaven and fate came the logical attempt to decipher the secrets of the predetermined course of events in order to help man attain well-being and avoid calamity" (Yang 1961: 250). Confucius made several statements to indicate that he thought that the predetermined course of events was knowable, and the Doctrine of the Mean explicitly asserts this to be so. In this connection, no better testimony to the Chinese conviction that one can know fate could be brought forward than the *I Ching*, but of course this is but one example out of many possible ones, including somatomancy itself. Western affirmations of the ascertainability of fate pursue the same logic as that of the Chinese and are just as numerous, but they will not be reviewed here.

What will concern us, however, is a comparison of the actual rationales used in divination—specifically, body divination.

The Macrocosm-Microcosm

One of the most striking of the premises held in common by both Chinese and Western physiognomists is that man is a microcosm of the universe. The Sinitic version of this doctrine was briefly reviewed in Chapter II but must be examined in more detail because of its close resemblance to the European version. Since the similarity of the doctrines may be conceded, the question that remains is whether this is due to chance or some common heritage from the ancient world, or even borrowing one from the other.

The analogies in both philosophic traditions are broad and are of two kinds: in the first, detailed correspondences are made between the universe or cosmos and the human body; in the second, correspondences are made between the society of the state and the human body. Our emphasis will be on the former, but it cannot escape us that to find the latter in conjunction with it may be more than a strong coincidence.

Not all theories of macrocosms and microcosms are concerned with envisioning man as a "little world" of the "great world," for there are such related views as the atomisms and monadisms, dealing specifically with portions of the universe apart from man (Conger 1922: xiii). Yet, through usage the microcosmic analogy has come to imply the idea of replication in man and it is only in this sense that it will here be employed.

A single example from Chinese writings may perhaps suffice to illustrate some of the tenets of the microcosmic doctrine. During the first Han dynasty or perhaps even earlier there appeared a physiological work, *Su Wen* (素問), compiled by an unknown author, in which the universal macrocosm is described in detail. Between heaven and earth is the median space where communication between the primordial Being and inferior things take place. Two superimposed wheels turn, one above the other in an inverse direction, in this space. This double gyration is regulated by the nine principal constellations and the seven celestial bodies. The upper wheel moves to the left and is that of the celestial Yin-Yang in flux, while the lower wheel moves to the right and has five sectors answering to the five natural agents. Each of the two alternating modalities—activity and passivity, lightness and darkness, masculine and feminine sex, etc.—is subdivided into three parts, with each of the modalities containing the germ of its opposite. Every thirty years the two wheels return to their respective positions at the point of departure and the movement recommences (Wieger 1927: 305–6). Just as the upper wheel, consisting of three Yin and three Yang, acts on the universal macrocosm it also acts on the human microcosm. To its action man presents his five viscera—heart, liver, lungs, spleen, kidneys—by which he participates in the five terrestrial natural agents. The heart, for instance, derives from the fire and presides over the formation of the blood, the circulation, and the animal heat. It answers to the influx heat, the orientation south, and the color red. The liver depends on the vegetal agent and presides over the good condition of the sinews. It answers to the influx wind, the orientation east, and the color blue-green. And so on with the lungs, spleen, and kidneys (*ibid*. 306–7).

In Europe, the first reference to a comparison between man and the universe appears in the writings of Plato, who also made the analogy between the state and the cosmos in his *Republic*. But we owe the term itself to Aristotle, who in his *Physics* refers to the "little world" when imputing motion not only to man but to the great world as well. Some scholars feel that the roots of the idea in Europe go back even further than this to the cosmogonic theory of Anaximenes of Miletus (fl. 545 BCE), as well as to Empedocles' view that in man we see a synthesis of all the elements constituting the universe. Democritus makes specific reference to the notion of the microcosm. The neo-Platonists perpetuated the doctrine. If further names from the ancient Mediterranean world are useful, those of Seneca, Philo Judaeus, Manilius (he assigned parts of the body to regions of the zodiac), and Galen come to mind.

Other writers of the Greek and Graeco-Roman worlds were Vitruvius, Plotinus, Porphyry, Chalcidius, Proclus, Hierocles of Alexandria, Hermes Trismegistos, Melampus, Macrobius, and Servius (cf. Conger 1922: 20–26).

During the reign of Constantine and his sons, Julius Firmicus Maternus of Sicily wrote *Mathesis*, a work of astrology, while he was still a pagan, and in it he spoke of one supreme god who made man, the microcosm, from the four elements (Thorndike 1923–58: I, 530).

Microcosmic theories found a place in Christian, Jewish, and Arabic theological traditions.

They appear, for instance, in the writings of the Church Fathers, without however occupying a prominent place, and sometimes only in order to be refuted. Clement of Alexandria wrote of man being a little universe, but for a century or two after his time the Church Fathers opposed microcosmic theories. However, as the Church gained strength there was not only less fear of microcosmic doctrines but even a tendency to incorporate them into the Christian system (Conger 1922: 29–36).

In the early middle ages Isidore, bishop of Seville (CE 560 or 570–636), described man as a microcosm (Thorndike 1923–58: I, 633), and subsequent patristic literature refers to the doctrine. Bernard Silvester wrote *Megacosmos et Microcosmos* (sometimes called *De Mundi Universitate*) during 1145–53, and his book had a considerable attraction for Saint Hildegard (d. 1179). Bernard may have received his inspiration from some Islamic epistles written in Iraq.

Later, both within Church circles and outside of them we meet with such names as those of Robert Grosseteste (c. 1175–1253), Albertus Magnus (1193–1280), and Nicolas Oresme (d. 1382) (*ibid.* II, 446, 577; III, 436).

In the 16th century the names come swiftly. Aside from Paracelsus (d. 1541), there must be included Leonardo da Vinci, Pompanazzi, Agrippa, and many lesser figures.

In the 17th century two names stand out prominently—those of Robert Fludd or Fluctibus (1574–1637) and Jacob Boehme (1575–1624), both of them mystics. Fludd published a two-volume work on the universe analogy called *Utriusque cosmi maioris scilicet et minoris metaphysica atque technica historia*. The second of the two volumes was never finished and is entitled "Microcosmi Historia," published in 1619. Figure 31 is one aspect of the universe analogy, and is taken from this work. Fludd took explicit interest in body divination (*ibid.* VII, 440). As for Boehme, a Protestant mystic, he represented man as fundamentally akin to the universe, which itself typifies the persons of the Trinity, and so gave man a basis for his reconciliation and mystical union with God (Conger 1922: 64).

Medieval Jewish philosophers were even more concerned with microcosmic theory than were Christian writers, and they made more extensive comparisons between the world and man. Their views more closely resembled Arabian theories than did the Christian ones (Conger 1922: 37–46).

The Arabs, of course, were just as much the recipients of the ancient Greek tradition of philosophy as were the early Christian writers. This tradition had come to them by way of Byzantium and became established when Islam was ascendant. The Arabs modified the Greek conceptions and gave particular prominence to the theory of man as a microcosm. Later, of course, the modified Greek ideas returned to the West. Most of the responsibility for the changes may be assigned to a religious sect formed at Basra (in Iraq) about 950 known as the Brethren of Sincerity. The Brethren assembled an *Encyclopaedia* made up of fifty-one treatises designed as a sort of supplement to the Koran. Much of this compendium, especially two of the treatises, is dominated by microcosmic theory. The parallelisms between man and the universe are worked out in great detail (Conger 1922: 46–50).

The relevance of all this to East-West connections is that when one grapples with the problem of the possible influence of Jewish and Arabian thought on Christian microcosmic theories, the question of a common derivation among these three must inevitably be raised. The answer suggested by one writer is applicable to the Chinese question. He thinks that while the Jewish, Arabian, and Christian traditions did not

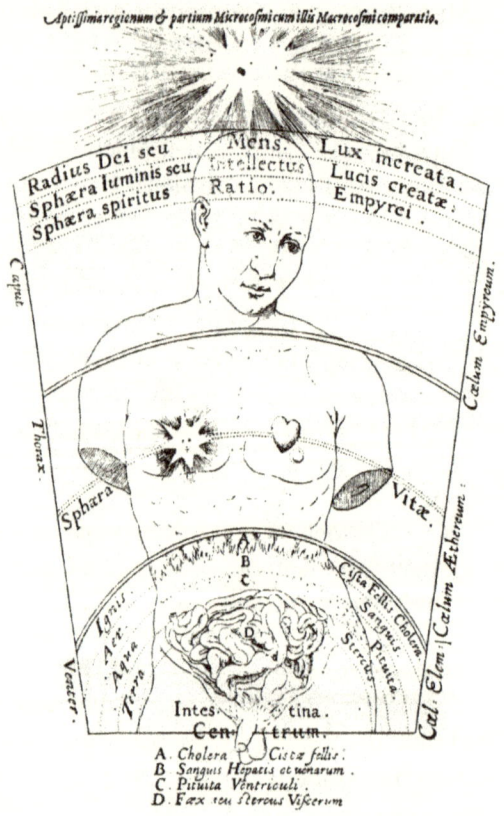

FIG. 31 A Western view of man as the microcosm. The cranium, thorx and belly are the seats of various qualities and are in turn associated with features of the universe. (From *Fludd, Utriusque cosmi historia,* 1617-21.)

develop in utter isolation, the similarities are most likely due to a common dependence upon philosophies older than any of them (Conger 1922: 36). There are scholars such as Berthelot (1885: 51) and von Lippmann (1919: 196, 666) who feel justified in saying that the macrocosm-microcosm theory originated in Babylonia, and if this is so it would not be too far amiss to look to that ancient land for the origins of the Sinitic version.

Setting aside the Babylonian hypothesis for the moment, it is advisable to examine Chinese parallels to the European universe analogy. For such resemblances we are indebted to Needham (1956–: II, 299–301), who points out that early writings on the subject of the macrocosm-microcosm were not very common in early Chinese writings because the analogy was so implicit in the whole world view of the Chinese; yet about 120 BCE a very explicit statement does appear, soon followed by others. The *Li Chi* and the *I Ching* also express the analogy, and there is continuous use of the idea for many centuries. Shao Yung (1011–77) almost parallels the Arabic Brethren of Sincerity in his physiological-geological comparisons.

The Chinese state-analogy, too, is similar in view to that of Plato and John of Salisbury.

A less explicit resemblance in the universe analogy of both China and the West is manifested in the correlative thinking employed in each place. Needham (*ibid.* 296–97) has pointed out that the correlative tabulations compiled by Agrippa of Nettesheim (1486–1535), Bruno (1548–1600), and Patritius (fl. 1593) are much like Chinese forms. Not only does he think that the European tabulations were largely Arabic and Jewish, he suggests that perhaps some inspiration came from the 3rd century BCE Chinese school of naturalists by way of India or over the Silk Road to Byzantium, Syria, and other parts of the Near East.

Yet Needham does not think that the Chinese universe analogy is philosophically similar to the form it took in Europe. He maintains that Europeans could only think in terms of either Democritean mechanical materialism or of Platonic theological spiritualism; a *deus* had to be found for a *machina*. When the living animal organism was projected on to the universe, Europeans were always impelled to find the "guiding principle" because they were dominated by the idea of a personal God or gods. In contrast, the Chinese never took this path, expressly avoiding the idea of any *spiritus rector*. To them, the observed phenomena could be accounted for well enough by the parts, in their organizational relations, whether of a living body or of the universe (*ibid.* 301–3).

Chinese microcosmic theory differs considerably from that of the West in another major respect. The macrocosm-microcosm analogy has a tendency to lead to divination, as it certainly did in opposite sides of the Eurasian continent. But only in the West did this notion establish a link with astrology. In the Greek and Graeco-Roman world, the earth as well as all things and living creatures could be assigned to either the various planets or to the signs of the zodiac—or both. As a microcosm, man is a replication of the divisions made of the world. Therefore, there is astral influence in his morphology and psychic powers (Bouché-Leclerq 1899: 83, 311–18).

Returning to the question of Babylonia as the common source of all universe analogies, nothing conclusive can be settled upon. However, it is interesting that Needham (1954–: II, 301) is intrigued by a suggestion from a French writer (Berthelot) to the effect that the whole conception of a macrocosm-microcosm may have been derived from the methods of divination used in high antiquity, wherein sacrificial animals were used to foretell the future. In one variant of the practice, the animal or its parts are divided into spaces and used as a microcosm of the expanse of the heavens; the divination depends on the appearance of "signs" in one spatial division or other. He notes that the Babylonians, Shang Chinese, Etruscans, and Romans all practiced animals sacrifice. However, he does not assign priority to one people or another. If we bear in mind the antiquity of Babylonian civilization as compared to that of other places involved, it would seem to be implied that in point of time, at least, it may have priority. This does not settle the question of genetic relationships but it would be at least one point in favor of Mesopotamia in any argument regarding sources.

If all these traditions, which certainly manifest a good deal in common, do have a common origin, such as in Mesopotamia, they diverged to a large extent in the course of time, especially when China is compared with the Mediterranean and Atlantic regions. Despite such differences, the fundamental principle is remarkably the same in East and West. Writing on this matter, Needham says: "If anything in Europe was analogous to ancient and medieval Chinese thinking in terms of cosmic pattern or organism, it was this doctrine..." (*ibid*. 294). Of this there can be little doubt.

The Doctrines of Signatures

An interesting corollary of the universe analogy is the premise that man contains in his physiognomy the signs of the external world which betray his inner character and destiny. In Europe, this began as an aspect of the Paracelsan "doctrine of signatures" in plants, according to which plants indicated by their external appearance the diseases for which they were remedies.

The doctrine soon went beyond this and became the physiognomy of all things. In 1584 Gerald Dorn, a Paracelsan, recognized four species of signatures, among them being physiognomy and chiromancy (Thorndike 1923–58: v, 635). Another Paracelsan, Oswald Croll, said that a doctor should be acquainted with chiromancy, for the lines of the hand indicate cures suited to that individual (*ibid.* 651). In 1676 Helvetius (Jan Frederik Schweizer), physician to the Prince of Orange, wrote a book in which among other things he expounded on the thesis that the features of one's physiognomy are signatures of other things (*ibid.* 470). But even before that the French philosopher Jean Belot had said: "It is a certain thing that every human being when he is born has in some part of the body the mark of the sign or planet that governed at the hour and the instant of his conception and nativity, which marks are to be found in the parts of the body which are referred to those signs and planets..." (Belot 1654: 219). Belot was arguing particularly about the moles of the body, which have a bearing on the individual's relationship to the universe.

Chinese physiognomics implicitly and explicitly affirm that the body contains signs of the universe external to it. However, this does not take exactly the form of the doctrine of signatures as originally conceived of in European medical circles and then extended to include more than plants. The idea of signs is most likely not an idea that one tradition borrowed from another but is probably an inevitable outgrowth of the macrocosm-microcosm principle, once it is accepted.

Harmony and the Mean

Turning now to parallels with the Chinese doctrines of harmony and the mean, there are obvious counterparts in Western philosophy and specific applications in Western physiognomy.

The Belgian statistician and astronomer, L. A. J. Quetelet (1796–1874) made explicit what physiognomists in Europe had been contending for some time when he formulated the theory of the "average man." The basic tenet of the *homme moyen* doctrine is that the ideal mental-moral-aesthetic man is what he is because he embodies the least deviation from the average of the population. When a person varies from this average he is inferior in mentality, morality, and appearance, in proportion to his deviation (Quetelet 1835).

The average man doctrine finds expression in old and to some extent contemporary medical belief that ugliness is somehow a manifestation of constitutional inferiority. Thus the physician-biotypologist, George Draper, says in his book, *Disease and the Man* (1930: 59) that there is an ancient German medical adage to the effect that ugliness indicates a poor prognosis. He adds that in patients in a hospital ward "the average standard of beauty in the ordinarily accepted sense is surprisingly low," and interprets this as follows: "It is as though ugliness, being an expression of bad modelling in respect of features and body proportions, expressed in the morphological panel a sort of genetic bungling." By this he means that the organism seems to be badly designed and that illness is final evidence of the unsuccessful adaptation to the environment. The same idea is expressed in the writings of other biotypologists, such as Viola and Montessori, and is explicit in the writings of many physiognomists, some of whom repeat the allegation that during the Middle Ages there was a judicial precept to the effect that if, of two men brought to trial for the same crime, it should be impossible to prove which of the two was guilty, then the uglier of the two was to be hanged (cf. Ellis 1890: 87).

Approaching the ideal not from the point of view of beauty but of constitution, Galen had long ago said in his *Hygiene* that if the exact means of all the extremes were in all parts of the body, this would be the best to observe as being the symmetry most suitable for all activities (Galenus 1951: 20–21).

The Arabic physiognomist, Fakhr al-Din al-Razi says enough in his *Kitab al-Firasa*, written in 1209, to show that the Arabs held views similar to those under discussion. Here again we return to the aesthetic ideal: "The perfection of the body depends on its beauty, just as imperfection is due to ugliness, and the seat of both beauty and ugliness is in the face" (Mourad 1939: 115).

The idea of the mean is of course typically associated with the name of Aristotle, who emphasized to the traditional Greek notion that virtue is the mean between two extremes.

This is essentially what the translation of the title of the Chinese essay, *Chung Yung*, impiles, for *chung* is "centrality" and *yung* is "normality," suggesting the fundamental moral idea of moderation, balance, and suitableness. Before the time of Aristotle, Confucius had spoken of a Mean and described the superior man in these terms. There is some disagreement as to exactly how the expression *chung yung* was used by him. One writer suggests that if he indeed did use the word he meant it like the Middle Way of early Buddhism, which was then being worked out in India, "and if we sense his meaning aright, he was well touching upon a theme which the Greeks, in the person of Aristotle, far 'across the roof of the world,' were soon to place at the center of their ethics" (Noss 1956: 360).

Without implying that Aristotle derives his idea of the mean from Chinese sources, Fung (1937: 371–72) points out a certain resemblance, namely, between what the *Chung Yung* calls a "timely" mean in human affairs and what Aristotle would call "relative" and not absolute. Aristotle's mean is one that serves as a guide for human emotions and actions, and is different according to the time, place. and persons involved, so that there can be no fixed rules that will always serve as a mean. The *Chung Yung* speaks of a timely mean, says Fung, of exactly the same sort. In pointing out this resemblance, Fung does not help us resolve the question of affinities. Elsewhere he has said that the Chinese doctrine differs from that of Aristotle only in its religious import (Fung 1934: 172–73).

E. R. and K. Hughes (1950: 56) express themselves more strongly about this difference when they say that the Way of the Common Mean-in-Action is not equatable with the Western ethical philosophy term, "the doctrine of the mean," because the latter has no great inspirational force to it.

Theriology

Turning our attention now to the theriological premise, whereby men are analyzed in terms of their morphological resemblances to animals, it would seem at first sight that here there is a firm connection between Sinitic and Western physiognomics; but while the principle is undoubtedly the same, one wonders what the Chinese were actually thinking of in applying this principle to the classification of human beings. For neither the descriptions nor the drawings of features which are associated in appearance with this or that animal species seem to bear much resemblance to these particular animals. The animal labels given to a morphological feature seem to be more symbolic than actually suggestive. Admittedly, analogies made between men and mythical animals, such as the dragon, unicorn, and phoenix, are purely arbitrary. On the other hand, analogies with real animals ought to have some morphological validity, which they seldom do.

In contrast to this, the animal analogies made by Westerners, from Polemon, Adamantius, and the Pseudo-Aristotle to Giambatista della Porta and Samuel Fuchsius, have at least a modicum of credibility, even though requiring some stretch of the imagination by both artist and reader. Figures 32 and 33 from a famous Renaissance work illustrate how a certain skill in caricature can go a long way.

Not surprisingly, for they were influenced by the early Greeks, the Arabs too have pursued the doctrine of human-animal resemblances. Mourad (1939: 11) says that when this was done the symbolic correspondences with animals and their moral attributes was not a random one. Certain animals have certain qualities, virtues, and vices. In Egyptian, Indian, and Greek mythological symbols, fish represent man's desires, insects his life of activity and productivity, and reptiles his unscrupulousness and capacity for deceit. In the medieval bestiaries and volucrairies, and in collections of fables, a distinction was made between beasts and birds, the beasts representing the passions of the flesh, while the birds represent those of the spirit.

As an aside, the human constitutionalist, William H. Sheldon, in one of his later works, *Atlas of Men* (1954), used animal names to label his 43 somatotype subsections, some of these being: walking stick, wasp, flycatcher, little falcon, big falcon, great owl, eagle, stingless mosquito, heron, little cat, great cat, supercat, sandpiper, rabbit, airedale, horse, bull, kiwi, anteater, ox, seal, porpoise, walrus, and hippopotamus. Here, in a serious investigation of body types and their relationship to temperament, delinquency, and other expressions of constitution, we find a persistence of theriologic names and more than a mere system of nomenclature.

The only conclusion that can be drawn from examining theriologic counterparts in China and Europe is that if the premise has a genetic connection it must be an ancient one, for in each region it diverged along differing lines and came to bear not much more than a superficial resemblance.

Some hints of theriology are alleged to be found in the *Kama Sutra* of Vatsyayana, a shadowy figure who lived between the 1st and 6th centuries of the present era. This Indian writer, who limits his comments to the sexual organs alone, says: "Men are classed according to the size of the lingam: hares, bulls, stallions. Women are classed according to the size of the yoni: gazelles, mares, elephants" (Vatsyayana 1885: 27). This is hardly a convincing passage, however.

Genetic Connections

FIG. 32 Western theriology: the ovine man. Various sheep-like features reveal various sheep-like qualities. (From Porta, *De humana physiognomonia*, 1601.)

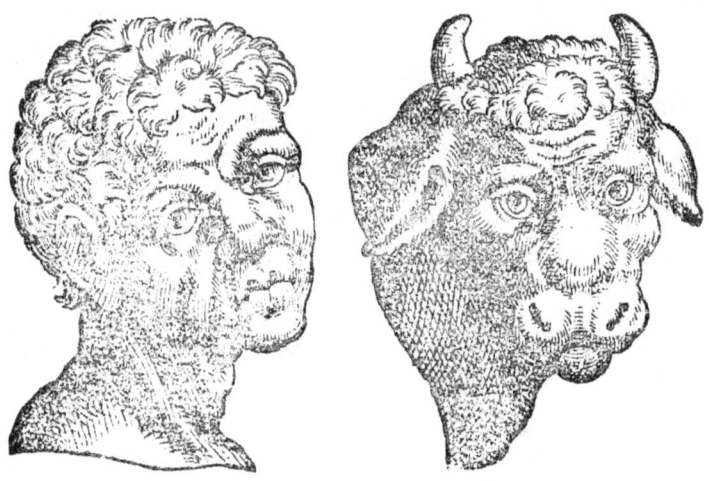

FIG. 33 Western theriology: the bovine man. Various cattle-like features reveal various cattle-like qualities. (From Porta, *De humana physiognomonia*, 1601.)

It is a different story, however, with certain Mesopotamian materials, but before turning to them it is necessary to clarify some misconceptions. Some writers seem to have confused teratology—the study of congenital malformations, monstrosities, or serious deviations from the normal type of organisms—with animal resemblances among normal human beings. For instance, Boissier (1911: 39 n. 1) and Conteneau (1938: 133) after him cite an example of incipient theriology occurring in *Cuneiform Texts from Babylonian Tablets, &c., in the British Museum* (Part XXVIII, 1910). They refer specifically to Plate 29 in that publication, reproduced here as Figure 34, in which reference is made to a baby born with the "eye of a lion."

No need to single out a single instance, however. Cuneiform inscriptions, including those from the British Museum as well as elsewhere, are filled with references to babies born with some animal feature or other, but these tablets also contain omens derived from the birth of sheep, cows, dogs, pigs, goats, and other animals. Some of the omens connected with humans refer to children born with six toes, or with the eye of a lion, a serpent, a demon, and so on. One of the tablets enumerates various omens to be derived from the condition or absence of different organs in a new-born child. As E. A. Wallis Budge writers in his introduction to the above-mentioned *Cuneiform Texts*, the tablets "include portents taken from the phenomena of animal as well as of human parturition; and the extraordinary character of many of the composite offspring described can only be explained as referring to events which might take place in dreams" (p. 3). Thus, these signs are not truly physiognomic, for they refer to omens affecting the king and the state rather than to signs of personal destiny or inner character.

Nevertheless, the birth omens do contain obvious seeds of theriologic physiognomy, and an authority in this field states explicitly that Greek and Roman physiognomics "is to be carried directly back to the birth-omens of Babylonia and Syria" (Jastrow 1914: 50). Such omens go back to c. 1600 BCE and are based on older oral tradition (Leichty 1966: 131–32).

If one includes motions and gestures, as many ancient and modern writers, Chinese included, are wont to do, the examples could be greatly expanded, for the omen lists show resemblances to many kinds of animals, with predictions concerning personal happenings, danger, death, success in ventures, and so on (Conteneau 1940: 207).

But there is no need to rely on either birth-omens or motions and gestures, for there are abundant examples of straightforward animal

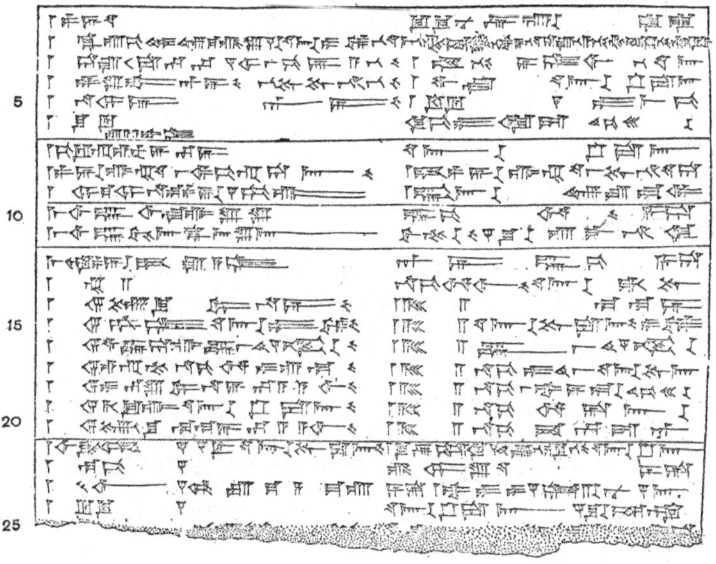

FIG. 34 A Babylonian birth omen tablet. The beginnings of theriologic physiognomy may be traced back to teratological birth omens. (From *Cuneiform Texts from Babylonian Tablets, &c., in the British Museum*, 1910.)

comparisons of the standard sort in Babylonian tablets. They are recorded in the publications of Kraus (1935, 1939, 1947). Here are some examples from his monograph, *Die physiognomischen Omina der Babylonier* (1935): "If he has a bull's neck, he will have great joy" (p. 61). "If he has lion-hands he will become rich, he will win trust. (That means) his hands are very muscular" (p. 63). "If he has duck-feet he will become powerful. (That means) his feet are broad and are covered with earth" (p. 63).

From all this we may assume that Mesopotamia was the source of all theriologic physiognomics in the Old World.

Chapter VII

EAST-WEST DIFFERENCES

Whereas in the preceding chapter the stress has been on the similarities to be observed between the somatomancy of the Western cultures and that of China, the present emphasis is on the differences in these traditions. By making a contrast of this sort it will be possible to make inferences regarding the extent to which genetic connections are validly supported by the evidence.

Chinese Concepts Absent in the West

This section, taking up the Chinese concepts which appear to be absent in the West, will perforce be short, for where these rationales do exist (China) they have already been discussed in detail, and where they do not exist (the West) there is little that one can say beyond denying that there are parallels in logic between the two.

The concepts limited to China are: (1) Five Elements, (2) Yin-Yang, (3) the trigrams, (4) *chi* and *li*, and (5) the Heaven-Man-Earth triad.

The first guiding principle in Chinese somatomantic interpretations is the Sinitic concept of the Five Elements and their use in deciphering the predetermined course of Heaven. Combined with the Yin-Yang premise, the idea of elements formulated "a frame of reference for interpreting the operation of the supernatural forces in the sky, the rise and fall of a dynasty, life and death, health and sickness, poverty and prosperity, divination, palmistry and physiognomy, astrology, chronomancy, and geomancy" (Yang 1961: 252). By consulting omens and this frame of reference, one could give supernatural explanations not only for natural phenomena in the universe but intimate events in the life of the individual as well. Heaven and fate, through this theory, became concrete expressions that men could grasp.

Let us see if the Chinese concept of the elements can be used to advance the theory of a connection with the West. The Greek theory of the elements of course comes immediately to mind. Needham (1954–: II, 245–46) has made a comparison of the two. The original number of elements recognized by the Greeks seems to have been three. Later, Anaximander (c. 560 BCE) distinguished the usual four—earth,

East-West Differences

fire, air, water—as well as a fifth, the *apeirom*, or non-limited. This fifth element does not have any parallel to the Chinese conceptions. Needham (*ibid.* 244) thinks, in fact, that the elements of the Chinese and those of the Greeks are not the same thing. He thinks that *hsing* should not properly be translated "element" because the five-element theory, so called, is really an effort to reach a provisional classification of the basic properties of material things. These properties would only be manifested when undergoing change.

However, he concedes that it is in this very idea of action and change that the Greeks sporadically showed some resemblance in their theory to that of the Chinese. For instance, Pherecydes of Syros (c. 550 BCE) claimed, in a manner reminiscent of the theory of the mutual conquest as formulated by the Chinese Naturalists, that the elements warred with each other. In the hands of Aristotle, earth, fire, air, and water became qualities: the dry, the hot, the cold, and the moist. These elements were capable of changing one into the other, and constantly did so. Another parallel is in the association made by Pherecydes and Empedocles of each element with a god. The Chinese similarly associated supernatural beings with each element. Nevertheless, we must conclude with Needham when he says: "In general one may say that while there are certain similarities between the Greek and Chinese theories of the elements, the divergences are still more striking, and it seems unnecessary to assume any transmission" (1954–: II, 245–46).

He is likewise skeptical of Chavannes' hypothesis that the Chinese derived their elements from neighboring Turkic or Hunnish people about the middle of the first millennium BCE. In examining this proposal (*ibid.* 246) he finds it relies a good deal on a passage in the *Shih Chi* or Book of Records, which does not even mention elements. He thinks it is just as plausible to picture the general cosmic system of fives as going from the eastern coastal states of Ch'i and Yen westward to the backward state of Ch'in.

Any intimation of foreign influence in the Chinese concept of the Five Elements is likewise rejected by the sinologist, Arthur Waley (1934: 109–10), who sees no similarity in the meanings of the Greek and Chinese words for element. The Greek word for element literally means "steps," while the Chinese *hsing* means "to walk," "to go," "to set in motion," to operation," "conduct"—never "a step."

If another authority may be cited to discount any suggestion that the theory of the Five Elements is of anything but Chinese origin, the views of Alfred Forke are cogent. He goes into the Turkic theory in more detail than does Needham, repeating some earlier statements on the subject by de Saussure; but he adds an elaboration of his own to the effect that it would be unlikely that the Turkish tribes in the 4th or 5th centuries BCE (when Chavannes alleges that they gave China the theory) were sufficiently developed culturally to be able to teach the Chinese much (Forke 1925: 242–44).

The ancient Sinitic concept of the Yin and Yang, to which we now direct our attention, has no European equivalent. This concept, described earlier in the chapter on the logic of interpretation used by Chinese physiognomists, envisions two interacting energy-modes which produce everything in existence; things in the physical world are differentiated not by matter but by the way they act. The origin of objects is to be attributed to mutations out of preceding states of existence. Nothing in Western somatomancy bears any evidence of a principle similar to this. Indeed, the concept is foreign to Western thought.

It may not even be equated with Zoroastrian dualism, let alone derived from it. In comparing the Chinese with the Iranian concepts, Waley (1934: 112) goes straight to the heart of the matter when he reminds us that whereas the Yin and the Yang are two complementary facets of existence, the light and the darkness of Zoroastrianism represent good and evil, respectively, and they are in eternal conflict. He concludes that "it is very difficult indeed to imagine that even the most confused and distorted account of Persian religion could have given rise to the *Yin-Yang* system as we know it in China." To this Needham (1954–: I, 154 n. b.) adds that the dualism of Manichaeism was even stronger than that of Zoroastrianism, from which it was derived, and was just as foreign to China as to Christendom, both of which opposed it.

Forke (1925: 221) compares the Yin and Yang not to two enemy powers but to "a married couple which generate all living things." This author also considers the great similarity between the Yin-Yang doctrine and the physical view of Anaxagoras, who saw two masses separating out from chaos: the thick and the thin, the cold and the warm, the dark and the bright, the moist and the dry (all fundamental attributes of the Yin and the Yang); but whereas the Chinese see these two substances as fire and water, Anaxagoras sees them as ether and air. Forke also sees analogies with the primogenial elements of Parmenides; but he finds a much less close relationship with Pythagorism, despite some remarkable agreements, saying that Pythagorism is in its essence entirely different from the Chinese doctrine (*ibid*. 221–23).

The Sinitic trigrams can be dismissed more summarily than the Five Elements or the Yin-Yang; they have no applicability to Western body divination. The trigrams are of course an aspect of the general Chinese view that all the world is in a state of interaction, and philosophers worked the concept of the Five Elements and Yin-Yang into the diagrams so as to express their general view of the universe as a system of flux. During the Ch'in or the Han a comprehensive system of cosmology emerged from this combination of concepts, with the first two of the Eight Diagrams being equated with the Yin and the Yang. Western cosmology neither gave nor received this concept. It has no parallel.

The Sinitic concepts of *ch'i* and *li* likewise are not found in Western physiognomy. The notion of *ch'i* goes back at least to Mencius, who believed that within each person there is present a vast-flowing vital energy, a sort of élan vital. The Neo-Confucianists took this concept and extended it to say that when *ch'i* interacts with *li*, the rational principle, then the Yin and Yang energy-modes are produced, and from the interaction of the latter the Five Elements are produced in turn. Admitting that Western physiognomy embraces no such doctrine as the *ch'i*, does this mean that the concept is foreign to the philosophy of the West? The answer is that despite the resemblance of *ch'i* to the Greek *pneuma*, these two are not the same. This is the conclusion that Needham came to after contending with the question: "I need not again insist on the untranslatability of this word, which has connotations similar to the Greek *pneuma*, and to our conceptions of a vapour or gas, but which also has something of radiant energy about it like a radioactive emanation" (1954–: II, 369 n. d.). As for the inseparable concept of *li*, it seems to have no specific parallel in the philosophy of Western scholars.

The Heaven-earth-man triad developed by the Han philosophers and incorporated to some extent into Sinitic physiognomy also has no firm parallel in Western body divination, unless we see it as a variant of the macrocosm-microcosm theory. The closest approximation to the triad of which I am aware appears in the previously cited work, *Utriusque cosmi* (1617–21), by the English mystic theosophist, Robert Fludd, who constructed a cosmology on the premise that God is the fountainhead, the end, the sum of all things. There are three worlds: the archetypal world, the macrocosm, and the microcosm, or God, earth, and man. Man's head is the equivalent of the angelic sphere, his breast of the ethereal sphere, and his belly of the elementary sphere occupied by the earth and planets. Fludd was an explicit advocate of the microcosmic theory, but his triad seems to have had no influence from or upon Chinese philosophy.

Western Concepts Absent in China

Certain concepts present in Western body divination fail to appear in its Sinitic counterpart and provide further reason to doubt that the two traditions are simple outright borrowings from either a common source or from one another. These are (1) astrology, (2) the humors, and (3) phrenology.

Certainly the outstanding difference between Chinese and Western physiognomics is in the great use made of astrology by the latter. In contrast, the Chinese version of somatomancy is not truly astrological at all, for while the Chinese have had a long tradition of adherence to astrology they have never felt impelled to combine it with the physical features of human beings.

Before proceding further, it will be profitable to make some terminological and conceptual clarifications. "Natural" astrology is what is nowadays referred to as "astronomy"; it is not truly divinatory even though it may predict movements of planets and stars. With this we shall not be much concerned.

Contrasted to this is divinatory astrology, and while this is generally referred to in the literature simply as "judicial" astrology it seems advisable to follow the terminology used by Neugebauer (1945: 14), who reserves the term for its public uses. In judicial astrology, he say, "celestial phenomena are used to predict the imminent future of the country or its government, particularly the king," from halos of the moon, eclipses, the approach or invisibility of planets, and so on. Contrasted to this is "genethlialogical"—or, as it is more commonly called, "genethliacal"—astrology, which "consists in the prediction of the fate of a person determined by the constellation of the planets, the sun, and the moon at the moment of his birth." Neugebauer is right in pointing out that genethliacal astrology is comparatively late and is preceded by the more generalized judicial form.

The Chinese, although they received the idea of astrology from the West, were more independent in the course they took with respect to the observation of the stars than they were in their interpretations. Their judicial astrology has a striking similarity to that recorded in cuneiform tablets (see Needham 1954–: II, 351–54), but there is much difference in what it was in the heavens that was being observed. These differences may be briefly reviewed to show that it was here rather than in prognostication that the Chinese showed independence of mind.

From the beginning the Chinese did not share in the Babylonian interest in the heliacal risings and settings of the stars; instead, they paid attention to the circumpolar constellations which never rise and set. Their defining stars were mostly equatorial, not ecliptic. They were divided into twenty-eight radiating divisions separated by hour-circles. Such hour-angle segments did not form a zodiac, for the moon and the sun did not move among the defining stars. Prognostication was therefore little dependent on what star or constellation was in the ascendant at the particular time relating to the terrestrial events in question. Furthermore, many of the constellations known to the Babylonians were not recognized as such by the Chinese, while on the other hand many groups of fixed stars recognized by the Chinese were not differentiated by either the Babylonians or the Greeks (Needham 1954–: II, 351). These are major differences in method, and they are enough to suggest why the pseudo-science of astrology may be said to have been sufficiently different in China and the West as to deny any more than what anthropologists call "stimulus diffusion"—a process in which the idea of a cultural invention is received by one people from another but given a new form.

Less different than the form and method of astrology was the use to which it was put. Let us examine this aspect of its development.

Genethliacal astrology was relatively late in coming to China. It began to make its appearance in the first century of the present era—during the Han dynasty, seven centuries after the first documented appearance of physiognomy itself.

The transition from judicial to genethliacal or horoscopic astrology had already been made in Babylonia, but not a good deal earlier. An authority (Eisler) is cited by Needham (1954–: II, 351–53) to the effect that we do not have horoscopes for individuals in Mesopotamia, which was Hellenized at the time, until the years 176 BCE and 169 BCE. This may be a century too late, for Neugebauer (1945: 16 fn. 61) mentions seven horoscopes as being preserved from Mesopotamia, all of which were written in the Seleucid period and four of which are dated as 233 BCE, 235 BCE, 258 BCE, and 263 BCE, respectively, making the last one the oldest horoscope in the world. But seven horoscopes are not many.

Evidence that astrology during the Chinese Han was not directed toward the individual but was used for political purposes has been accumulated by Eberhard (1957), who says that this was based on the Chinese assumption that portents of nature indicated that the normal harmony between celestial and terrestrial actions had been disturbed by human beings; indeed, the portents served as a warning of Heaven that something was amiss in the administration of government. Specifically, the assumption was made that the emperor was personally responsible for the calamities of nature. So astronomy was political in function; it was used as a tool by Chinese scientists interested in antidynastic and revolutionary movements against the government. Astronomers, astrologists, and meteorologists were motivated more by an interest in politics than science. The members of the Han bureaucracy exercised an institutional right to criticize the ruler, and they did this by blaming him for a calamity or portent, and in this way induced him to change his attitude. They did not hesitate to fabricate portents for this purpose.

In the light of these findings, we are perhaps justified in concluding that the Western mating of astrology with physiognomy did not diffuse to China, whose own astrology seems to have come from Mesopotamia or elsewhere in the Hellenic world, but with its specific techniques or its genethliacal character. The Chinese appear never to have thought on their own of applying astrology to the human body. And so it has remained. Any use of horoscopic astrology at the present time would appear to be a very recent and deliberate borrowing from the West.

What can we say of astrology throughout European history and of its specific connection with physiognomy?

European astrology is of course a direct outgrowth of Babylonian and Assyrian astrology, which was itself a formalization of the ancient belief that human life and destiny lie in the power of celestial influence. During the middle of the first millennium BCE astrology spread westward to the Greeks and Egyptians and then to the Romans. At that time the distinction had not yet been made between natural astrology, which was the crude astronomy of those times, and judicial and horoscopic astrology, which sought to understand the effects of the stars on human destiny.

When astrology came to be incorporated into Christian theology it had already undergone important changes at the hands of the Greeks and Egyptians. In the divinatory sphere the Greeks had made provision for the individual's interests and not the general public's alone, and the Arabs and Kabbalists accepted and preserved what the Greeks passed on the them. It is even possible that horoscopic astrology was developed by the Greeks and introduced to Mesopotamia during the Hellenic period (Neugebauer 1945: 15).

Why did the early Church accept astrology? Because even though it came from the pagan realm it gave expression to certain views of the world which it favored. In astrology the Empedoclean doctrine of the four elements, as well as Aristotle's theory of the *quinta essentia* again asserted itself. The Stoics founded their physics on the Empedoclean-Aristotelian theory (although they were hesitant about the fifth essence), and on this they based their religion. Almost from the start Christian circles had found the Stoic hypothesis much to their liking, preferring it to the rival atomic concept invented by Leucippus and Democritus and embraced by the Epicureans. The Epicurean doctrine lacked the mystical appeal so urgently demanded in theology by the emotions. Moreover, Christianity favored the moral creed of the Stoics, going so far as to question whether the Epicureans had any morals at all. Emotion rather than reason, then, doomed the atomic theory in favor of the four element theory. Finally, since the terracentric hypothesis fit in with their spiritual and ethical philosophy, the Christian theologians and philosophers rejected any theory which did not place man in the center of the universe (O' Connell and Henry 1915: xi–xiv).

And so during the early Christian period the desire for easy systematization, as well as the need for harmony and mysticism, fused these various elements into one consistent view of the world. The earth, which occupied the center of the universe, was made up of the four elements—fire, water, air, earth—these being made up of the four qualities—heat, dryness, cold, moisture. It lay between the four points of the compass, experienced four seasons, and was refreshed by the four winds of Heaven. The earth was populated by a race of beings whose physical health was controlled by the four humors (blood, phlegm, yellow bile, black bile) and whose moral health was linked with the four cardinal virtues (prudence, temperance, fortitude, justice). This pleasant symmetry was further elaborated by conceiving of the earth as surrounded by eight concentric spheres bearing the seven planets and the fixed stars. Beyond this lay the outer or crystalline sphere, which set all the other spheres in motion at their respective velocities. Finally, beyond and above all else was the "third heaven," or abode of God. This satisfying and convincing theory was embraced by pagan Greeks and Romans as well as by Christians. It persisted into the Renaissance (O'Connell and Henry 1915: xiv–xvi).

The opening of the 14th century in Europe found magic and experimental science as inextricably interwoven as they had been for the previous few centuries. The great minds of the day were continuing as much as ever to sanction astrology and the occult. With the prestige of both the Thomist and Scotist (Duns Scotus) schools of philosophy in accord in accepting astrology, it takes little stretching of the imagination to discern the atmosphere of the times. Only a few men, notably Nicolas Oresme in the latter half of the century, spoke out in protest. Not only did he warn the world against astrology but, it is of special interest for us to know, he specifically attacked the genethliac aspect of physiognomy, including its chiromantic variant. But he was opposing something too deep a part of the times. Astrology continued on.

Spreading to all fields of thought and activity, it became the master discipline of the times. For instance, it became strongly linked with medicine on the grounds that, as the planets and humors were linked with one another, celestial influences had to be taken into consideration in the treatment of disease. Even during the 14th century, when medicine was beginning to feel the Hippocratic revival, it had to contend with the simultaneous revival of astrology. The calendar had to be consulted before one dared administer a drug or open a vein.

Polemics against astrology increased during the latter part of the 15th century in Italy. Marsilio Ficino, the most influential exponent of Platonism of his time, expressed his belief that while the stars might influence the body they were subservient to man's saving gift of free choice and to the providence of God. His young contemporary, Pico de la Mirandola, wrote an attack on astrology that was to become a model for later critics in different parts of Europe. In the 16th century, there appeared many more assaults, notably by Agrippa, Scepper, Calvin, van Hemminga, Frischlin, Pereyra, and Fra Alessandro. But the number of defenders exceeded that of the disbelievers and included some illustrious names, not only in science but letters, politics, and philosophy as well. Moreover, they tended to present their cases more convincingly and with greater erudition (Allen 1941).

Enjoying much prestige and responding to a psychological need of the times, it is no wonder that astrology came to dominate almost completely the physiognomics of the Renaissance. During this period, despite the popularity of Della Porta's theriologic approach, natural physiognomy had less appeal than its more occult sidereal manifestation. If astrology and physiognomy found themselves bedfellows, they were not strange bedfellows as long as one accepted the nexus between the planets and the bodily features. For Europeans astro-physiognomy was a variant of the doctrine of signs. The stars influence the person and implant in him signs reflecting that influence. Astro-physiognomy was an indirect way of discovering how the stars shape one's character and destiny.

The notion of astro-physiognomy is, as we have seen, of great antiquity and predates the Renaissance by at least two millennia. It had been set forth quite clearly in some Babylonian tablets which told the future through facial features.

But it remained for medieval and later Europeans to develop it, their sources coming from the classic world. One of these was Ptolemy (fl. 127–141), the Graeco-Egyptian mathematician, astronomer, and geographer, who wrote about astro-physiognomy in his *Tetrabiblos*, a work which circulated not only in the original Greek but Arabic and Latin translations as well. He describes the physiognomies resulting from each of the planets (Ptolemaeus 1820: 149–52). Galen (c. 130–c. 200) too makes reference to the astrological component in physiognomy, saying that it is the greater part (Galenus 1821–33: XIX, 530); but his remarks are so brief that they could not have been the source of any influence.

Sextus Empiricus (late 2nd century CE). in his "Against the Astrologers" (1949: 323–71), makes some remarks about astral physiognomy. This famous physician and skeptic philosopher exerted much influence.

Another source was Hippolytus, who may have derived much of his information from Sextus Empiricus. Hippolytus (d. c. 236) was a Christian theologian who became the first antipope. In his *Refutation of All Heresies* he gives us a surprisingly detailed account of the twelve zodiacal physiognomies, with their associated temperaments (Hippolytus 1868: 86–93). He himself of course was not a diviner; in fact his book is directed against all magic and divination.

Bouché-Leclerq (1896: 318–26) provides other instances from the Graeco-Roman world.

Notwithstanding, astral physiognomy was not much developed in the ancient Mediterranean area.

But later the Arabs made extensive use of it, according to Sarton (1924–48: III (1), 271), who says that they "went especially far in this direction." However, Mourad (1939: 8–9) maintains that Arab writers have adhered to a "natural" course of investigation, and that only occasionally, as in the instance of al-Dimashki (d. 1326–27) can

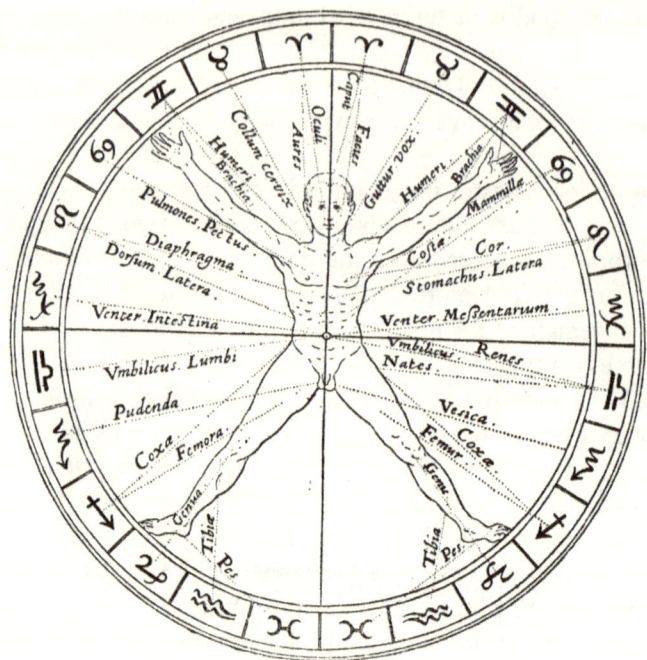

FIG. 35 Western astro-physiognomy: the whole body. Each part is connected with a sign of the zodiac. (From *Fludd, Utriusque cosmi historia*, 1617-21.)

one find in their writings a relationship between physiognomy and astrological morphology. The truth lies between these two views, for other Arabic writers were sometimes astral minded.

In medieval Europe the astrological approach to the study of physiognomy took several forms. In some instances the whole body was correlated. One example is to be seen in Figure 35. Not all schools associated the stars and the parts of the body in the same manner, some of the discrepancies being due to the increase in knowledge regarding the functions of the organs. According to one system, the seat of Mercury is the liver; that of Saturn, the brain; that of Venus, the genital organs and the belly; that of Mars, bile, blood, and the kidneys; that of the Sun and of the Moon, either the right or the left eye (depending on one's sex); and that of Saturn and Mars, the ears. In accordance with ancient Greek and Roman precedents, even the constellations were linked with the body, but this innovation never attained as much significance in the history of astro-physiognomy.

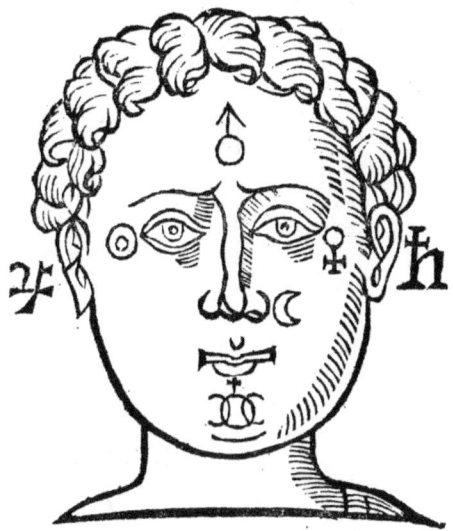

FIG. 36 Western astro-physiognomy: the face. Features of the face are connected with the planets. (From *Belot, Ouvres*, 1654.)

Sometimes, the parts of the face alone were studied. A sample may be seen in Figure 36. Again, it should be remembered that there has been some variation in the way the features are correlated with the planets. Thus, while the book from which this figure is taken (Belot 1654) assigns the left ear to Saturn and the right ear to Jupiter, Ptolemy assigns them to Mars and Saturn, respectively (Ptolemaeus 1820: 154).

More often, however, than either the whole body or the face, it was the hand or the forehead which was scrutinized. These approaches were so specialized that they acquired their own names: chiromancy, or divination from the hand, and metoposcopy, or divination from the forehead.

There is every indication that the study of the palm did not at first have an association with the stars. This came later. Even in its classic form it always made some allowance for "natural" rationales.

Chiromancy deals in large part with the lines of the palm; these are not linked with the stars. However, the five fingers and especially the seven mounts or excrescences of the palm are so linked. Named after the planets, they denote those qualities which have been traditionally associated with the mythological beings after whom the planets were named. The mount of Jupiter, for example, indicates religion, ambition, love of honor, and felicity, for these go with that particular god. Should

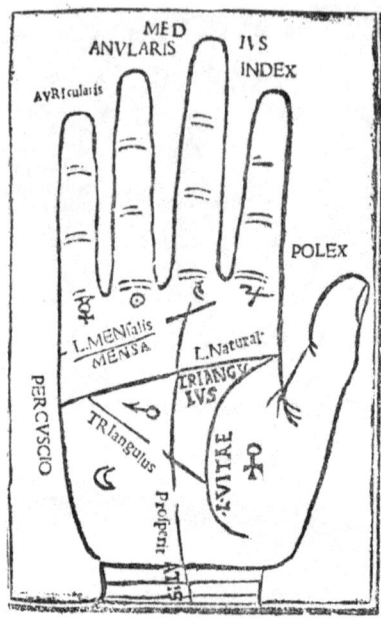

FIG. 37 Western astro-physiognomy: the hand. The parts of the hand are connected with the planets. (From *Corvus, Excellentissimi et singularis viri*, 1520.)

a mount be highly developed, it would indicate an excess of the quality it represents, so in the case of Jupiter it would be interpreted as superstition, pride, and a tendency to madness. Should the mount be very weak or even absent, then the qualities it stands for would be absent, which in the case of Jupiter would mean irreligion, indifference, shyness, lack of dignity, and sadness. Not all systems identify the lines and the mounts in the same way, but there is some degree of consistency in this regard. Figure 37 shows how Corvo named the mounts and main lines of the palm in a small book published in 1520.

The origins of palmistry are obscure. We can dismiss as absurd the statement made by Giles (1904: 985) that the origin of palmistry in China "has been assigned to prehistoric times—the third millennium before Christ." Verbal tradition is notoriously unreliable, and in any event we know that the Chinese study of the hand has never been astral.

We may also ignore the various alleged references to palmistry in the Old Testament, these having neatly been disposed of by Heron-Allen (1892: 55–58), himself a non-astrologic palmist.

As for Babylonia, Contenau (1940: 351) says that there is "little chance" that it ever existed there.

Another authority, Boissier (1905–6: I, 131), gives it as his opinion that the Babylonians did not practice it, but if they did they gave it a secondary role. He does note, however, that a provocative similarity exists between the rules and terminologies used in European chiromancy and in Babylonian entrail divination, or extispicy. "The terms hepatic line, cephalic line, mensal line, etc., used by the chiromancers of the Middle Ages, is an indication that this vocabulary borrowed much from that of extispicy" (*ibid.* 132). In comparing palm lines in some illustrations found in Jean Belot's book on palmistry with some lines occurring in cuneiform tablets, he finds the resemblance striking. One wonders if palmistry may have started out in Mesopotamia in a natural form and then received its astral element in the hands of others, perhaps in the outside Hellenic world?

Ancient Greek references to palmistry are worthy of notice. In his *Historia Animalium*, Aristotle made some brief remarks on the connection of long-livedness and short-livedness to certain lines of the palm, but in doing so he made no references to the stars (Aristotle 1965–: I, 53). We must, however, ignore a treatise, the *Chyromantia Aristotelis*, which is indeed astral but was not published until 1490, in Ulm. The work, like many others of its kind attributed to the Greek philosopher, is regarded by most authorities as being spurious.

An obscure Hellenic writer named Melampus, who probably lived in the 3rd century BCE, authored a treatise in Greek in which he gave planetary significance to the hand (Franz 1780: 482–85). This work is of considerable importance as it establishes a good baseline for the appearance of astro-palmistry.

Further evidence of the antiquity of palmistry in the Mediterranean is afforded by a now-lost treatise on the subject by Artemidoris Daldianos of Ephesus (fl. c. 138–80). Artimidoris lived in Lydia at the time of the Antonines—Roman emperors of the 2nd century CE.

Hellenistic palmistry in its astral form, then, goes back at least to the 3rd century BCE and probably a few years before that. It would not be surprising to discover that it originated somewhere in the Hellenic world, for we are well aware of the Greek inclination to personalize divination in general and astrology in particular. It is significant that India, with its strong tradition of astral palmistry, received its judicial or genethliacal astrology from the Greeks in the early centuries of our era; therefore, it could hardly have been the place of origin of astral chiromancy.

There have been preserved in Latin a large number of medieval manuscripts in which palmistry is treated as a distinct subject, art, or science (Thorndike 1965: 674–706). These attest to the importance of chiromancy before the period of the Renaissance had yet set in. Some medieval manuscripts on chiromancy have been attributed to Albertus Magnus (1193?–1280) and while their genuineness has never been demonstrated they afford additional evidence of the preoccupation with the palm.

Metoposcopy, which is the other elaborated form of astral physiognomy, was created during the Renaissance by the famous and controversial Italian mathematician, philosopher, and physician, Girolamo Cardano. In his book, *Metoposcopia* (1658), he divided the forehead into seven horizontal bands, named after the planets and partaking of the anthropopsychic and other characteristics of the deities after whom the planets themselves had been named. Cardano was interested in lines, not in bumps or mounts. The location, direction, length, and color of the lines with reference to the horizontal bands provide the clues to fortune and character. Figure 38 may be consulted to see how Cardano mapped out the forehead.

European astro-physiognomy took other forms but none of them were as systematic or popular as these.

Chinese physiognomics has no counterparts of these various kinds of European celestial physiognomy. Sometimes there seem to be resemblances but they are superficial and in any event relate to the "natural" aspects of physiognomy rather than the astral ones.

Take the palm, for example. Where Europeans name the mounts after the planets, the Chinese name them in terms of their locations in the areas of the trigrams of the *I Ching*. (The three at the base of the fingers have special names.) Of course, it is interesting that both systems agree in assigning significance to the mounts, but the point here at issue is the use of astrology. Where the Chinese look upon the elevation at the base of the small finger as K'un, the Europeans see it as Mercury. Where the former call the elevation below the thumb K'en, the latter call it Venus, and so on. In passing it is interesting to see Arlington (1927: 233) berate the Chinese for not recognizing the Mount of the Sun, for the Chinese may be better observers of the human palm than the Europeans; they see only three elevations at the base of the four fingers, whereas Europeans, possibly in their desire to get all seven planets into the picture, have traditionally recognized four elevations. The Mount of the Sun allegedly exists at the base of the third finger.

East-West Differences

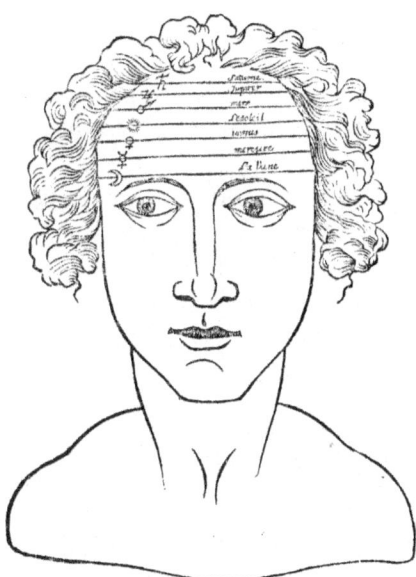

FIG. 38 Western astro-physiognomy: the forehead. The forehead is mapped out into horizontal planetary bands. Its wrinkles are considered significant. (From *Cardano, Metroposcopia,* 1858.)

It is puzzling, moreover, to read Arlington's remark that "The difference between foreign and Chinese chiromancy is that the latter is astrologic, not scientific," for in his article comparing the two he proceeds to speak of the European mounts in terms of the planets and nowhere mentions any Chinese reliance on astrology. This is especially brought out in his figure 1, comparing Western and Chinese maps of the hand. It is the former that has labels which are named, at least in part, after the planets; the Chinese map contains only the trigrams, which have nothing sidereal about them. Admittedly, Arlington is not himself interested in astro-physiognomy, for he belongs to the 19th century D'Arpentigny-Desbarolles school of palmistry, which studies the whole hand, without reference to planets. But his article is on Western chiromancy, not chirgnomy, as the "natural" method is called. His article is highly ethnocentric and must be read with caution.

The forehead affords still another illustration of the differences under discussion. Certainly the Chinese have made note of the lines of the forehead, but they have not elevated this to a separate art or associated it with the stars. They consider forehead lines to be among the several lines to be found throughout the whole face (cf. Figures 7, 8, and 9).

Two other branches of European astro-physiognomy, not previously discussed, may now be considered. These are neomancy and onychomancy.

The Chinese do not have a sidereal neomancy, even though they have a great interest in moles.

European neomancy (sometimes distinguished from nevology, which is natural rather than star-linked) is based on the premise that the heavenly bodies leave their imprints in the form of moles or other kinds of nevi on that part of the body to which each of the planets belongs. The place of these imprints depends on the conditions surrounding the time of one's birth.

Neomancy asserts that for every mole on the face there is a corresponding mole on the rest of the body, especially the torso; the location of the facial mole depends on the location of the body mole. As many as 100 potential moles on the face, ears, and neck have been correlated with a like number of the body. Here is a single example of the neomantic approach and its interpretation of a given kind of mole:

> LXVIII. A Mole appearing on the lower corner under the hinder part of the right Eye, from the Temples, as in the first figure and number (68) indicates another on the right side the Ribs, and designs the man cruel and furious: if of honey colour, he is more temperate: if red, he is addicted to martial affairs, and full of revenge: if it be black, he shall either be the death, or cause the death of some man: if as a Lentil, he is bold. It shows a woman to be vain and proud: if she have it black, she will be the cause of the death of some one to the hazard of her own life. This mole is of the nature of *Mars*, assigned to the *Caput Herculis*, a Star of the third magnitude (Saunders 1671: 328).

Additional European writers, other than the one from whose writings the above quotation has been extracted, have written extensively on moles, showing similarly the correspondences between facial moles and those on the body. Cardano, from whose posthumous work, *Metoposcopia* (1658), the drawing in Figure 39 has been taken, is the most prominent. He illustrates his principles through 151 facial sketches which not only relate the moles to the signs of the zodiac but tell where each facial mole is found to be equated with a body mole. Lodovico Settala or Septalius wrote a later book on moles, *De naevis* (1605) in which he maintained that though moles and other markings of the skin appear scattered in a haphazard way all over the

East-West Differences

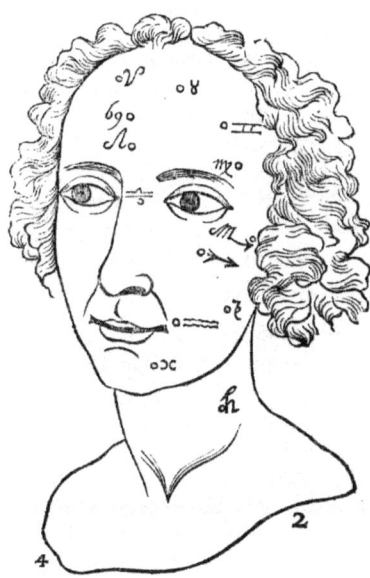

FIG. 39 Western astro-physiognomy: the moles. Moles are generally unfavourable indicators. (From *Cardano, Metroposcopia*, 1858.)

body, they nevertheless are distributed according to a definite order, based on astrological rules. Filippo Finella or Phinella, in his *Libri tres naevorum* (1633), relates moles not only to the planets but also the signs of the zodiac, and like Cardano, Settala, and Saunders he indicates where each facial mole is accompanied by a mole elsewhere on the body. Interestingly enough, Finella takes the position that the human will is free and that the stars cannot do more than indicate; they cannot compel.

Contrasted with this, the Chinese interest in moles is not sidereal, nor does it make reference to the face-body correspondences referred to above. In these respects it is close to the oldest of all extant works on moles—that of the Greek, Melampus (3rd century BCE) (Franz 1780: 501–8).

The Chinese share in the generally pessimistic European interpretations of moles, but not to the extent of Cardano, or especially the German, Philipp Mäyens, who has left us some medical writings of astro-physiognomic character. In his *Chiromantia et Physiognomia Medica* (1739) Mäyens says that moles and blemishes "never portend something good, but always misfortune and disease" (pp. 111–12).

The Arabs were familiar with Greek writings on moles. Mourad is in error when he says, "Divination through nevi did not constitute a part, it seems, of the divinatory methods in use among the Arabs" (1939: 37). In support of this he says that Masudi (956), Abshihi (1446), and Ibn Khaldun (1406) do not mention this method among the divinatory arts which they cite. However, we know that Ibn abi-l-Rijal (fl. 1016–40), a Muslim astrologer who was active in Tunis, wrote a physiognomic treatise on nevi (Sarton 1927–48: I, 715–16). He was widely known in Europe as Abenragel (also Albohazen, Alboacen) and was frequently cited as an authority on moles by medieval and Renaissance physiognomists. According to Sarton (*ibid.* III [1], 960) he combined the study of moles with astrological ideas. Another Arabic writer to discuss moles was the Palestinian man of letters and historian, Khalil Ibn Aibak al-Safadi (c. 1297–1363), who imputed prophetic significance to birthmarks according to their position on the body (*ibid.* III [1], 271, 960).

As for onychomancy, neither the Chinese nor the Europeans have paid a good deal of attention to the markings of the fingernails. Nevertheless, we must note that the astrological difference crops up once again when these are considered. European onychomancy is sidereal in that the black and white markings so often found in the fingernails are believed to result from the four humors, whose action is in turn influenced by the stars. The Chinese interest in the fingernails is free of astral concepts; instead, it is content to interpret the nails in terms of their size and softness. However, the Chinese do link the nails with the muscles, liver, and gall bladder.

We now turn briefly to the concept of the four humors, already tentatively alluded to in the above discussion on astrology. Most likely the theory of humors stemmed from or was inspired by those Greeks, such as Pythagoras and Empedocles, who had developed the hypothesis of the four elements. Originally, it maintained that four body fluids—blood, phlegm, yellow bile, and black bile—determine man's health. Hippocrates, of course, was a well-known exponent of the idea, saying that an imbalance in the humors results in pain and disease; but although he developed what is probably the earliest recorded typology of human morphology he did not base it on the humoral principle. In the 2nd century of the Christian era, Galen expanded the idea so as to say that each humor was at the basis of each of the four basic temperaments—sanguine, phlegmatic, choleric, and melancholic, or buoyant, sluggish, quick-tempered, and dejected. The Greeks seem

East-West Differences   155

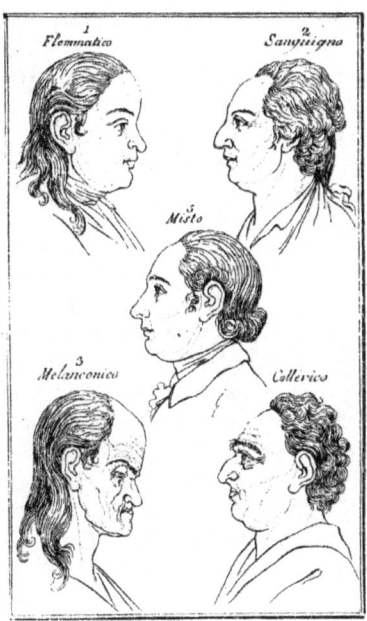

FIG. 40 Western humoral physiognomy. Galen popularized the theory of humors, which persisted into 19th century medical circles. (From *Plane, Fisiologia*, 1803.)

never to have based a morphological typology on these four humors, but some of the Renaissance astro-physiognomists did, among them being Belog, Peruchio, and Pujasol, whose works did not appear until the 17th century. The humors have had a persistent place in modern physiognomy, possibly because of a certain air of plausibility given to them since the discovery of the function and importance of the endocrine glands. It is interesting that classical Arabic physiognomics apparently makes no use of humors, even though the theory of these body fluids was well known to the Arabic world. Figure 40 shows how the humoral types of men were represented in a work published in 1803.

The Chinese have nothing corresponding to the humoral theory, so that here again a distinction between Sinitic and Western manifestations of the art of body divination may be made.

Phrenology is still another development in European physiognomy with no counterpart in China. The resemblance between phrenology and the reading of the "pillow bones" is purely superficial, and in any event does not stem at all from a common theoretical base. The

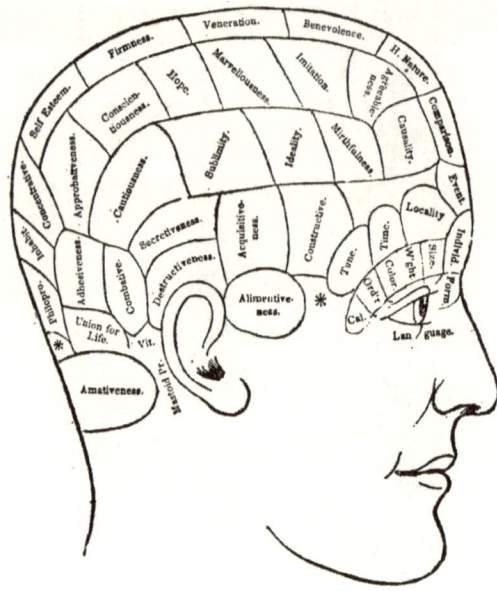

FIG. 41 Western phrenology. Originally based on a scientific hypothesis of localized brain function, it quickly degenerated into popular characterology. (From *Fowler, Practical Phrenology*, 1840.)

originator of phrenology was the Swabian medical philosopher Franz Joseph Gall (1758–1828), and his approach was scientific rather than mantic. His doctrine was based on the premise that every mental faculty is represented by a particular cranial protuberance, its size being an indication of either a small, moderate, or large development of the underlying cerebral region, where the seat of the locality is located. A necessary assumption made by this theory was that each part of the brain has a special function. As Davies (1955: 3–64) has pointed out, Gall's doctrine became considerably changed in the hands of his brilliant but erratic disciple, Spurzheim, who was in fact the originator of the very term, "phrenology." It went from bad to worse in the hands of various European enthusiasts, receiving its greatest popular appeal but lowest credibility when commercialized by the Americans, Orson Squire Fowler and his brother, Lorenzo, whose publications for the laymen were astoundingly successful from the commercial point of view. Figure 41 shows how these brothers mapped out the head phrenologically.

The rationale of Chinese occipitomancy is not at all clear but certainly it has no resemblance to the theoretical basis of phrenology, which may have been in error but was within the bounds of scientific speculation. We cannot accept as valid the implications of the statement by Giles (1905: 180–1) that "The Chinese undoubtedly believe the outer configuration of the skull to be dependent upon the shape of the brain within…" Giles mistakenly confuses pillow bone divination with phrenology. Indeed, at times he uses the term phrenology as a synonym for the whole of physiognomy.

One does not encounter the usual correlative thinking in Sinitic occipitomancy. This, however, does not mean it is free of arbitrariness. Both phrenology and physiognomy are interested in character reading; they diverge greatly in the degree to which they make prognostications regarding one's fortune. In its most ignominious form, phrenology was made astral but by that time it had been so discredited that it had fallen into oblivion. Even as an astral form of physiognomy it of course has no genetic connection with occipitomancy.

Chapter VIII

AN HISTORICAL SYNTHESIS

We now return to the question that was posed in the opening sentence of Chapter VI: Is there some sort of genetic connection between Chinese body divination and that of the West? Up till here we have restricted ourselves to pointing out resemblances and differences, and it is now time to assemble these comparisons into a coherent whole. Before doing so, it may be of some usefulness to review some of the principles involved in making an historical reconstruction where the written record has no direct relevance or is altogether lacking.

Theoretical Considerations

Anthropologists, especially due to the influence of Franz Boas (cf. Boas 1896), have insisted that in making comparisons between two cultural traits for the purpose of arriving at decisions concerning their manner of origin, the data must be comparable and not superficially alike.

There can hardly be any doubt that this first requirement has been filled. The *hsiang shu* of the Chinese is equatable with the *summa alamdimu* of the Babylonians and Assyrians, the *physiognomonia* of the Greeks, the *firasa* of the Arabs, and *physiognomia* of the medieval Europeans. However, to admit that they are alike does not answer the question as to what makes them alike.

One might postulate that the likeness is due to a common working of the human mind. This would be in areement with the supposition, popularized by Adolf Bastian, that independent developments in culture take place because of "elementary ideas" (*Elementargedanken*), these being in turn an aspect of the psychic unity of mankind. Bastian, however, did not insist that all similarities were due to such independent developments; he merely insisted on the recognition that such a process must be reckoned with in the reconstruction of culture history.

Nevertheless, the psychic unity idea, which was incorporated into the unilinear scheme of the classical evolutionists, seems hardly sufficient to explain the resemblance of Chinese physiognomics to that of the manifestations found in areas to the west. In order for it to be tenable, it would be necessary to show that somatomancy had developed in every other culture which had attained the same approximate developmental level as ancient China, but as we have seen it was absent in ancient Egypt (until introduced later from Greece). It should be added that it was absent from such civilizations as those of the Mayas, the Aztecs, and the Incas, all of which had their urban communities.

Another school of anthropology has long maintained that cultural similarities are due to borrowing or cultural diffusion. In extreme form, as in the hands of G. Elliot Smith and W. J. Perry, it insisted that all culture worthy of the name came from a single source—Egypt and the Fertile Crescent. Without accepting this radical point of view, other diffusionists maintain that most instances of cultural likeness can be attributed to borrowing.

Diffusion theory demands that one of the essential conditions for proving historical connection between cultural traits is continuity of distribution. For the Mesopotamian area, the geographic facts show this continuity of culture in general and physiognomics in particular existed with Europe and the Arabic world, and even India. A gap of a sort exists between China and western Asia, but of course we are aware of the intercourse that took place along the old Silk Road. Our earlier review of this question seems to warrant the conclusion that no barriers to diffusion existed among the various civilizations concerned.

Donors and Borrowers

We have been depending to a large extent on similarities in logic to link differing physiognomic traditions with one another. It is more difficult in tracing diffusion to deal with ideas rather than material objects, but this is what must be done, as somatomancy does not have a paraphernalia requiring the use of artifacts. A comparison of these ideas or rationale has already been made and to them we must return. For easier comparison, these are presented in succinct form in Table 5.

If phrenology, which is a development of the 19th century in Europe, is ruled out, it would appear obvious that there is a Greek-Arabic-European tradition. Every concept found in one system has a concomitant in each of the other two. The evidence of history makes this resemblance out to be due to more than commonality of principles alone, for fortunately it can be demonstrated that the Arabs borrowed directly from the Greeks, and the Europeans from both the Greeks and Arabs. A genetic connection may thus be said to exist, beyond a shadow of a doubt, among these three.

The next step is to inquire into the possibility of a connection between the Greek tradition and its Arabic and Greek derivatives, on the one hand, and the Mesopotamian, on the other. History cannot come to our assistance here, for there is no written record to show that Greece actually borrowed its somatomancy from the Assyro-Babylonians. However, the evidence of the logical principles involved strongly suggests a connection. Excepting only the concept of the four humors and possibly also the idea of harmony and the mean, the Mesopotamian tradition is like that of the Greek-Arabic-European. It is especially linked to them by the principle of judicial astrology—an idea of sufficient distinctiveness to lead us to suppose that it was not independently invented twice.

In contrast to this, Chinese physiognomics, while apparently allied to all the others, shows enough distinctiveness to merit consideration as a system of considerable independence. Although it possesses the concepts of destiny, macrocosm-microcosm, harmony and the mean, and theriology, it nevertheless has developed each of these in ways that are somewhat Sinitic.

In addition to the sinitization of traits held in common, the Chinese further show their independence by endowing their physiognomics with such distinctively Chinese features as the Five Elements, Yin-Yang, Eight Trigrams, *ch'i* and *li*, and the Heaven-Man-Earth triad.

The great distinctiveness of Chinese body mantic is not, however, sufficient to establish this system as having had an entirely independent source, for in some of the key premises the resemblances to Western systems are too close to warrant as assumption of separate origins. Nevertheless the differences are sufficiently great as to indicate either that the borrowing from the West took place in remote times, when Western physiognomics was still generalized and had not emerged from its nascent state, or that only the idea and not the substance of the art was borrowed. Both of these possibilities could be true.

TABLE 5
Physiognomic Premises According to Varying Systems

Premise	System				
	Mesopotamian	Greek	Arabic	European	Chinese
Destiny	+	+	+	+	+
Microcosm	+	+	+	+	+
Harmony-Mean	?	+	+	+	+
Theriology	+	+	+	+	+
Astrology	+	+	+	+	0
Humors	0	+	+	+	0
Phrenology	0	0	0	+	0
Five Elements	0	0	0	0	+
Yin-Yang	0	0	0	0	+
Trigrams	0	0	0	0	+
Ch'i and Li	0	0	0	0	+
Triad	0	0	0	0	+

Key: + = present; 0 = absent; ? = uncertain or unknown

Mesopotamia would seem to qualify easily as the source of the whole idea of the body mantic, with no claim from Egypt being possible. Cuneiform tablets from the library assembled by the last great Assyrian king, Assurbanipal (d. 626? BCE), are copies of much older writings and clearly contain within them some lists of somatomantic interpretations. Kraus (1935) has written a monograph on the subject and we may select a few examples from it to illustrate the point: "A man will die from thirst if the wrinkles on his forehead show the form of the sign ZA" (p. 6). "If the hair of his head is long, his days will be long; he will be poor" (p. 6). "If there is a pimple at the left or right side of her upper lip, she will have plenty of food" (p. 7). "If the hair of his head is full and his lips red, he will suffer from grief and difficulties" (p. 77). "If the hair of his head is like a bear's hair, there will be no rival for him in the palace" (p. 81).

So, although adumbrations of physiognomics appear in the writings of Homer and Aristotle, and such men as Pythagoras and Socrates are said by other Greeks to have made practical use of the art in sizing up people, priority rests with the Mesopotamians, whose writings on the subject are not only older but more specific and systematic.

As for Chinese body mantic, despite apocryphal statements alluding to a Neolithic era, it cannot lay claim to anything as ancient as the cuneiform examples from the Tigris-Euphrates Valley.

If the Chinese were indeed the borrowers, they must have received the idea of body divination at a time when the Western systems had not yet incorporated astrology into their physiognomics, for the Chinese system contains nothing astral. The time of course would have to be prior to 626 BCE, for we know that at least a simple kind of physiognomy was then present in northern China. This period is a favorable one for our theory, for we know that at that time astrology was still judicial or public rather than personal in character in Mesopotamia, the first horoscope being dated at 263 BCE.

This argument is supported by other facts. The Chinese received astronomy from the Tigris-Euphrates Valley by stimulus diffusion—as a suggestion without specific astronomical knowledge. They received, in addition, a system of astrologic prognostication of the judicial or public sort. Not until the time of the great skeptical philosopher, Wang Ch'ung (CE 27–97), did they begin to apply astrology to individuals, as the Greeks and Babylonians had begun to do before that time, nor did they ever incorporate genethliacal astrology with physiognomy, as had been done in the West.

The absence of the Greek humoral theory in China would seem to indicate any of several possibilities, the first being that the concept of the four humors appeared too late in Greece to have been present when the Chinese were first becoming acquainted with physiogomics. The humoral theory can trace its beginnings back to at least the 6th century BCE, but it was not really developed as a physiognomic concept until the time of Galen in the 2nd century of the Christian era. Another possibility is that if the Chinese had ever heard of the four humors, even after they had developed some system of body divination, they rejected them as incompatible with their own notions of philosophy and physiognomics. A third possibility seems most likely: the Chinese borrowed nothing from the Greek physiognomists, having been influenced instead by the Mesopotamians.

Stimulus Diffusion

In advancing the idea of stimulus diffusion as the process whereby the Chinese took over the suggestion of body divination and then developed it along their own distinctive lines, we are able to account for diversity in the midst of unity. The unity may be said to exist in the overall tradition of physiognomics, wherever it may be found, and rests on the one obvious and dominating feature that characterizes somatomancy: belief that educated scrutiny of the human body can reveal facts concerning a person's character, potentials, and future condition. The diversity, on the other hand, exists in the special turn given by the Chinese to the supporting rationales of somatomancy, as well as to the new rationales which it added from its own philosophic system.

That the Chinese gave body divination a Sinitic style need not be unexpected. The theory of stimulus diffusion adopted above recognizes that when an idea spreads to a recipient culture, it will be developed more or less as if it were an invention of the borrower. To the extent that the recipient culture differs from the donor, it will modify the borrowed trait. If the difference is overwhelming, as it was not indeed in this instance, an idea may be rejected out of hand because it is too alien to be integrated into the culture as a whole. Actually, physiognomics is a complex of traits rather than a single trait, and some of its specific aspects were undoubtedly rejected or even lost in the process of transmission.

It is interesting that none of the five distinctly Chinese philosophic concepts, all of which are ancient, ever became incorporated by the civilizations of the West. Possibly they were too alien to those cultures and therefore could not be reinterpreted so as to become integrated into their world view.

India

The role of India relative to body divination in China has hardly been touched upon in these pages, mostly because the historical record is so sparse and physiognomic literature so scant as to preclude the formulation of definitive conclusions. Nevertheless, India is not entirely a wasteland without value in our quest for enlightenment in matters of historical development. Indeed, it provides the most cogent example of a clear-cut borrowing of a physiognomic premise. This premise is found in Indian sutras and is implied by the grotesque morphological features which are said to characterize great men.

Enormous stature is one of the features of Indian origin found in ancient Chinese official annals. For instance, in the *San Kuo Chih* (History of the Three Kingdoms), edited during the Chin dynasty by Ch'en Shou, it is said that Hsien Chu or Liu Pei, the founder of the Minor Han dynasty, was 7 feet 5 inches tall. The same stature is attributed to Kao Tsu, the founder of the Han dynasty, and to Liu Hsien-chu. But Emperor Hsüan is said to have been 8 feet 3 inches tall, and Emperor Wen only three inches less than that. Not to be outdone by these dimensions is Emperor Yü, described in the official annals as 9 feet 6 inches tall (cf. Dschi 1949: 96–97). Even taking into account that the ancient Chinese foot is less than the English one by about two inches, these statures are formidable, to say the least.

Another characteristic, which physical anthropologists would associate with apes rather than man, is the enormous arm length of great men. Hsien Chu, Liu Hsien-chu, Kao Tsu, Emperor Hsüan, and Emperor Wen, all mentioned above, are said to have had arms extending beyond their knees—an infra human trait if ever there was one.

There are also statements in these and other sources to the effect that certain great men in Chinese history had two pupils in each eye, or two elbows in each arm, or four breasts. Other strange features are: hair that reaches the ground, dragon faces, tiger noses, ox heads, snake heads, coalescent teeth, and bird beaks. In addition, some men could see their own ears.

Less taxing to credulity are: teeth as white as jade, big ears, broad foreheads, sun-shaped bones on the forehead, long heads, hillock-like heads, high cheek bones, shining eyes, huge eyes, high noses, and beautiful beards.

Hiän-lin Dschi (1949) has taken up the question of the relationship of these traits to the thirty-two marks and eighty secondary marks of a great man often mentioned in the Buddhist canon, as well as similar but less minutely described criteria in the Brahmanistic and Jainistic canons. He shows that in the Eastern Han, Wu, Western Chin, Eastern Chin, Earlier Sung, Sui, and T'ang dynasties, spanning the period CE 25–906, we find translations into the Chinese of various Buddhist canons, and in them the marks of great men are minutely described. The sutras are not always consistent with one another in the order in which the marks are described, and sometimes they repeat, but for the most part they are alike.

We must agree with Dschi that there is a genetic connection between the Indian and Chinese marks of a great man, and that India was the source of these traits. But although he has chosen to stress the mention of these traits in the official annals for the Three Kingdoms, the Chin Dynasty, and the Northern and Southern Dynasties, covering the years CE 221–581 (these annals should be distinguished from the translations of Buddhist canons mentioned in the preceding paragraph), he is well aware that some of the same traits are mentioned several centuries earlier. He briefly discusses such earlier works as Hsün Tzu's *Against Physiognomy* and Wang Ch'ung's *Lun-Heng*, their authors having lived c. 298–238 BCE and c. CE 27–100, respectively.

The source of the Chinese morphological traits under discussion was probably Buddhistic, despite the fact that the traditional date of the introduction of Mahayana Buddhism into China is CE 65. It had probably penetrated there from Central Asia and Bactria many years, perhaps centuries, before then. This should mean that the Chou and Han philosophers mentioned above could after all have been treating with physiognomic traits introduced by Buddhism. The source might even have been pre-Buddhistic but still Indian. Dschi himself (*ibid*. 101–2) is inclined to see Central Asia as the intermediary in this movement, saying that Buddhist works translated long ago into central Asiatic languages also mention the thirty-two marks; but he offers no evidence to support his belief that this was the route, although other writers have often said much the same thing.

India cannot be said on the basis of these data to have been the source of earliest Chinese body divination, which goes back at least to the 7th century BCE, before Gautama was born. There can be no doubt, however, that whatever the Chinese took from an indigenous Indian source assumed a Chinese flavor.

Summary

Summing up, body mantic probably originated in Mesopotamia, and at a time well before the reign of Assurbanipal. It incorporated such concepts as those of destiny, the microcosm, and theriology. Despite the antiquity of the astrology in the Tigris-Euphrates Valley it seems that astral interpretations did not find their original expression in this area but were borrowed at a comparatively late time from elsewhere.

To the Mesopotamian basics, the Greeks added the doctrine of harmony and the mean, as well as the theory of the four humors, which however probably first had to await the elaboration it eventually received at the hands of Galen during the 2nd century of the present era. Quite possibly it was in the Hellenic world outside of Mesopotamia that the astrological ingredient was developed, at a time before or contemporaneous with Melampus in the 3rd century BCE It could hardly have originated in India, which received its astrology from Greece at a time when astro-physiognomy had already been developed in the Hellenic world.

The Arabs accepted all that Greek body divination, with its Mesopotamian and Hellenic features, had to offer, and although adding nothing essentially new, nevertheless made numerous refinements. They preserved Hellenic physiognomics from oblivion during the span of centuries from the decline of ancient Greek culture until about the 13th century.

The Europeans of the Middle Ages, stimulated towards the latter part of that period by the discovery of classic literature on body divination, especially the Arabic version of it, were chiefly borrowers who added no basically different concepts until the emergence of phrenology and the theory of cerebral localization under Gall and Spurzheim early in the 19th century. However, activity was marked during the period of the Renaissance, when somatomancy received its greatest support from the intelligentsia. While the Europeans did not originate astro-physiognomy, they hypertrophied the astral doctrine beyond anything that had appeared in the past or was destined to develop in the future.

Meanwhile, the Chinese had borrowed the idea of physiognomy, probably from Mesopotamia, many centuries prior to the 7th century BCE, which is not only the time when body mantic is first mentioned in Chinese literature but also the time when most of the cuneiform tablets pertaining to the subject had been copied from even more ancient records for Assurbanipal's great library. Geographic boundaries did not prevent the absorption of ideas by China from the Western regions, for we know that there was ample traffic and communication between the East and the lands to the far west even before the establishment of the Old Silk Road.

Nevertheless, the Chinese steadily developed a physiognomics of their own, with several indigenous features that never diffused to the West. These included the Five Elements, Yin-Yang, the trigrams, *chi* and *li*, and the Heaven-Man-Earth triad. These concepts were intimately related to the religio-philosophical ideas that had developed over the centuries at a time, for the most part, prior to Confucius. There is no evidence that Chinese body divination owes anything to the Greeks or even to modern Europe, except for very recent times. It never incorporated the humors or astrology, and while it embraced the idea of the mean and harmony, there is no evidence that this came from the Greek or Hellenic world. Chinese somatomancy achieved its greatest glory in the Sung period, being a synthesis of all that had gone by before. While it was directly influenced by certain Buddhistic concepts of apparent Indian origin, it seems to have been little effected by India.

Our reconstruction has perforce been diffuse because the kinds of close similarities desirable in delineating historical origins and movements are lacking. It is only in extreme instances of similarity, such as one sees in the Indian criteria of the great man, that the verdict for diffusion is categorical and unchallengeable. Such instances are not otherwise forthcoming, and in their absence we must make do with a tentative historical scheme.

Chapter IX

FUNCTION

The near-ubiquity as well as the great antiquity of divination as a general phenomenon has already been alluded to in this volume, so it would be redundant to dwell again upon these points. It now remains, from an interpretation of the Chinese materials on body divination, to try to understand what function is served by somatomancy and to see if that function is matched elsewhere in the world where it is found. For the very persistence of body divination offers a challenge for the social scientist as well as the psychologist. It must fill an important individual need, else it would have disappeared long ago in conformance with the principle that has been called "extinction through non-reward."

Personal Divination

Mantic systems may be divided into those which serve the state, community, or society and those which serve the person. Some systems may be used to serve both. Body divination is completely personal in essence and has never been used for public purposes. It is not the only mantic form used solely for the individual, however, for in primitive societies as well as civilized ones other personal forms are not uncommon. What distinguishes it from the rest is that it uses the human body as a vehicle to answer questions concerning the unknown.

The personal nature of its scope may be seen in Mesopotamia, where predictions were made by the Babylonians with respect to life expectancy, financial condition, family life, manner of death, relationships with people, lawsuits, and attitude toward the tutelary deity (Franz 1935: 10).

The appearance of body divination in China may have been part of a general shift away from public divination towards private quests for answers. If a shift of this kind could be shown to have been a reality it would be valuable to us because it would encourage us to look for the broader changes with which it was concomitant. But did such a change really occur?

Some observations by C. K. Yang in his *Religion in Chinese Society* (1961) reassure us on this point. Divination in China, he says, was at first essentially public, with important political functions. During the Shang dynasty, 1523–1027 BCE, we encounter the first systematic Chinese writing, and he points out (p. 107) that these were on oracle bones and recorded divination on matters of war and peace of the Shang state. Then, as in the ensuing Chou era, 1027–256 BCE, divination was conducted by official priests and nobles.

> The control of divination was apparently one of the early means of political leadership, for it imparted a sacred character to political decisions and facilitated their popular acceptance. Through divination, political decisions became commands of the gods (Yang 1961: 107).

Yang says that divination became a private religious practice in later years. His remarks would seem to lend support to the argument that social concomitants have something to do with the applications of divination in general and somatomancy in particular.

One of those concomitants could well have been social and political change.

Conditions Arousing Concern

In turning our attention to the question of changes in Chinese society we enter into the sphere of interpretation. We begin our search for the conditions that arouse especial concern in the individual, and while a variety of them will have to be considered, it is best to begin with the notion of mobility.

We know that an era of continual and deepening change took place in China with the beginning of the decline of the feudalistic system during the Chou dynasty. Following upon the relatively more stable Shang period, the Chou years witnessed great turbulence and flux.

Indirect evidence indicates that body divination made its presence felt in this era. The clue is contained in a brief work, *Against Physiognomy*, written by the great Confucian, Hsün Tzu, during the Chan Kuo (Warring States) period of the Chou dynasty. In this essay he specifically attacks one T'ang Chü of Liang (a former state in which present Nanking is located) as representative of the rising trend of body divination. His argument is twofold. The first reason he advances is briefly stated in a single sentence: "Physiognomy did not exist in ancient times; a student should not consider it" (Hsün Tzu 1928: 67).

Then, leaving this recourse to the conservative prejudice against anything new, he proceeds to show contradictory instances provided by historical figures. Some great men have been short and others have been very tall. One official had a body seven feet in height and a face three feet long and three inches wide. (Even allowing for the fact that the ancient foot was shorter than the present English one, the "figures" are impressive.) A man who was the virtual ruler of Ts'u was bald and his left leg was longer than his right. Hsün Tzu goes on to give several other instances to show lack of consistency in the traits held by great men who were kings, dukes, ministers, and philosophers. Confucius, for example, is described by a character of ambiguous meaning that could be translated as either rumpled square, hairy in the face, or two eyed. Such anomalies as great facial hairiness, said Hsün Tzu, or dwarfness, hunchback, hairlessness of face, lameness, paralysis, and two pupils in one eye, have been found in able figures in history. On the other hand, the two tyrant emperors, Ch'ie and Chou, "the greatest criminals in the country," were very tall, attractive, and handsome. Hsün Tzu's conclusion is that a man should be judged by his "heart" (mind) and even more by his principles.

The implication of his remarks is that divining from the body had begun to expand in late Chou times. Some credence may be given this suggestion by the fact that the *Shen Hsiang* makes no mention of any earlier authority than T'ang Chü, the very object of Hsün Tzu's blast. And, as has already been noted, the first historical reference to physiognomy associates it with an incident that occurred in 626 BCE.

If the assumption is valid that physiognomy was prevalent in the Ch'un Ch'iu and Chan Kuo periods, it becomes pertinent to inquire into the characteristics of these two Chou eras in order to discover if there was something present in them that was congenial to the somatomancic art.

One cannot escape noticing that these times were days of great although gradual change, marked by the rise of considerable social and individual mobility.

A book by Cho-yun Hsu, *Ancient China in Transition* (1965), is in fact devoted to demonstrating the thesis that a great transition took place during the second and third phases of the Chou dynasty. These two phases, the Ch'un Ch'iu (Annals) period, 722–464 BCE, and the subsequent Chan Kuo (Warring States) period, 463–222 BCE, were destined to set the pattern of Chinese political institutions, social relationships, and world view for many centuries to come.

Hsu has made novel and extensive use of documentary sources in demonstrating Chinese social mobility, which he has focussed upon as a built-in index of the stability of a stratified society. He has compiled statistics relative to: social stratification; the increasing importance of ministers in various activities; the concentration of ministers in big families; the increasing percentage of persons of obscure origins in the list of outstanding personel compiled by the ancient historian Pan Ku; frequency of wars in the Ch'un Ch'iu period (38 peaceful years out of 259), as well as the Chan Kuo period (89 peaceful years out of 242), and so on. He has documented changes not only in social stratification but politics, economics, and ideology as well.

He finds that following upon the rigid stratification of Chinese society under a rule by feudal lords in the earliest of the Chou periods, the next two periods of the dynasty witnessed not only a reduced stratification but the possibility of movement between strata. Transition by an individual became increasingly easy as the Chou dynasty approached its end. Mobility in an upward direction was possible at many levels. The *shih*, the lowest segment of the ruling group, composed of officials, warriors, and stewards of the noble households, bestirred itself in the Ch'un Ch'iu period and began to assume greater and greater roles in politics, even to the extent of commanding armies and leading rebellions. Their power and influence rose still higher in the Chan Kuo period, when they were transformed into a virtually new group within a new type of state, "in which the ruler wielded despotic power and ministers could be brought into and discharged from a bureaucratic system that selected and promoted competent men and rejected the unqualified" (pp. 105–6). The ministerial class also moved upwards during the Ch'un Ch'iu period, gaining rewards in the form of land and slaves, and so increasing its power relative to the rulers and even eclipsing them. Many ministers stood to benefit from wars and consequently some of them encouraged them. Commoners, too, were also able to rise upward into public service as a reward for their support during the intrastate disturbances among nobility during this time. Another group, the merchants, who had once been little more than dependents of noble households, came to possess as much material wealth and importance as rulers and ministers, even though their social status remained that of subjects and commoners.

There of course had to be some downward mobility in the face of these changes, says Hsu, and the ones who came to be affected during the Ch'un Ch'iu period were the higher aristocracy. Fewer and fewer sons of rulers shared automatically in the power to rule. The rulers of states possessed only nominal sovereignty, and as a class were degraded in function. In fact, during the Chan Kuo period the hereditary aristocracy was ruined by the struggle for power and the nobles class disappeared. During this same period the ministerial class, which had previously gained great power, saw the majority of its members sink to the bottom of the social scale because of the interfamily struggle for power.

By the end of the Chou dynasty the Confucian ideal that a man should have humanitarian views, a moral conscience, and the ability to carry out his convictions, had gained such acceptance that a new concept of the outstanding man had become firmly fixed. He was one who owed his superiority not to hereditary rank but to personal qualities. Perhaps Confucius had been inspired in this direction as the result of witnessing the sudden ascents and declines of his contemporaries and becoming aware of the inequities of his society. Be that as it may, Hsu concludes by saying, "The idea of selecting only the best men for public service led to the philosophy of giving every man a fair chance to rise in the social scale" (p. 180).

Another study, *Social Mobility in China* (1966) by Yung-teh Chow, a sociologist, further attests to the centuries old tradition of mobility in China. Although concentrating on the 1940s, the author reminds us of the antecedents of the more recent shifting in positions of individuals, as well as families and status groups. Following upon the Chou dynasty, the king of Ch'in unified China for the first time, abolished feudalism, and placed administrative power in the hands of a centrally appointed bureaucracy.

> Thus was created the vitally important official gentry class, which in most later periods was the effective ruling group in China and which, though it tended to be self-perpetuating as a status group, never achieved individual hereditary rights in the government posts it held. The orthodox ideology of this group was Confucianism. During the later dynasties the gentry's position and qualifications became formalized through the imperial examination system (Chow 1966: 2–3).

The point is that after the empire came into being under the Ch'ins, the mobility already begun at the close of the Chou dynasty became one in which the passing of government examinations provided an entrée into the gentry. One could be born into a gentry family, but to become an official one could obtain the appointment only through one's own efforts, especially after the establishment in the middle of the 7th century of the nation-wide competitive imperial examination system, which made possible the selection of "an intellectual elite, even of obscure origin, once every three years" (Chow 1966: 4–5). Social mobility was given a tremendous incentive under this system. To it must be added another factor, the breakdown of feudalism, after which it was possible for anyone to become emperor by capturing the throne. But the old gentry persisted until the advent in 1911 of the Republic, when the old imperial examination system was abolished and a new gentry, recruited from the peasantry, came into being. With the Emperor gone, the warlords took his place, and of course this gave new opportunities for upward mobility. Although Chow's research concerns itself with but a single county in the province of Yunnan in the 1940s, his use of life histories and detailed social statistics for that county supports the implication that the whole nation had long endured a kind of social rise in which the individual could improve his position through his own efforts.

A third book, *The Ladder of Success in Imperial China* (1962), by Ping-ti Ho, further shows the inevitable consequences of the mobility initiated in Chou times. Even through the author is mostly interested in social mobility in the Ming and Ch'ing times, 1368–1911, he reaches back into a more remote time. The book is essentially a study in socioacademic mobility within a context of general mobility, and its more systematic data deal with entry into officialdom as one particular kind of social mobility. The author resorts considerably to the compilation of statistics, and quantifies as much as possible from government documents, local histories, biographical series, and genealogies. His most systematic sources are the lists of *chin-shih*, or holders of the highest academic degree, who almost automatically became officials of middle rank. However, he also analyzes lists of holders of intermediate and elementary academic degrees.

He recognizes that the roots of Ming-Ch'ing mobility are traceable to a tradition emerging from the Chou era. The Confucian idealists, the disciples of a school of political strategy expressed in the book the *Kuan-tzu*, the followers of Mo-tzu, and the Legalists, had all adhered to the idea of an unequal or hierarchical society in which there should be a sharp demarcation between the ruling and ruled classes. But their social views differed vastly from one another, encompassing in some instances a unitary state and an authoritarian society (the Legalists) and in others the time-honored feudal system (the Confucianists). The disagreement was in resolving the basic antithesis common to all ancient social ideologies: society is necessarily hierarchical, yet a hierarchical society can not survive indefinitely unless its inherent injustice is either eliminated or in some way greatly alleviated. Eventually, by the 3rd century BCE at the latest, the various schools of thought found a common formula in their social ideologies—the principle of individual merit. Great diversity attended the definition of merit as seen by the various schools, but at least the doctrine was established that ruling class membership should be determined on the basis of individual virtue. Eventually, the Confucian school's view, that social equity comes from educational equity, won out.

The implications of all this for social and individual mobility ought to be apparent. China since the time following Confucius has consistently placed emphasis on individual qualifications, thus instigating efforts to rise above the social condition into which one is born.

If the collapse of Chou feudalism favored social mobility, and if Confucianist theory, which continued to be influential for many centuries to come, viewed social status as something achieved rather than ascribed, with the virtuous being wealthy and honored and the unworthy poor and humble, why should there be uncertainty and insecurity? Should not those human beings who are superior in intelligence, ability, and morality rise inexorably to the top in the natural social hierarchy?

For various reasons, the answer is in the negative. The actual system of stratification wandered from the ideal pattern as such theorists as Hsün-tzu and Mencius had envisioned it. To be sure, during the late Chou period of the Warring States many men with humble backgrounds did become high officials, such as generals and chancellors, and during the Han period the recommendation system came into being, with offices bestowed in principle on the basis of merit; but between the ideal and the real there was much discrepancy. One could not be at all sure that his personal endowments insured rise in status. This was apparent to the ancients themselves, who were puzzled by the failure of a man such as Confucius to hold a post commensurate with his great virtue and ability. Two Han scholars, Wang Fu and Wang Ch'ung, wrote explicitly on the subject, with the latter attributing the discrepancy to the fact that "opportunity is not always there when one seeks to enter upon an official career" (Ch'ü 1957: 238–39).

The recommendatory system, instituted during the Han, was not always administered in accordance with its stated aims. It had been designed to recruit government officials on the basis of merit, with provincial and local officials being regularly required to recommend deserving men. To understand the reasons for its ultimate failure requires an understanding of the so-called gentry state, to which we now turn very briefly.

Gentry society began with the medieval period of Chinese history, which commences with the Han. It was a society devoid of aristocracy and nobility. Eberhard, in his book *Conquerors and Rulers: Social Forces in Medieval China* (1965) lists as its criteria not only leisure, non-productive, literacy, and high status, but also a class of rulers in contrast to the uneducated and primarily inactive commoners (p. 43). The gentry invested its wealth in land. Its members either served as officials or lived on their estates as junkers.

There was a discrepancy between the theory—that this was an open society—and the reality, which was that on the whole it was a closed society made up of four classes, of which the gentry formed one. Ideally, anyone could enter into the ranks of the open society, except such unfree persons as slaves, professional soldiers, professional musicians, and dancers, as well as, in some periods, merchants, shopkeepers, and artisans. In practice, then, social rise, which was frequent at first, became extremely unusual (Eberhard 1965: 212).

One reason for the inability to move into the gentry class was economic, for to become an official in the city required an education which could only be paid for by families able to hire a tutor. The country home was the chief economic support of the family. Helping to weld the gentry into a closed society were rules of behavior observed by its members. These rules created differences in behavior, language, gestures, and morals from those of the lower classes (*ibid.* 44–45).

The gentry class was extremely stable and preserved itself until the advent of the Communist regime. It maintained suitable rules of marriages, for it was class conscious and deterred as much as it could any movement between the classes.

The recommendatory system of the Han and subsequent dynasties naturally suffered under such a society. Aside from the problem of agreeing on what constituted "merit," there was the difficulty of preventing the recommendation of already existing minor officials and their descendants, as well as scholarly families. The system was not synonymous with the whole era of the gentry state, however, for it was abandoned when the Han dynasty collapsed. Instead, a new official was appointed for each prefecture who was charged with the responsibility of seeking out and placing able men of the area into nine grades for the purpose of bureaucratic recruitment. This system, too, was unfortunately abused, and after three centuries of political division the T'ang dynasty came into existence and instituted the competitive civil service examination system. Examinations were necessary to earn the various scholarly titles and degrees. Because it was a more objective system than that based on recommendations, it became permanently institutionalized (Ho 1962: 10–17).

The civil service examination system did not provide quite the upward mobility claimed for it. Much of this was due to the actual exclusion of many classes of people from the right even to take the examinations. Only the gentry and the farmers were admitted. Excluded were merchants (0.3 percent of the total quota were finally admitted in very late times), sons of criminals, monks, non-Chinese, and certain others. Moreover, candidates had to be recommended by local authorities according to a severe quota system (1:7,000,000 for one of the three categories in the Earlier Han period). There was corruption in favor of the gentry, and in the 10th century degrees could be bought at fixed prices without any examination. The gentry was also favored by a privilege granted to officials who had served three years: they could secure appointments of relatives to positions at court. Finally, the sons of the gentry were at an advantage over other boys by their favored position in the admission of students to the state schools and in their ability to get education in private schools or by hiring tutors (Eberhard 1962: 22–26).

So, while the Confucian theory that social stratification should be based on the difference between mental and physical labor continued to be effective for many centuries, there remained considerable uncertainty that one could actually move into the class that he deserved. In fact, sumptuary laws came into being which hardened the difference between the ruled and the rulers. These laws were designed to give legal privileges to officials, and to insure their prestige and style of life. The government wanted to stabilize society by assigning to each class its definite position in the society, and went so far as to specify the garments that should be worn by the various classes. Also, it forbade marriage between members of different classes. The ruled—scholars, farmers, artisans, merchants, butchers, and others—were definitely inferior and were discriminated against in varying degrees, depending on the occupational group, for different occupations were endowed with different degrees of prestige. In fact, the lowest stratum, made up of the "mean people," formed virtually a caste; slaves, prostitutes, entertainers, government runners, and certain others could not marry into the other strata of the ruled class. The "mean people" were not allowed to take the civil service examinations (Ch'ü 1957: 245–49; cf. Eberhard 1962: 10–22). Restrictions were not removed until after Sung times, especially between 1450 and 1720.

Perhaps the picture of the hardening of class lines depicted above is misleading. The creation of the gentry class did after all do away irrevocably with feudalism. While the gentry tended to be self-perpetuating as a status group it never gained individual hereditary rights in the government positions it held. Some of the social mobility that had characterized later Chou times did persist.

The relevance of this to body divination may now be clarified. While it may have been true that the recommendation and competitive examination systems did not in fact allow much penetration of the lower classes into the gentry, there was nevertheless considerable opportunity for relocation among the gentry itself. One could advance his status even if it was done through irregular application of the channels for advancement. The fluidity within the gentry was bound to create a certain degree of uncertainty in its members. Not all of those who were recommended or who took the examinations were given official positions. Passing the examinations might be followed by many years of waiting for an opening, and in the end the candidate might never live to acquire a bureaucratic office. Then of course there was the more basic anxiety preceding this uneasiness—the anxiety as to whether one would pass the examination at all. The classic physiognomic writings of the later Sung period were built on a foundation erected in medieval times, and both the earlier and later books and essays show that physiognomics was directed towards the gentry class and its concern over the attainment of political office. In traditional China, political position carried not only great status but economic advantage as well. Levy (1953–54: 170) reminds us that the gentry were expected to depend for income on the perquisites of political office and the absentee ownership of land.

If the declining social mobility of the medieval period prevented physiognomics from achieving a wider base than it did, other factors worked simultaneously against its conceptual advancement. When the Han dynasty collapsed CE 220, there followed three centuries of confusion, social change, and intellectual agitation. Much of China, especially in the north, came under the rule of foreigners, and China experienced its first partition. Many kingdoms, each with its own dynasty, rose and fell. The San Kuo or Three Kingdoms existed simultaneously (221–65), to be followed by an uneasy reunification under the Chin, which itself experienced a Western phase (265–317) and an Eastern one (317–479). It was the Huns who, attacking the Chinese, had brought the Western Chin dynasty to an end. In addition to them, Turkic, proto-Mongolic, and Tibetan pastoral nomads set up a 260-year rule in the Yellow River Basin. Even the south underwent turmoil (cf. Eberhard 1960: 107–65). Natural calamities combined with social and political disintegration to worsen matters. History records 619 calamities between CE 220 and 589. Understandably, a "drowning humanity" reached out for relief and found it to some extent in Buddhism (Yang 1961: 115–17).

But Buddhism was not congenial to physiognomics. It was a world rejecting religion whose overriding goal was that of salvation. Man, it taught, is by nature greedy and angry and he must seek a total escape. With such an outlook, Buddhistic thinking hardly concerned itself at all with body divination.

Physiognomics also had to contend with the rational and skeptical Confucianists, who could not accept it and who indeed attacked it, with the notable exception of Wang Ch'ung (b. CE 27)

Nor were the Taoists of much help during these times, for having gone through their formative philosophical phase they had now become preoccupied with magical means for achieving eternal life for people.

The medieval period, then, was one of conceptual stagnation for body divination. Its appeal and perhaps to some extent its practice were circumscribed by hardening class lines.

Following the close of the T'ang dynasty a new era of "modern times" was ushered in by the brief Five Dynasty period (907–60), to be followed by the sophisticated Sung dynasties. This era endured a thousand years and, contrary to some earlier theories, had social mobility (Eberhard 1962: 265). Ping-ti Ho has dealt with the Ming and Ch'ing phases of this mobility in his previously cited work, *The Ladder of Success in Imperial China*, but as we have already summarized his methodology and findings they will not be gone over again here.

It was in this modern period that body divination enjoyed its classic expression. Its conceptual aspects achieved their most brilliant synthesis. Although there is no direct means of gauging the extent to which somatomancy was practiced, indirect evidences lead us to assume that it enjoyed its greatest vogue during these times. Many books on the subject were written, among them the influential *Ma-i Shen Hsiang* and its derivative, the *Shen Hsiang Ch'üan Pien*.

Physiognomists obviously flourished among the gentry, as an inspection of the treatises on physiognomy readily reveal. The reasons are most likely to be found principally in the solace afforded to men who were uncertain about their careers and all the human situations dependent upon status. As long as the ideal persisted that one could become a general, a courtier, or even a prime minister, there would be the hope that a divinatory analysis would reveal one's chances of being the successful aspirant. Official position of course was not the only problem of these persons but it must have been one of the most pressing of all. The gentry undoubtedly had in addition all those further concerns—economic, marital, familial, physiological—that beset men everywhere.

In this connection it must be remembered that body divination was only one of the many mantic recourses available to and popular with the Chinese. It happened, however, to be particularly appropriate for personal kinds of anxieties. Whether it assumed a vulgar form for the lower classes of people cannot be determined, for we do not know of any popular publications except in recent times; but it would be safe to assume that there were common practitioners who took on humble clients for a modest fee. The concerns of such clients might not be characterized by the problem of public office, yet there would be considerable overlapping in other respects.

Areas of Concern

If our thesis is correct—that divination is a response to areas of concern, anxiety, and cognitive frustration—it is appropriate to look into the responses given by Chinese physiognomy to the morphological indicators within the individual so that we may see if there is any pattern.

I have attempted to do this by means of a statistical sampling from the *Shen Hsiang Hui Pien*, a physiognomic compilation in four volumes published in 1843. The sampling procedure involves recording visible morphological units, their characteristics, and the corresponding interpretations regarding destiny and character. It is only with the interpretation of the physical units that we shall deal, and not with the units as such or with their mode of interpretation.

While a certain degree of subjectivity must necessarily enter into this analysis, the "responses" to the inquiries being ill-defined, overlapping and not at all wholly comparable to one another in kind value, a certain degree of objectivity is nevertheless assured. I have limited myself to visible morphological units only and not included anything based on abstraction and intuition, such as one gets in dealing with color, *ch'i* (cf. Greek *pneuma*), and *shen* (spirit), which in any event I do not consider to be truly somatomantic even though the Chinese include them as part of the art of physiognomy. Further objectivity is achieved by dealing with manifest content rather than depth analysis.

The total number of responses recorded from the *Shen Hsiang Hui Pien* is 546, a fairly large and at the same time well balanced set because the book is a representative one that combines the seventy three known schools of physiognomy—or so the compiler, Kao Wei-ching, tells us. The compilation embodies the cumulative judgments of many centuries, and while it is undoubtedly weighted towards the later dynasties it at the same time has its roots in the earlier ones. So, though it cannot be said to speak for China as an unchanging and social entity, it makes an approximation to it.

Based on a consideration of the nature of the responses, I have divided them into two major groups. One deals with the positive side of human concern, telling us about the favorable things that people wish to be true or to have happen. The other deals with the negative side, showing the undesirable things that are apt to be associated with persons.

Under these two major divisions, several kinds of human concern are listed. In general they emanate from the raw material rather than an *a priori* scheme. Where responses extracted from the book are closely allied, even though they may have different labels they have been combined so as to increase the degree of distinctiveness between one unit and another. The relative importance of one area of concern as compared with another is indicated in terms of total recorded frequence of occurrence and their corresponding percentages.

The positive side of human concern is shown in detail in Table 6. From this it is seen that the Chinese place great value on receiving honor, attaining office, acquiring wealth, and having a long life. These four desirable things constitute almost sixty-three per cent of the frequency of occurrence of all items. If the first three of them (honor, office, wealth) are seen as facets of an ambitious striving for ascendancy, they then make sense as being consistent with the high value the Chinese have placed throughout history on ameliorating one's position socially, economically, and politically.

The rags to riches theme permeates "numerous Chinese novels, short stories, operas, shadow plays, and legends" (F. Hsu 1953: 144). Books such as the *Shen Hsiang Hui Pien* as well as its many antecedents were obviously written for a stratum of society which envisioned the possibility of improvement of one's standing. They write about the attainment of such positions as that of a royal attendant, a king's advisor, a general, a governor, or even a cabinet minister. Some signs they proclaim to be attributes of a lord or marquis; others they assert are indicative of the winning of wealth and fame. The road to success is often envisioned as being achieved through admission to the literati-bureaucratic group, which means acquiring the highest examination honors, a future sometimes predicted in responses to physiognomic signs, especially as seen in the lines of the palm. Commenting that entry into officialdom may be the most important aspect of social mobility in imperial China, Ho (1962: 92) has written: "There can be little doubt that traditional Chinese society considered entry into the ruling bureaucracy the final goal of upward social mobility."

Table 7, which treats of the negative side of human concern, would seem to indicate that the Chinese regard poverty as the most undesirable aspect of human life. Shortlivedness, harm to or loss of relatives, viciousness or aggression, and lack of relatives or friends follow in that order.

Table 6
Areas of Concern as Seen in Physiognomic Responses: Positive

Response*	Frequency	Frequency Per Cent	Cumulative Frequency Percentage
1. honor..................................	47	20.9	20.9
2. attainment of office...............	41	18.2	39.1
3. wealth.................................	32	14.2	53.3
4. longevity.............................	21	9.3	62.6
5. intelligence.........................	15	6.7	69.3
6. blessed happiness.................	13	5.8	75.1
7. success...............................	9	4.0	79.1
8. prosperity...........................	8	3.6	82.7
9. prominence and fame............	7	3.1	85.8
10. many brothers.....................	7	3.1	88.9
11. good character.....................	4	1.8	90.7
12. family................................	3	1.3	92.0
13. landownership.....................	2	0.9	92.9
14. serene life and business..........	2	0.9	93.8
15. filial piety..........................	2	0.9	94.7
16. protection from family...........	2	0.9	95.6
17. strong character...................	2	0.9	96.5

*Also, one each: have servants, good luck, generosity, beautiful wife, no criminal penalties, no worry, become fat, become monk.

Compared to the positive outcomes or responses, the negative ones are not only more varied but more numerous (321 compared to 225). The greater variability may simply be a function of larger numbers of responses, but the larger numbers themselves need interpretation. Frankly, they seem to be contradictory to the general impression that one gets from the usual works on physiognomy, especially the *Shen Hsiang Ch'üan Pien*, written earlier and furnishing most of the descriptive materials used in the present book. Perhaps the *Shen Hsiang Hui Pien*, used for our statistical analysis, was compiled in an era of growing pessimism, when China had become a second-rate power dominated by foreign governments and incapable of meeting the material needs of an expanding population.

Do the results conform to general expectation? Within limits, yes. We must make a distinction between any general concerns held by the people and those which are expressed through body divination. It may well be that other forms of divination are better suited for handling certain kinds of inquiries and anxieties besetting the individual.

Specifically, one would expect to find divination especially suited to concern over health and life. If we look at Table 6 and 7 it is obvious that with respect to longevity it holds fourth rank in the table of positive responses (21) and second place in the negative list (28). Combined, these exceed any other combination of responses except wealth (32) plus poverty (52).

Yet sickness is barely mentioned. Perhaps this is because it is subsumed by longevity, of which it is an indirect expression. On the other hand, perhaps body divination is not an appropriate instrument for forecasting illness—a strange possibility, for it would seem highly plausible for physiognomic inspection to take on the characteristics of clinical diagnosis, as it does indeed in European somatomancy.

Family matters, as one might expect, are solidly reflected in the responses. Reference is made to harm to or loss of relatives (23), no relatives and friends (22), homelessness (8), many brothers (7), family (that is, having one) (3), fear of wife (3), filial piety (2, surprisingly little), protection from family (2), and so on. If little prognostication is made as to whether or not one will have a large family, a thing greatly desired by the Chinese, it may be linked to the age at which clients consult physiognomists, who might be reluctant to make a prediction when the client's procreative life is already far advanced or already behind him.

Table 7
Areas of Concern as Seen in Physiognomic Responses: Negative

Response*	Frequency	Frequency Per Cent	Cumulative Frequency Percentage
1. poverty..................................	52	16.2	16.2
2. shortlivedness.........................	28	8.7	24.9
3. harm to or loss of relatives.........	23	7.2	32.1
4. viciousness; aggression.............	22	6.9	39.0
5. no relatives and friends.............	22	6.9	45.9
6. meanness; lowness...................	18	5.6	51.5
7. failure (business, family)...........	17	5.3	56.8
8. bad character...........................	17	5.3	62.1
9. unluckiness.............................	14	4.4	66.5
10. criminal penalties.....................	11	3.4	69.9
11. hardship.................................	11	3.4	73.3
12. stupidity.................................	10	3.1	76.4
13. non-success............................	9	2.8	79.2
14. lecherousness..........................	9	2.8	82.0
15. homelessness..........................	8	2.5	84.5
16. bad death................................	7	2.2	86.7
17. worry.....................................	4	1.3	88.0
18. litigation................................	3	0.9	88.9
19. fear of wife.............................	3	0.9	89.8
20. uncertainty.............................	3	0.9	90.7
21. raised by another family............	3	0.9	91.6
22. often victimized......................	3	0.9	92.5
23. betrayal.................................	2	0.6	93.1
24. no office................................	2	0.6	93.7
25. jealousy.................................	2	0.6	94.3
26. no help from family or Heaven....	2	0.6	94.9

*Also, one each: lifelong sickness, no affinity with opposite sex, trouble in general, cunningness, family not forthcoming early, being a servant, being a concubine, lack of steadiness, weak character, pompousness, mother must be changed, scared often by water, divorce, childlessness, without blessing, landless.

Love, as well as the war between the sexes, is scarcely reflected in the responses. There is some explanation for this. It is not that the Chinese stifle sexual attraction, for after all there are the pornographic and erotic novels, as well as erotic paintings and the illustrated sex-technique books for householders. But for the Chinese, "love" is a term that has never been respectable, and the emphasis on man-woman relations has been that of procreation. The Chinese way of life subordinates individual feelings to group requirements, "while sex and all activities associated with it must be restricted to the compartments of life where it is socially appropriate" (F. Hsu 1953: 37–38).

In art the artist bases his craftsmanship not on the study of the nude as in Europe but on the study of the landscape. He portrays the human figure naked rather than nude, in terms of deromanticized realism rather than idealism or naturalism. To the traditional Chinese the nude is immoral. Erotica art exists, but while no traditional family would have thought of furnishing a house without a collection of erotic paintings, these were stored rather than displayed (Gluck 1961: 412–21).

If sexuality is infrequent in Chinese art, it is very plain in pornography. Works of pornography are never enjoyed or displayed in public, but in private they are viewed together with husbands, wives, sweethearts, or prostitutes without any feeling of guilt. The Chinese regulate sex by compartmentalizing it into specific areas where the need to feel reserve is not necessary (F. Hsu 1953: 21–23).

It is this compartmentalization which causes the Ch'ing dynasty *Shen Hsiang Hui Pien* to avoid love and sex and any hint of the romantic. The separation was less rigidly observed when the earlier, Ming dynasty *Shen Hsiang Ch'üan Pien* was published, for here we find much allusion to man-woman relations, as the reader can see for himself by turning back to Chapters III, IV, and especially V of the present volume. But even here there is no precipitous rush into these matters, which in any event concern not affairs of the heart but for the most part the difficulties of the relation between husband and wife.

This restraint began in the wake of the events that took place in the 13th century, when the Mongols established their military rule over entire China. Previous to that, as Gulik has shown in his highly authoritative and well documented book, *Sexual Life in Ancient China* (1961), the Chinese had for 2,000 years freely talked and written about sexual matters. The germs of prudery came into existence when the Chinese made efforts to keep their sexual life a secret from all outsiders.

Fearful of having their women-folk importuned by the conquerors, householders who had Mongol soldiers billeted on them kept their women secluded from them as much as possible (Gulik 1961: 245–46). During the Ch'ing (Manchu) dynasty this prudery was once more intensified, again as the result of foreign occupation.

The later books on physiognomy may be contrasted with one mentioned by Gulik, *T'ai-ch'ing-ching* said to be an ancient work cited by a Sui dynasty book in which the physiognomy of a woman suitable for the exercise of sexual intercourse is delineated (*ibid.* 149–51).

In conclusion, our analysis of the responses, though it lacks precision and a rigorous methodology, is provocative. Imperfect as it may be, it nevertheless seems to reflect the function of Chinese body divination. A form of supernatural practice can only continue to persist if it has some kind of sociocultural function in a society, otherwise it will die out.

The analysis described above should help strengthen my thesis that the function of Chinese body divination is mainly to provide individuals with information concerning their potentials and future life. The way in which they envisage these potentials and destiny reflect not only the general concerns of all people but the particular ones of the Chinese in a given time and place. In view of the great amount of literature on the subject and the prestige accorded physiognomists throughout history, it can hardly by doubted that body divination has long fulfilled an important function in Chinese life. If in contemporary times that role has declined it will have been because supernaturalism in general has everywhere lost ground in the modern setting.

Functional Parallels in Europe

In Europe body divination flourished in an historical and social context approximating that of China, and experienced pulsations comparable to it.

The initial European appearance of the practice was in ancient Greece. It took root there, if my interpretation is valid, not only because it had received a heritage of culture in general and divination in particular from Mesopotamia but also because conditions were such that it found functional usefulness there.

The Mesopotamian situation itself has a bearing on the interpretation of the functional value of all kinds of divination and is worth alluding to before examining the Hellenic conditions. It has been interpreted in a provocative fashion by the Frankforts (1946), who see a nexus between the hypertrophy of the mantic arts and the nature of the physical environment. They contrast this with the relative paucity of divination in Egypt, where the physical environment offered a sharp contrast.

According to their reasoning, both the Egyptians and the Mesopotamians, living agricultural lives in small urban centers, agreed on certain fundamental assumptions: the individual is part of society; society is imbedded in nature; and nature is but the manifestation of the divine. The Egyptians, however, had a different world view. They conceived of the gods as powerful without being violent, and saw nature as an established order, with the divine Pharoah sitting on the throne ensuring that between nature and society there would always be a harmonious integration. These features were possibly connected with the regular natural rhythms along the Nile. In contrast, the Mesopotamian gods assigned a mere mortal to rule men, and their divine favor might be withdrawn from him at any time. Here man was more subjected to decisions he could neither measure nor influence. In Mesopotamian texts there are "overtones of anxiety which seem to express a haunting fear that the unaccountable and turbulent powers may at any time bring disaster to human society." For this reason the king and his counsellors looked for portents on earth and in the heavens which might manifest changes in divine grace, so that catastrophe might be anticipated and therefore possibly averted. These features, say the Frankforts, seem to be related to the more irregular natural setting of the Tigris and Euphrates rivers.

If stability and predictability discouraged the development of divination in Egypt, so did the orientation of the religion towards the afterlife. It is one of the arguments of the present volume that great preoccupation with life after death is not conducive to mantic efforts. In Egypt the cult of the dead, with its hope of endless life, dominated the thinking of the people more than it had ever done in any other religion. The cult of Osiris reflected the prevalent belief that happy immortality awaited the living upon death. Mortuary customs prevailed which were designed to preserve the body as an abode for the *ba* and the *ka*—the soul and the ghostly double, respectively. In contrast to this the Mesopotamians saw death as putting a virtual end to the personality, and so they had little preoccupation with the afterlife. Upon death, the individual went to a shadowy, dust-filled place under the earth and there he remained, without being punished for evil or rewarded for virtue. These differences in perspective must have had opposing repercussions relative to divination. The Mesopotamians were much more preoccupied with their present life and its problems, and found astrology and other forms of divination congenial to the allaying of their anxieties.

However much Mesopotamian conditions were conductive to the rise of divination, they did not particularly favor the development of body divination, a completely personal mantic art requiring for its existence the emergence of the individual from his ties with the natural and social world. Individualism implies self-reliance, self-containment, privacy, and man's awareness that he is a separate and independent entity. It places value on a certain lack of restraint on the individual. Mesopotamia did not have this.

Periclean Athens saw the beginnings of individualism in the Western world, with Epicureans giving expression to the doctrine that the individual was the unit on which society is based. That is why astrology became genethliacal in the hands of the Greeks, whereas it had been public in the hands of its donors, the Babylonians. The Romans, who never developed physiognomics to the same extent as the Hellenes, clung mostly to highly developed forms of public divination because their greater adherence to Stoicism did not encourage the independence of the individual.

During the Middle Ages which followed upon the classic period of European history there was less scholarly preoccupation with body divination than in the past, and what had been developed in this respect by the Greeks would have been lost to the world if it had not been preserved by the Arabs. One could dismiss the decline of physiognomics in part as a casualty of the times, for while this may not have been the kind of "dark ages" once attributed to it, a general retrogression had struck European culture. Beginning with the disintegration of the West Roman Empire in the 4th and 5th centuries, the medieval period endured in some places until into the 15th century, after which it gave way almost imperceptibly to the Renaissance and modern times. During that time Christianity preserved civilization as best it could in the face of new waves of invasions.

If factors other than cultural retrogression conspired to diminish the importance of body divination in the Middle Ages, what were they?

One of them was medieval Christianity itself, with its emphasis on other worldliness and divine providence. As far back as the 2nd century the Gnostics had embraced a dualism of spirit versus matter. They saw the material world as utterly vile and degrading, and not at all of God's doing. Jesus, they said, had pointed the way for the miserable human souls to liberate themselves of the enslavement of the flesh and the material world, and to enter into pure spirituality of being. Thus, Gnosticism was a plan of salvation. This was only one manifestation of abnegation of the world.

After Christianity had become the imperial state religion of Rome, monasticism as a technique of abnegation gained rapid growth, with monastaries springing up everywhere both in the East and West. In the medieval period monastic piety was given its greatest expression by the Benedictines, Dominicans, and Franciscans. Along with monasticism there went a certain degree of mysticism. When in solitary meditation, the monk tried to purge himself of evil and unite his soul in ecstacy with God and the saints. The influence of Augustine (354–430), who had considered the world of the spirit to be far more consequential than that of the flesh, permeated the Scholasticism of the times. In the 13th century Thomas Aquinas taught that the individual can only attain eternal life through the theological virtues—faith, hope, and love—which come from God. Medieval mysticism, which was both individual and cultic in form, pursued the belief that the mystic vision of God was possible not only in the next world but here on earth. An especially powerful manifestation of salvationism was that of medieval millenarism, a chiliastic doctrine offering solace to the poor by presenting them with phantasies of a terrestrial Paradise—a Heavenly City on earth which would come about through a sudden miraculous event completely transforming the world and purging it of suffering and sin.

The tendency in the Middle Ages, then, was to try to rise above the formal and external limits of human experience and to confront God directly. In an ambience of this kind, as we have already suggested for Buddhism, body divination found itself hindered because of its own emphasis on this life as it actually exists.

Yet somatomancy was not an inconsequential force even during this period of European history. An article on chiromancy in late medieval Latin manuscripts shows how prevalent were the writings of this kind of divination even when people were so oriented towards a transcendent world (Thorndike, 1965).

Medieval Christianity acted as a check in another respect, too. With its doctrines of providence and predestination it insisted that one's life and future were out of the hands of the individual and in the hands of a divine determining action. One's eternal destiny is determined by God. Dogma of this sort did nothing to encourage recourse to divination of any kind, let alone somatomancy.

Individual freedom and assertiveness, which had first emerged in ancient Greece and to a lesser extent Rome, was inhibited not only by the Christian emphasis on total commitment to God but equally as much by a new complex of economic, social, and political forces having a bearing on the mobility, or relative lack of it, which was possible for the individual. As it is our contention that social mobility and body divination have a functional connection, it is necessary to consider the pattern of life in the Middle Ages, which unfortunately can only be done here in a sketchy way.

After the dissolution of Charlemagne's empire, the characteristic European form of social and political organization became that of feudalism, based agriculturally on the manor system. In feudalistic society there existed a strict division into social classes: nobility, clergy, peasantry, and in later times burgesses. Under the manorial system on which the political economy was based the peasants worked the land which their lord granted them to use in exchange for fixed dues in kind, money, and personal services. The rights of cultivation were usually heritable among the peasants, who were either serfs or villeins. Serfdom was a condition of hereditary semibondage, the serf usually having been descended from slave status to a condition in which he was not free. Villeinage differed to some extent from serfdom in that the villein was usually a man who had descended from full freedom to half-status and was personally free.

While the concept of feudalism has been challenged by some historians, largely as the result of the difficulties encountered when trying to discover common ingredients in its alleged manifestations elsewhere in the world, there is no doubt of its reality as a sociopolitical system. Its main features—a rural economy and the dispersal of power in a variety of semi-independent domains—were not conducive to social mobility and individual freedom. Communications were either poor or virtually lacking, and geographic movement was severely circumscribed. The person was hemmed in by restrictive rules and obligations that affected all aspects of life. One's role was so fixed in the social order that classes resembled castes. One pursued a calling that was deemed to have been set in Heaven by God, and it was hereditary.

The Church, which became the central and most influential social institution, did provide an important avenue of social mobility to able young men from the lower classes, but such upward mobility was always limited to a few. In any event, internal stratification within the Church was related to that of the general society. The upper clergy came mostly from the upper classes, being closely connected with the nobility by ties of blood; the lower clergy were drawn from the lower classes and had inferior status (O'Dea 1966: 75).

A positive consequence of the lack of freedom in the Middle Ages was that it endowed a person with a certain security. He was not alone and isolated. This is exactly the point made by Erich Fromm in his *Escape from Freedom* (1941), in which he argues that individualism is gained at a price, for it makes a man isolated and therefore anxious and powerless.

Fromm says that life for medieval man had a meaning which left no place or need for doubt, because from the moment he was born a person had a distinct, unchangeable, and unquestionable place in the social world. A man, whether a peasant, craftsman, or knight, was identical with his role in society. Because the social order was thought of as a natural order, with man a part of it, it gave him a feeling of security and of belonging. Competition was relatively little. Being born into a certain economic position gave assurance of a livelihood determined by tradition (Fromm 1941: 41–42).

The feudal and manorial systems declined for a variety of reasons which will not be explored here. Decline came early in Italy and later to other countries of Europe, some of which never saw the complete disappearance of feudalism and the manor until fairly recent times. The close of the Middle Ages took place gradually but is generally thought of as coming about with the historical developments which brought the Renaissance into being, and with it modern times.

The Renaissance has been dated, defined, and described in many ways, arousing heated controversy and even some denial of its very reality. Much of the disagreement centers around the question of its originality, with one school of thought insisting that all the ingredients of the period were already to be found in the Middle Ages. Perhaps the seeds were there, but as Sarton has said the baby had not yet been delivered. We shall take the position that the latter event took place in the 14th century, although there are many prominent authorities who would assign it to the 15th instead. Also, contrary to some, we shall extend its duration into the 16th century, thus extending its span so as to include the beginnings of the period of the Reformation.

The nature and role of religion in society always has a bearing on the receptivity extended to personal divination, and we may proceed to examine their place in the Renaissance by referring to an allegation made in 1860 by Jacob Burckhardt in his now famous and provocative *Die Kultur der Renaissance in Italien* to the effect that the Italians had reverted to paganism. This view has now been discredited and there are even writers who insist that Renaissance man was even more religious than medieval man. This may be so, but certainly he was religious in a different way. World denial was now no longer one of the dominant themes of Christianity. The Protestant Reformation made it possible to turn away from world rejection. It declared that salvation was potentially available to anyone, regardless of his station or calling. It successfully institutionalized the idea that salvation is not to be found in any kind of withdrawal from the world but rather in the midst of wordly activities. The world is the theater of God's glory and the place in which to fulfill his command (Bellah 1964).

In focussing attention on the here and now, religion lost much of its traditional function for those who constituted the elite of Renaissance society. A vacuum was created into which it was possible for personal types of divination to step in, and that is why somatomancy reached its climax in this particular period of European history.

The reason the role of the Church underwent such considerable change was that although it had succeeded in the past in integrating a society that was based on an agrarian and feudal system, it failed when confronted by a society now composed of a large proportion of urban, commercial, and industrial groups. Among the upper classes in the more developed and affluent cities of Italy there appeared a fast-growing secular spirit that deliberately preoccupied its members with the pursuit of worldly goods. They were not concerned with ascetic otherworldliness or with the view that the world is a vale of tears. Indeed, they were reluctant to accept the counsel of the clergy or to let the Church control social and economic functions which they felt were better handled by their own state governments. This secular development soon spread to northern Europe (O'Dea 1966: 87–88).

Obviously the traditional ideas of the Middle Ages were incapable any longer during the Renaissance of providing life with a satisfactory meaning. One could experience and represent life, said Petrarch, without reference to Christological concepts. Erasmus found permanence and stability in human factors that a man could himself perceive. Much of the secularized view of life was an inheritance from the Graeco-Roman world, especially as Cicero and Seneca had expressed it, and leaned heavily on Platonic and Neo-Platonic philosophy for its justification.

The enormous popularity enjoyed by body divination during the Renaissance did not come about only because of a new world view. There was great fluidity in all aspects of culture and social organization, and this jarred the individual even further out of a comfortable pattern of expectations.

The Renaissance was a culture of a wealthy upper class and was marked in Italy by despotism. There as elsewhere it went along with the rise of a powerful money class. Caste distinctions were ignored, and social stratification among the masses too was shaken. A symptom of the times were the *condottieri*, mercenaries and soldiers of fortune who flourished in an Italy torn by strife between the forces of the Holy Roman Empire and the Pope, between the emerging cities and the feudal overlords. From the 13th to the 16th century, these men dominated warfare, influenced politics, and often carved out states and principalities for themselves. Often they came from humble backgrounds.

As a consequence of these and other changes, the Renaissance saw the emergence of man to full awareness of himself as a separate entity. This theme was first formulated by Burckhardt (*The Civilization of the Renaissance*, 1944: 81–103) and has generally been adopted by historians of the period.

If an expression of this awareness is needed, a modest example is that of the great demand for portraits at the beginning of the 15th century. Another would be the large number of highly personal biographies and autobiographies written in Italy during the Renaissance. Nothing like Benvenuto Cellini's egotistical life history, Girolamo Cardano's introspective self analysis, or Luigi Cornaro's optimistic account of his use of diet to attain the age of the centenarian, could have been written in the Middle Ages.

The implications of the heightening of individualism has not escaped the attention of the psychologist, Erich Fromm, who draws some provocative conclusions relevant to our interests.

Fromm sees the man of the Renaissance as torn from the "primary ties" which had connected medieval man with the Church and his social caste. The Renaissance capitalists, for example, were not happy and secure; they were anxious and insecure. Each step in the direction of growing individuation threatened people with new insecurities, for it meant growing isolation and thereby growing doubt concerning one's own powerlessness and insignificance as an individual (Fromm 1941: 36).

Another way of perceiving the plasticity of the times is through the idea of the *secretae naturae*—a doctrine that saw nature as holding untold secrets which could be unlocked by man if only he applied the right key. The alchemists are one of the best examples of the devotion lavished upon this optimistic belief. Says one writer,

> For five centuries, from the fourteenth to the eighteenth, the most gifted students of nature, the most devoted experimentalists and pioneers in chemistry believed passionately in the existence of an elixir of life, a substance which could resurrect the dead and cure all disease, bring perfection to the crippled, restore permanent youth to the senile, bring wisdom to the foolish and virility to the impotent. In addition to these grandiose powers it could also transmute the base metals into noble, silver and gold... (Graubard 1953: 238).

While to the man of the Renaissance nothing seemed to be impossible in this world, with its secret forces at work, these forces appeared to him to be both chaotic and miraculous. Says Groethuysen (1935), the inclination not to deny the possibility of any imaginable phenomenon caused man to feel that he lived in a world where all was in continuous flux, and only chance ruled. In the face of this, since he could not master Fortuna, all that one could do was adapt himself to her. This could be done through clever calculations, by looking for typical and recurrent regularities.

And, if the thesis of this chapter is correct, it could be done through divination.

Groethuysen (*ibid*). cautions against accepting the pursuit of wonders as indicative of the development of a secular view of the world in a modern sense, for the requisite scientific conditions simply did not exist. It was a question of deciding in favor of one form of belief in miracles as against another, one miracle being rejected while another was recognized. Only with the advent of modern scientific consciousness, delineating between reality and fiction, did a new conception of the world come into being. So, while the new scientific spirit did make progress it did so only slowly.

Yet it cannot be ignored that science was having some effects and by forcing a reconsideration of past ideas added further to the unsettling conditions of the times. Copernicus and Galileo, for instance, had destroyed the ancient terracentric concept of the universe, with all that this implied for the undermining of scholastic dogma and theology.

Recapitulation

In pursuing the kind of comparative analysis of body divination that has been used in these pages, it is at once apparent that the attempt which has been employed to establish generalizations of both historical and functional nature is an ambitious one fraught with many perils. It begins first by investigating the phenomenon as it manifests itself especially in one culture during a particular era, that of Sung China, and then widens its inquiry so as to encompass similar manifestations in Mesopotamia, ancient Greece, the Arabic world, and medieval and Renaissance Europe, with occasional reference to India.

Comparison on so vast a scale is perhaps more piquant than the small-scale, highly controlled comparisons being advocated nowadays by anthropologists, but it is also filled with greater risk. He who undertakes to look for universals must contend with poorer controls than the person who limits himself to a single area whose societies are historically related and whose common culture makes it possible to provide controls against which variables may be tested.

Perhaps a more limited comparison, in both time and space, would have yielded more meaningful results than a broad one. Even though the goals would have been narrower and the achievement less fascinating they would have been better fulfilled. Research design comes closer to the experimental when the scope of inquiry is limited.

Yet the broader goal was chosen as a more stimulating means of achieving a better understanding of the history and role of body divination. Refinements can come later, even at the risk of negating some of the conclusions that have been arrived at in this volume. For example, it would be good to see how *firasa* operated among the Arabs when they were in their greatest ascendancy. The records for such research are fairly ample, although they would require considerable scholarly background for their interpretation. Ancient Greece, too, is well known and would make further inquiry than we have undertaken here a rewarding study.

Previous research on my own part had hitherto been confined to Europe, primarily of the Renaissance period. It is now glaringly apparent to me that this had provided too narrow a vista for the proper examination of body divination in its wider aspects. In retrospect, European somatomancy now seems far less important and original than it did before I explored its occurrence elsewhere in the world, and some of the particular social concomitants of this mantic art now have narrower applicability than I had supposed. Happily, however, the fundamental hypotheses have borne up quite well, but this a matter of judgment on my part that the reader may wish to evaluate for himself.

The historical emphasis given to this inquiry has proven to be invaluable in the results it has yielded. Among social anthropologists it has usually been the fashion to spurn history and historical reconstruction in favor of so-called functional analysis; but the truth of the matter is that function is often best revealed through the insights provided by tracing historical relationships and observing changes in social contexts throughout time. Elsewhere (Lessa 1968) I have an article whose emphasis is on the pulsations of Chinese history and the changing social contexts in which Chinese body divination has found expression throughout the centuries. Body divination in China seems to rise and fall with increase and decrease of social mobility and personal insecurity. This thesis is not exactly new, for anthropologists have long understood that all forms of divination, not somatomancy alone, are a response to cognitive frustration. But it is hoped that this hypothesis has now been given ample demonstration with respect to physiognomics, a narrow and highly personal kind of mantic activity which has been consistently ignored by social scientists.

One of the most valuable by-products of the historical inquiries made in this book was not foreseen before the work was begun. I had supposed that body divination arises independently wherever the social concomitants—individualization, insecurity, urbanization, sophistication—are just right. But I am now convinced that these conditions are not enough. They may yield personal mantic devices of various kinds, but not necessarily body mantic, which apparently originated in one place, Mesopotamia, and then spread to most of Eurasia. However, diffusion would not have taken place if social and phychological conditions had not provided the kind of receptivity that is mandatory for the incorporation into the culture of somatomantic ideas. An example of the failure of the proper social conditions alone to produce somatomancy in the face of lack of contact with an already existing tradition would be the native Americans of the higher centers of New World civilization. I know of no evidence that personal divination of the somatomantic kind ever existed among them.

Perhaps the present investigation will induce similar but independent research on the part of social scientists and historians of science. It would be good, too, if it were to inspire functional study among contemporary peoples who still practice the art in all seriousness.

There are such peoples, even though they are rapidly losing interest in the face of scientific advance and technological achievement.

Finally, I have not discussed the relationship of body divination to the field of human constitution, except in a most cursory fashion in these pages and in an article published in 1952. The connection is a fascinating one which if adequately explored could lead to even better insights into both the psychology of insecurity and the search for what people understand to be the truth of things.

BIBLIOGRAPHY

PRIMARY SOURCES

Ku Chin T'u Shu Chi Ch'eng (古今圖書集成) (Complete Collection of Ancient and Contemporary Books). Compiled by Ch'en Meng-lei (陳夢雷) and others. "Palace Edition." Peking: 1728.

Ma-i Hsiang Fa (麻衣相法) (The Physiognomy of Ma-i). Compiled and edited by Lu Wei-chung (陸位崇) from the original work by Ch'en T'uan (陳摶). Hsin Tsu, Taiwan: Tsu Lin Book Company, 1958.

Sien Hsiang Ch'üan Pien (神相全篇) (Complete Work on Physiognomy). Collected by Ch'en T'uan (陳摶), revised by Yuan Chung-ch'e (忠徹) or Yuan Liu-chuang (袁柳). 13 vols.; Published by Yun Ching T'ang, 1793.

Sien Hsiang Hui Pien (神相彙篇) (Compilation of Physiognomy). Compiled by Kao Wei-ching (高味卿). Shang Yang: Chiang Tso Hsu Lin (江左書林), 1843.

PRINTED WORKS

ALLEN, DON CAMERON. *The Star-Crossed Renaissance: The Quarrel about Astrology and Its Influence in England*. Durham, N. C.: Duke University Press, 1941.

ARISTOTLE. *Historia Animalium*. "Loeb Classical Library." Translated by A. L. Peck. 3 vols.; Cambridge: Harvard University Press, 1965–.

ARLINGTON, LEWIS C. "Chinese versus Western Chiromancy," *The China Journal*, 7: 170–75, 228–35; 8: 67–76, 1928.

BELLAH, ROBERT N. "Religious Evolution", *American Sociological Review*, 29: 358–74, 1964.

BELOT, JEAN. *Les Ouvres de M. I. Belot...contenant la chiromance, physionomie, l'art de memoire de Raymond Lulle...*Derniere édition, revûë, corrigée & augmentée de divers traités. 2 pts.; Lyon: Claude de la Riviere, 1654.

BERTHELOT, MARCELLIN P. E. *Les origines de l'alchimie*. Paris: Georges Steinheil, 1885.

BODDE, DERK. "Types of Chinese Categorical Thinking," *Journal of the American Oriental Society,* 59: 200–19, 1939.

BOISSIER, ALFRED. *Choix de textes relatifs à la divination assyro-babylonienne.* 2 vols.; Geneva: Henry Kündig, 1905.

———. "Iatromantique, physiognomonie et palmomantique babyloniennes," *Revue d'Assyriologie et d'archéologie orientale,* 8: 33–39, 1911.

BUDGE, E. A. WALLIS, editor. *Cuneiform Texts from Babylonian Tablets, &c., in the British Museum.* Part XXVIII. London: British Museum, 1910.

BURCKHARDT, JACOB CHRISTOPH. *The Civilization of the Renaissance.* Translated by S. G. C. Middlemore. London: Phaidon Press, 1944.

BURKHARDT, V. R.. *Chinese Creeds and Customs.* 2 vols.; Hong Kong: The South China Morning Post, 1953–55.

CARDANO, GIROLAMO. *Metoposcopia.* Paris: Thomas Iolly, 1658.

CHANG, KWANG-CHIH. *The Archaeology of Ancient China.* New Haven: Yale University Press, 1963.

CHAO, WEI-PANG. "The Chinese Science of Fate Calculation," *Folklore Studies.* 5: 279–315, 1946.

CHENG, TE-K'UN. *Archaeology in China.* Vol. 1, *Prehistoric China.* Cambridge: H. Heffer & Sons, 1959.

CHOW, YUNG-TEH. *Social Mobility in China.* New York: Atherton Press, 1966.

CH'Ü, T'UNG-TSU. "Chinese Class Structure and Its Ideology," in John K. Fairbank, editor, *Chinese Thought and Institutions.* Chicago: University of Chicago Press, 1957.

CONGER, GEORGE P. *Theories of Macrocosms and Microcosms in the History of Philosophy.* Ph. D. Dissertation. New York: Columbia University Press, 1922.

CONTENEAU, GEORGES. *La Medicine en Assyrie et en Babylonie.* Paris: Maloine, 1938.

———. *La Divination chez les Assyriens et les Babyloniens.* Paris: Payot, 1940.

Bibliography

CORVUS, ANDREAS. *Excellentissimi et singularis viri in chiromantia exercitatissimi Magistri Andree Corvi Mirandulensis.* Venice: Georgium de Ruscinibus, 1520.

COULING, SAMUEL. *The Encyclopædia Sinica.* Shanghai: Kelly and Walsh, 1917.

DAVIES, JOHN D. *Phrenology: Fad and Science—A 19th Century American Crusade.* New Haven: Yale University Press, 1955.

DAY, CLARENCE BURTON. *Chinese Peasant Cults: Being a Study of Chinese Paper Gods.* Shanghai: Kelly & Walsh, 1940.

DE LACOUPERIE, TERRIEN. *Western Origin of the Early Chinese Civilisation from 2,000 B. C. to 200 A. D.* London: Asher & Co., 1894.

DORÉ, HENRI. *Researches into Chinese Superstitions.* 11 vols.; Shanghai: T'usewei Press, 1914–38.

DRAPER, GEORGE. *Disease and the Man.* London: Kegan Paul, Trench, Trubner & Co., 1930.

DSCHI, HIÄN-LIN. "Indian Physiognomical Characteristics in the Official Annals for the Three Kingdoms, the Chin Dynasty and the Southern and Northern Dynasties," *Studia Serica,* 8: 96–102, 1949.

DUBS, HOMER H. *Hsüntze: The Moulder of Confucianism.* London: Arthur Probsthain, 1927.

EBERHARD, WOLFRAM. "The Political Functions of Astronomy and Astronomers in Han China," in John K. Fairbank, editor, *Chinese Thought and Institutions.* Chicago: University of Chicago Press, 1957.

———. *A History of China.* 2nd ed., revised; Berkeley: University of California Press, 1960.

———. *Conquerors and Rulers: Social Forces in Medieval China.* 2nd ed., revised; Leiden: E. J. Brill, 1965.

EGERTON, CLEMENT, translator. *The Golden Lotus.* A translation, from the Chinese original, of the novel, Chin P'ing Mei. 4 vols.; London: Routledge & Kegan Paul, 1939.

ELLIS, HAVELOCK. *The Criminal.* New York: Scribner & Welford, 1890.

FAIRSERVIS, WALTER A., Jr. *The Origins of Oriental Civilization.* New York: New American Library, 1959.

FINELLA (PHINELLA), FILIPPO. *Libri tres naevorum.* Antuerpiae: Plantin, 1633.

FLUDD, ROBERT. *Utriusque cosmi maioris scilicet et minoris metaphysica atque technica historia.* 2 vols.; Oppenhemij and Francofurti: aere J. T. de Bry, Typis H. Galleri, 1617–21.

FORKE, ALBERT. *The World Conception of the Chinese.* London: Arthur Probsthain, 1925.

——, translator and editor. *Lun Heng.* Part 1. *Philosophical Essays of Wang Ch'ung.* Translated and annotated by Alfred Forke. Leipzig: Otto Harrassowitz, 1907.

FRANKFORT, HENRI and HENRIETTE. "The Emancipation of Thought from Myth," in Henri Frankfort et al., *The Intellectual Adventure of Ancient Man.* Chicago: University of Chicago Press, 1946.

FRANZ, JOHANN GEORG FRIEDRICH. *Scriptores Physiognomoniae veteres...* Altenburg: Gottlob Emanuel Richter, 1780.

FROMM, ERICH. *Escape from Freedom.* New York: Rinehart & Co., 1941.

FUNG, YU-LAN. *A History of Chinese Philosophy.* Translated by Derk Bodde. Vol. 1, Peiping: Henri Vetch, 1937.

——. *A Short History of Chinese Philosophy.* Edited by Derk Bodde. New York: Macmillan Co., 1948.

GALENUS. *Prognostica de decubitu ex mathematica scientia.* Volume 19 of *Opera Omnia,* edited by Karl Gottlob Kühn. 20 vols; Leipzig: Cnoblochii, 1821–33.

——. *A Translation of Galen's Hygiene* (*De santitate tuenda*). By Robert Montraville Green. Springfield III.: Thomas, [1951].

GILES, HERBERT A. *A Chinese Biographical Dictionary.* Shanghai: Kelly and Walsh, 1898.

——. "Palmistry in China," *The Nineteenth Century and After* 56: 985–88, 1904.

——. "Phrenology, Physiognomy, and Palmistry," in *Adversaria Sinica,* Series 1. Shanghai: Kelly & Walsh, 1905.

GLUCK, JAY. "Sex in the Art of the Far East," in *The Encyclopedia of Sexual Behavior.* Edited by Albert Ellis and Albert Abarbanel. 2 vols.; New York: Hawthorn Books, 1961.

GRANET, MARCEL. *La Pensée chinoise*. "L'évolution de l'Humanité" series. Paris: La Renaissance du Livre, 1934.

GRAUBARD, MARK. *Astrology and Alchemy: Two Fossil Sciences*. New York: Philosophical Library, 1953.

GROETHUYSEN, B. "Renaissance," in *Encyclopaedia of the Social Sciences,* Editor in Chief, Edwin R. A. Seligman. Volume 13, pp. 278–85. New York: Macmillan Co., 1935.

GULIK, R. H. van. *Sexual Life in Ancient China: A Preliminary Survey of Sex and Society from ca. 1500 B. C. till 1644 A. D.* Leiden: E. J. Brill, 1961.

HEDIN, SVEN. *The Silk Road*. Translated by F. H. Lyon. New York: E. P. Dutton, 1938.

HERON-ALLEN, EDWARD. *A Manual of Cheirosophy*. 6th ed.; London: Ward, Lock, Bowden, & Co., 1892.

HIPPOLYTUS. *The Refutation of All Heresies*. Translated by J. H. Macmahon. Ante-Nicene Christian Library, edited by Alexander Roberts and James Donaldson. Edinburgh: T. & T. Clark, 1868.

HIRTH, FRIEDRICH and W. W. ROCKHILL, translators and annotators. *Chau Jukua: His Work on the Chinese and Arab Trade in the Twelfth and Thirteenth Centuries, Entitled Chu-fan-chi.* St. Petersburg: Imperial Academy of Sciences, 1911.

HO, PING-TI. *The Ladder of Success in Imperial China: Aspects of Social Mobility. 1368–1911.* New York: Columbia University Press, 1962.

HODOUS, LEWIS. *Folkways in China*. London: Arthur Probsthain, 1929.

HSU, CHO-YUN. *Ancient China in Transition: An Analysis of Social Mobility, 722–222 B. C.* Standford: Standford University Press, 1965.

HSU, FRANCIS L. K. *Americans and Chinese: Two Ways of Life*. New York: Henry Schuman, 1953.

HSÜ TSU. *The Works of Hsüntze*. Translated with notes by Homer H. Dubs. London: Arthur Probsthain, 1928.

HU, SHIH. *The Chinese Renaissance*. Chicago: University of Chicago Press, 1934.

HUDSON, G. F. *Europe and China: A Survey of Their Relations from the Earliest Times to 1800.* London: Edward Arnold, 1931.

HUGHES, E. R. *The Great Learning and the Mean-in-Action*, New York: E. P. Dutton & Co., 1943.

HUGHES, E. R. and K. *Religion in China.* London: Hutchinson's University Library, 1950.

JASTROW, MORRIS. *Babylonian-Assyrian Birth Omens and Their Cultural Significance.* "Religionsgeschichtliche Versuche und Vorarbeiten," 14 Band, 5 Heft. Giessen: Alfred Töpelmann, 1914.

KRAUS, FRITZ RUDOLPH. *Die physiognomischen Omina der Babylonier.* "Mitteilungen der Vorderasiatisch-Aegyptischen Gesellschaft," 40 Band, 2 Heft. Leipzig: J. C. Hinrichs'sche Buchhandlung, 1935.

——. *Texte zur babylonischen Physiognomatik.* "Archiv für Orientforschung," Beiheft 3. Berlin: Privately printed, 1939.

——. "Weitere Texte zur babylonischen Physiognomatik," *Orientalia*, series 2. 16: 172-206, 1947.

LEGGE, JAMES, translator. *The Chinese Classics.* Vols. 1-2, 2nd ed., rev.; Oxford: Clarendon Press, 1983-95. Vols. 3-5, London: Henry Frowde, 1865-72.

LEICHTY, ERLE. "Teratological Omens," in *La Divination en Mésopotamie ancienne et dans les régions voisines.* Bibliothèque des Centres d'Études superieures spécialisés. Paris: Presses Universitaires de France, 1966.

LESSA, WILLIAM A. "Somatomancy: Precursor of the Science of Human Constitution." *Scientific Monthly*, 75: 355-65, 1952.

——. "Chinese Body Divination." in *Folk Religion and the Worldview in the Southwestern Pacific.* The Keio Institute of Cultural and Linguistic Studies. Keio University, Tokyo, 1968.

——. "The Context of Chinese Body Divination" in *Themes in Culture: Essays in Honor of Morris E. Opler*, Zamora, Mario D., J. Michael Mahar, Henry Orenstein, eds., Kayumanggi Publishers, Quezon City 1971.

LEVY, MARION J., Jr. "Contrasting Factors in the Modernization of China and Japan," *Economic Development and Cultural Change*, 2: 161-97, 1953-54.

LI, CHI. *The Beginnings of Chinese Civilization*. Seattle: University of Washington Press, 1957.

LIPPMAN, EDMUND O. VON. *Entstehung und Ausbreitung der Alchemie*. Berlin: Springer 1919.

MAVENS, PHILIPP. *Chiromantia et Physiognomia medica...wie auch... Chiromantia curiosa...*. 2nd ed.; Dresden and Leipzig: Gottlob Christian Hilscher, 1739.

MAYERS, WILLIAM FREDERICK. *The Chinese Reader's Manual*. Reprinted from the original edition [1874]. Shanghai: Presbyterian Mission Press, 1924.

MOURAD, YOUSSEF. *La Physiognomie Arabe et le "Kitab Al-Firasa" de Fakhr Al-Din Al-Razi*. "Collection des éscrites Medico-Psychologiques Arabes." Paris: Librairie Orientaliste Paul Geuthner, 1939.

NADEL, SIGFRIED F. *The Foundation of Social Anthropology*. London: Cohen & West, 1951.

NEEDHAM, JOSEPH. et al. *Science and Civilisation in China*. 7 vols.; Cambridge: University Press, 1954-.

NEUGEBAUR, O. "The History of Ancient Astronomy: Problems and Methods," *Journal of Near Eastern Studies*, 4: 1-38, 1945.

NOSS, JOHN B. *Man's Religions*. Rev. ed.; New York: Macmillan Co., 1956.

O' DEA, THOMAS F. *The Sociology of Religion*. "Foundations of Modern Sociology Series." Englewood Cliffs: Prentice-Hall, 1966.

PLANE, G.M. *Fisiologia, ovvero l'arte di conoscere gli uomini dalla loro fisonomia*. 2 vols.; Milan: G. G. Destefanis, 1803.

PORTA, GIOVANNI BATTISTA DELLA. *De Humana physiognomonia Ioannis Baptistae Portae Neopolitani*. Ursellis: Cornelius Sutoris, 1601.

PTOLEMAEUS, CLAUDIUS. *The Tetrabiblos; or, Quadripartite of Ptolemy, Being Four Books Relative to the Starry Influences*. Translated by James Wilson. London: W. Hughes, [1820].

QUETELET, L. ADOLPHE J. *Sur l' homme et le Développement de ses Facultés, ou Essai de Physique Sociale*. Paris: Bachelier, 1835.

REICHELT, KARL L. *Religion in Chinese Garment.* Translated by Joseph Tetlie. New York: Philosophical Library, 1951.

SARTON, GEORGE. *Introduction to the History of Science.* Published for the Carnegie Institution of Washington. 3 vols.; Baltimore: William & Wilkins Co., 1927–48.

SAUNDERS, RICHARD. *Physiognomie, and Chiromancie, metoposcopie, the symmetrical proportions and signal moles of the body...* 2nd enl. ed; London: Nathaniel Brook, 1671.

SETTALA (SEPTALIUS), LODOVICO. *De naevis.* Mediolani, 1605.

SEXTUS EMPIRICUS. *Against the Professors.* "Loeb Classical Library." Translated by R. G. Bury. Cambridge, Mass.: Harvard University Press, 1949.

SHELDON, WILLIAM H. *Atlas of Men: A Guide for Somatotyping the Adult Male at All Ages.* New York: Gramercy Publishing Co., 1954.

THORNDIKE, LYNN. *A History of Magic and Experimental Science.* 8 vols.; New York: Columbia University Press, 1923–58.

——————. "Chiromancy in Mediaeval Latin Manuscripts," *Speculum,* 40: 674–706, 1965.

TING, SU. "Fortune Telling: A Study of a Most Advanced Form of Magic in Practice in China," *Asia,* 3: 428–37, 1953–54.

TS'AO, CHI-PEN. *Hsiang Jen Fa*(相人法)(The Method of Physiognomy). Hong Kong: Shanghai Book Store, 1965.

TSIEN, TSUEN-HSUIN. *Written on Bamboo and Silk: The Beginnings of Chinese Books and Inscriptions.* Chicago: University of Chicago Press, 1962.

VATSYAYANA. *The Kama Sutra of Vatsyayana.* Translated [by Richard F. Burton]. Benares: Kama Shastra Society, 1885.

WALEY, ARTHUR. *The Way and Its Power: A Study of the Tao Te Ching and Its Place in Chinese Thought.* London: Allen & Unwin, 1934.

——————. *The Nine Songs: A Study of Shamanism in Ancient China.* London: George Allen & Unwin, 1955.

WATSON, WILLIAM. *China before the Han Dynasty.* New York: Frederick A. Praeger, 1961.

WERNER, EDWARD T. C. *Myths and Legends of China*. New York: Farrar & Rinehart, [1922].

WIEGER, LEON. *A Short History of the Religious Beliefs and Philosophical Opinions in China from the Beginning to the Present time*. Translated by E. C. Werner. Hsien-hsien: Hsien-hsien Press, 1927.

WILHELM, RICHARD. *The I Ching, or Book of Changes*. Translated from the German by Gary F. Baynes. Foreword by C. G. Jung. 2 vols.: Routledge and Kegan Paul, 1951.

YANG, C. K. *Religion in Chinese Society: A Study of Contemporary Social Functions of Religion and Some of Their Historical Factors*. Berkeley and Los Angeles: University of California Press, 1961.

INDEX

A

Abenragel. *See* Ibn abi-I-Rijal
aboriginal Australia, 3
Abshihi, 154
Adamantius, 132
Against Physiognomy (by Hsün Tsu), 165, 169
Agrippa of Nettesheim, 125, 127, 144
Albertus Magnus, 125, 150
Alexander the Great, 115
Americans. *See* native Americans
Anaxagoras, 138
Anaximander, 136
Anaximenes of Miletus, 124
Ancient China in Transition (by Hsu), 170
animal types. *See also* theriologic principle; theriology
   body as a whole, 32-38 *passim*
   eyes, 56-59
   eyebrows, 59-63
   noses, 63-67
   mouths, 67-71
   ears, 71-74
anxiety, *see* concern
Anyang, 111-14 *passim*
Apology (by Apuleius), 120
Apuleius, 120
Aquinas, Saint Thomas, 122, 188
Arabic body divination, 8, 130, 145, 154, 155, 159, 160, 161
Arabic correlative tabulations, 127
Arabic interest in moles, 154
Arabs, 125, 166, 187, 194
Arabs in China, 116
Aristeas of Proconnesus, 115

Aristotle, 124, 130-31, 137, 143, 149, 162
Arlington, L. C., 84, 85, 90, 150, 151
Artemidoris Daldianos, 149
Assurbanipal, 161, 165, 166
astrologers, 120, 122
astrology, 1, 3, 29, 30, 84, 120, 124, 136
   genethliacal, 121, 140, 141
   judicial, 140, 141, 142, 143
   natural, 140, 142
   Chinese and Babylonian, 141, 162
   political function in China, 142
   in European history, 140, 142-45
   attacks against, 120, 144
   defense of, 144
astro-physiognomy
   present in the West, 140-53 *passim*
   absent in China, 140-42 *passim*
   dominant over natural physiognomy in Europe, 144, 145
Atlas of Men (by Sheldon), 132
Augustine, Saint, 122, 188
Australia. *See* aboriginal Australia
authorities on physiognomy cited in the *Shen Hsiang*, 11-12
average man theory, 129, 130

B

Babylonia. *See* Mesopotamia
back, 110
Bardesanes, 120
Bastian, A., 158

Index 207

beard, 71
belly, 109-10
Belot, J., 129, 147, 149
Bernard Silvester, 125
Berthelot, M. P. E., 127, 128
bibliographic sources on Chinese physiognomy, 9-11
birth omens, 134
Boas, F., 158
Bodde, D., 15, 27, 28, 30
Bôdhidharma. *See* Ta Mo
body as a whole, 32-38 *passim*
Boehme, Jacob, 125
Boethius, 121, 122
Boissier, A., 134, 149
Bouché-Leclerq, A., 128, 145
Brethren of Sincerity, 125, 127
Bronze Age, Shang, 112-14
Bruno, Giordano, 127
Buddhism and world rejection, 122, 178
Buddhism introduced into China, 117
Buddhistic marks of the great man, 164-65
Budge, E. A. W., 134
Burckhardt, J., 191, 192
Burkhardt, V. R., 6, 24

C
Calvin, John, 144
Cardano, G., 150, 151, 152, 153, 192
Cellini, B., 192
Chalcidius, 124
Chang Chung-yuan, 11, 56
Chang Hsing-chien, 12, 61, 64, 71
Chang Kwang-chih, 113
Chau Ju-kua, 116
Chavannes, E., 137, 138
Ch'en Hsi-i. *See* Ch'en T'uan

Ch'en Meng-lei, 10
Ch'en Shou, 164
Ch'en T'uan, 9, 10, 12
chest, 109
ch'i (matter energy), 26, 27, 139, 160, 161, 179
Childe, V. G.,
Chin Ping Mei. See *The Golden Lotus*
Chinese Creeds and Customs (by Burkhardt), 6
Chinese Reader's Manual (by Mayers), 27
chirognomy, 90
chiromancy. *See* palmistry
Chiromantia et Physiognomia Medica (by Mäyens), 153
Chow Yung-teh, 172
Chu Fan Chih (Records of Barbarous Peoples), 116
Chu Hsi, 27
chung (centrality), 24, 25, 130
Chung Yung (Doctrine of the Mean), 24, 25, 28, 122, 130, 131
Chyromantia Aristotelis, 149
Cicero, 192
class system in China, 172-77 *passim*
Clement of Alexandria, 124
comparative approach, 8-9, 194
concepts common to China and the West, 117-35
concepts (premises) compared, 161
concern (anxiety)
 conductive to divination, 7
 aroused by mobility, 169-79 *passim*
 areas, 179-85
 positive, 180-81

negative, 182-83
  sex and love, 184-85
condottieri, 192
Confucius
  on predestination, 6, 122
  on ancestry and employment, 14
  postdates Yin-Yang theory, 17
  postdates Five Element concept, 18-19
  postdates *I Ching*, 23
  on *chung*, 24
  aware of *ch'i* and *li*, 27
  Heaven as a personified predeterminer, 119
  failure to achieve proper status, 174
Conquerors and Rulers (by Eberhard), 175
Consolation of philosophy (by Boethius), 121
Conteneau, G., 134, 149
Copernicus, 193
Cornaro, L., 192
correlative thinking, 14-16
  number mysticism, 16
  Yin and Yang, 18
  numerical categories, 27-30 *passim*
  universe analogy, 127
  absent in occipitomancy, 157
Corvo (Corvus), A., 148
Couling, S., 24
Croll, O., 129
cuneiform script and tablets, 112, 134, 141, 149, 161, 162, 166
Cuneiform Texts from Babylonian Tablets, 134

D
D'Arpentigny, C. S., 90, 151
Davies, J. D., 156

Day, C. B., 6
De Lacouperie, Terrien, 117
De naevis (by Settala), 152
Democritus, 124, 143
Desbarroles, A., 151
destiny, 118-22, 189; *see also* fate; free will
determinism. *See* destiny
Dictionary of Chinese Mythology (by Werner), 5
Die Kultur der Renaissance in Italien (by Burckhardt), 191
Die physiognomischen Omina der Babylonier (by Kraus), 135
differences between East and West, 136-57
  Chinese concepts absent in the West, 136-40
  Western concepts absent in China, 140-57
different years of a lifetime, 30, 49, 51
diffusion of culture, 112, 113, 159
al-Dimashki, 145
Disease and the Man (by Draper), 130
divination
  importance of, 1-3
  as supernaturalism, 1
  antiquity of, 2-3
  function of, 3
  near-universality of, 3
  categories, 3-4
  public, 140, 168
  personal, 168-69
Doctrine of the Mean. *See Chung Yung*
Doctrine of signatures, 118, 129
Doré, H., 5
Dorn, Gerard, 129
Draper, G., 130

Index

Dschi, Hiän-lin, 164, 165
dualism of Chinese and Zoroastrians, 138
Dubs, H. H., 14, 23
Duns Scotus, 144
dynasties, Chinese, 2

E
ears, 71-74
Eberhard, W., 15, 142, 175-78
Egypt not source of body divination, 161
Egypt weak in divination, 186
Egyptians receive astrology, 142
Eight Schools (*pa hsüeh t'ang*), 29, 41, 43
Eight Diagrams. *See* Trigrams
elementary ideas (*Elementargedanken*), 158
Empedocles, 124, 137, 154
empirical method, 16, 31
Epicureans, 143, 187
Erasmus, 191
Escape from Freedom (by Fromm), 190
Europeans as borrowers, 166
examination system in China, 172-73, 175-77
eyebrows, 59-63
eyes, 56-59

F
face
    as a whole, 39-51
    lines, 51-56
Fairservis, W. A., Jr., 112, 113
Fakhr al-Din al-Razi, 130
famous men with anomalous features, 13
famous men with contradictory features, 14
Fang shih (occultists), 18
fatalism. *See* destiny; free will
fate, 5, 6, 13, 20, 27, 118-22; *see also* destiny; free Will
feudalism, 18, 172, 174, 177, 189-90
Ficino, Marsilio, 144
Finella (Phinella), F., 153
fingernails, 106
Firmicus Maternus, Julius, 122, 124
Five Elements, 19-21
    importance in divination, 5, 6
    importance in the Pah Tze, 7
    resonance of, 15
    macrocosm-microcosm theory, 17, 123
    mutual production principle, 19, 37
    mutual conquest principle, 19, 37-38
    control principle, 19-20
    masking principle, 20
    correspondences, 20
    body types, 21, 36-38
    interpretation of hexagrams, 22
    type of five-fold category, 28-29
    one of Six Treasuries, 29
    used by palmists, 85
    indigenous to China, 166
Five Planets (*wu hsing*), 29, 43
Five Sacred Mountains (*wu yüeh*), 29, 43, 45, 47
Five Senses (*wu kuan*), 28, 45, 47
Fludd, Robert, 125, 126, 139, 140, 146, 147
Folkways in China (by Hodous), 5, 6
foot, 106, 108-09
Forke, A., 13, 137, 138
Fortuna, 193
Four Rivers (*ssu tu*), 28, 43, 45
Four Schools (*ssu hsueh t'ang*), 28, 29, 41

Fowler, O. S. and L., 156
Fra Alessandro, 144
Frankfort, H. and H., 186
Frazer's laws, 7
free will, 119, 120, 121, 122; *see also* destiny
freedom, 120, 121, 189, 190
Frischlin, N., 144
Fromm, E., 190, 192, 193
Fuchsius, S., 132
function of divination, 168-196
    extinction through non-reward, 168
    Chinese-European parallels, 185-193
Fung, Yu-lan, 18, 25, 131

G
Galen, 124, 130, 145, 154, 162, 166
Galileo, 193
Gall, F. J., 156, 166
gentry in China, 172-79 *passim*
Giles, H. A., 4, 5, 10, 28, 148, 157
Golden Lotus, 30, 56, 63, 78, 80, 84
Granet, M., 15, 16, 17
Greek; Greeks, 2, 4, 26, 115, 116, 118, 124, 125, 128, 130, 131, 132, 134, 136, 137, 139, 141, 142, 143, 145, 146, 149, 153, 154, 158, 159-62 *passim*, 165, 166, 167, 179, 187
Greek-Arabic-European tradition, 159, 160
Groethuysen, B., 193
Grosseteste, Robert, 125
Gulik, R. H. van, 184, 185

H
hair of foot, 109
hair of head, 71
Hallstatt culture, 114

hand, 84-107; *see also* chirognomy; palmistry
    color, 85
    palm, 85-106 *passim*
    types of lines, 86, 88, 90-106 *passim*
harmony and the mean, 24-26, 118, 129-31, 160, 165
head, 39
heaven-earth-man triad. See *San kang*
Hedin, S., 116, 117
Helvetius (Jan Frederik Schweitzer), 129
Hemminga, S. van, 144
Hermes Trismegistos, 124
Herodotus, 115
Heron-Allen, E., 148
hexagrams, 18, 22, 23, 24
Hierocles of Alexandria, 124
Hildegard, Saint, 125
Hippolytus, 145
Historia Animalium (by Aristotle), 149
History of the Former Han Dynasty, 18
ho (harmony), 24-26,
Ho, Ping-ti, 173, 178
Hodous, L., 5
Homer, 162
Hsiang Fa Ju Men, 11
Hsiang Pien Wei Mang, No. II, 24
Hsiang shu (physiognomics), 7, 158
Hsiang Te Ch'i Ti-wu, 11
Hsiang Wu-te P'ei Wu-hsiang Ti-san, 11
Hsu, Cho-yun, 170
Hsü, Fu
    authority on physiognomics, 11
    on eyeballs, 56
    on eyebrow, 61
    on noses, 63

Index   211

on teeth, 70
on ears, 71
on bellies, 110
Hsün Tzu
    man is evil by nature, 14
    author of *Against Physiognomy*,
        14, 165, 169
    used some empiricism in attacking physiognomics, 14, 170
    social stratification, 174
Hu Shih, 5
Hughes, E. R. and K., 25, 131
humoral theory, 155, 162
Hygiene (by Galen), 130
Hymn of the Soul (by Bardesanes), 120

I
I Ching (Book of Changes), 6, 17, 22, 23, 122, 127, 150
Ibn abi-I-Rijal, 154
Ibn Khaldun, 154
India, 5, 110, 112, 115-17, 122, 127, 131, 149, 159, 163-67 *passim*, 194
individual merit, 173
individualism, 187, 190, 192
Isidore, Bishop of Seville, 125

J
Jablonski, W., 15, 16
Janse, O., 114
Jewish correlative tabulations, 127
Jewish macrocosm theory, 124, 125, 126
John of Salisbury, 122, 127

K
Kama Sutra (by Vatsyayana), 132
Kao, Wei-ching, 10, 180
Karasuk culture, 114
Khalil Ibn Aibak al-Safadi, 154

Kitab al-Firasa (by Fakr al-Din al-Razi), 130
Kraus, F. R., 135, 161
Ku Chin T'u Shu Ch'eng (Complete Collection of Ancient and Contemporary Books), 10, 52, 92
Kuan Lo, 11
Kuei Ku-tzu ("The Philosopher of the Demon George"), 11, 24
Kuo Lin-tsung, 11, 16, 71

L
Ladder of Success in Imperial China (by Ho), 173, 178
Legalists and hierarchical society, 173
length, 25
Leonardo da Vinci, 125
Lessa, W. A., 4, 8, 195
Leucippus, 143
Levy, M. J., Jr., 177
Lévy-Bruhl, L., 15
li (rational principle), 26, 136, 139, 160, 166
Li Chi, 112, 113
Li Chi (Record of Rites), 17, 127
libertarianism. *See* Free will
Libri tres naevorum (by Finella), 153
Lippmann, E. O. von, 127
lips, 69
Liu Hsin, 18
Lü Ch'ung-yang. *See* Lü Tung-pin
Lü Tung-pin, 11, 36
Lun Heng (by Wang Ch'ung), 13, 165
Lungshan (Lungshanoid) culture, 113

M
Ma-i ("Mourning Clothes"), 10, 12, 30, 32
Ma-i Hsiang Fa (The Physiognomy of Ma-i), 10

Ma-i Shen Hsiang, 10, 12, 178
Ma-i Tao Jen ("Hemp Clad Philosopher"). *See* Ma-i
Macrobius, 124
macrocosm. *See* macrocosm-microcosm
macrocosm-microcosm, 123-28
    Chinese microcosmic principle, 17, 33, 127
    analogy between universe and body, 123
    analogy between universe and society, 123
    Greek concepts, 124
    European concepts, 124-25
    Jewish philosophers, 125
    Arabic concepts, 125
    Babylonian origins, 128
    Chinese-West differences, 128
Manilius, 124
manorial system, 190
Masudi, 154
Mathesis (by Firmicus Maternus), 124
Mayas, Aztecs, Incas, 159
Mäyens, P., 153
Megacosmos et Microcosmos (or *De Mundi Universitate*) (by Bernard Silvester), 125
Melampus, 124, 149, 153, 166
Mencius, 6, 27, 119, 139, 174
Mesopotamia, 7, 110, 113, 128, 134, 135, 141, 142, 143, 149, 159, 161, 162, 165, 166, 168, 185, 186, 194, 195
Mesopotamians, 186-87
Mesopotamian tradition, 160
Metoposcopia (by Cardano), 150, 152
metoposcopy, 4, 39, 147, 150
microcosm. *See* Macrocosm-microcosm

microcosmic principle. *See* Macrocosm-microcosm
Middle Ages and decline of body divination, 187-90
ming. *See* fate
Minusinsk, 114
Mo-tzu and hierarchical society, 173
mobility in China, 170-77
mobility in Renaissance Europe, 192
Mohists, 118
moles, 11, 30, 39, 47, 74-80, 108, 109, 129, 152-54
Montessori, M., 130
Mourad, Y., 130, 132, 145, 154
moustache, 34, 71
mouth, 26, 28, 34-36, 67-69
Myths and Legends of China (by Werner), 5,

N
Nadel, S. F., 8
native Americans, 195
navel, 110
Near East, 113, 127
neck, 35, 109
Needham, J.
    correlative thinking, 15-16, 127
    number mysticism, 17
    five Elements, 19, 136, 137
    continuity of European-Chinese artifacts, 114-15
    Chinese and European universe parallels, 127
    macrocosm-microcosm and extispicy, 128
    dualism, 138
    ch'i, 139
neomancy. *See* moles
Neugebauer, O., 140, 141, 143
Nine Songs (by Waley), 6

Index 213

nose, 17, 26, 28, 34-35, 41, 43, 45, 47, 51, 63-67, 70, 78, 164

O
occipital bone, 80-83
occipitomancy, 80
Old Silk Road. *See* routes
onychomancy, 152, 154
Oresme, Nicolas, 125, 144
organs, sexual. *See* sexual organs
Origen, 122
origin of body divination, 160-61, 165

P
Pa kwa. *See* Trigrams
Pah Tze (Eight Words), 7
palmistry. *See also* chirognomy; hand
 very old in China, 84
 lacks astrology in China, 84
 as astro-physiognomy in Europe, 145-46
 European, 145-50
 origins, 148-49
Pan Ku, 18, 171
P'an Ku, the first man, 29
Paracelsus, 125
Parmenides, 138
Patritius, 127
pedomancy, 106, 108-09
Pereyra (Pererius), B., 144
Peruchio, [Le Sieur] de, 155
Pherecydes of Syros, 137
Philo Judaeus, 120, 124
phrenology, 39, 80, 140, 155-57, 159, 161, 166
Physics (of Aristotle), 124
physiognomy. *See also* body divination
 earliest record in China, 1

 antiquity in China, 18
Pico de la Mirandola, 144
pillow bones. *See* occipital bone
Plane, G. M., 155
Plato, 124, 127
Plotinus, 121, 124
Polemon, 132
Pompanazzi, 125
Porphyry, 121, 124
Porta, G. della, 132, 133, 144
Proclus, 124,
providence. *See* destiny
Pseudo-Aristotle, 132
psychic unity, 158
Ptolemy (Ptolemaeus), 145, 147
Pujasol, E., 155
Pythagoras, 154, 162
Pythagorism, 138

Q
Quetelet, L. A. J., 129, 130

R
raphe, 69, 70, 78, 118
recommendatory system, 174, 175
Refutation of All Heresies (by Hippolytus), 145
Reichelt, K. L., 6
religion, popular Chinese, 6
Religion in Chinese Society (by Yang), 4, 168
religiosity of the Chinese, 5-6
Renaissance, 7, 143, 144, 150, 154, 155, 166, 187, 190-94 *passim*
Republic (by Plato), 124
research aims and design, 7-9
Researches into Chinese Superstitions (by Doré), 5
Romans; Rome, 2, 7, 119, 128, 142, 143, 187, 188, 189

214   Ancient Chinese Body Divination

routes (between China and India and the West), 115-17 *passim*, 127, 159, 166

S

san kang (Trinity of the universe), 6
San Kuo Chih (History of the Three Kingdoms), 164
Sarton, G., 145, 154, 190
Saunders, R., 152, 153
Saussure, L. de, 138
scapulimancy, 2, 112, 113
Scepper, C., 144
secretae naturae, 193
secular spirit, 191
Seneca, 124, 192
Servius, 124
Settala (Septalius), L., 152, 153
sex and love minimized, 184
Sextus Empiricus, 145
sexual
    lines, 102
    organs, 132
Sexual Life in Ancient China (by van Gulik), 184
Shang culture, 5, 112-14
Shao Yung, 127
Sheldon, W. H., 132
Shen Hsiang Ch'üan Pien (Complete Work on Physiognomy), 9, 10, 12, 32, 92, 170, 178, 182, 184
Shen Hsiang Hui Hui Pien (Compilation of Physiognomy), 10, 179, 180, 182, 184
Shih Chi (Book of Records), 137
Siniticism, 5
Six Stars (*lu yüen*), 29, 43,
Six Treasuries (*liu fu*), 29, 39
size, 25-26
Smith, G. E. and W. J. Perry, 159

social milieu, 7
Social Mobility in China (by Chow), 172
Socrates, 162
somatomancy, 4
sources of Sinitic civilization, 112-17
Speculum Astronomiae (unknown author), 122
Spurzheim, J. G., 156, 166
stimulus diffusion, 141, 162-63
Stoics, 143
Su Wen, 123
Sung Ch'i-chiu, 12

T

Ta Mo, 11
Ta T'ung Fu, 12, 61
T'ai-ch'ing-ching, 185
T'ang chü, 11, 169, 170
Taoists and eternal life, 178
teeth, 69-70
teratology, 134-35
Tetrabiblos (by Ptolemy), 145
theriologic principle, 24; *see also* animal types, theriology
    in typing the whole body, 33-35
    in typing noses, 64
    in typing mouths, 67
    in typing ears, 71
    Arabs, 132
    confused with teratology, 134
    origin in Mesopotamia, 135
    overshadowed by astrology, 144
theriology, 24, 131-35 *passim*; *see also* animal types, theriologic principle
Thirteen Parts (*shih san pu*), 30, 47, 48
Three Essentials (*san ch'i*), 85, 87
Three Forces (*san ts'ai*), 28, 39, 41, 87
Three Sections (*san t'ing*), 28, 33, 41, 47

Index

Tigris-Euphrates Valley, 112, 162, 165, 186; *see also* Mesopotamia
Ting Su, 7,
toes, 108
tongue, 70-71
trade routes. *See* routes
Trigrams,
   Pah Tze reliance on, 7
   resonance and, 15
   application to body divination, 22
   explanation of, 22
   correspondences of, 22
   palm mapped into, 85
   palm explained by, 85, 87, 90, 91-92
   yin and yang present in, 23
   indigenous to China, 166
trinity of the universe. *See* san kang
Tso Chuan, 1
Twelve Temples (*shih erh kung*), 30, 45, 47, 87
Tzu Ssu, 26

U

ugliness, 130
Utriusque cosmi historia (by Fludd), 125, 126, 139, 146

V

Vatsyayana, 132
Viola, G., 130
Vitruvius, 134

W

waist, 110
Waley, A., 6, 137, 138
Wang Ch'ung
   author of "On Anthroposcopy" in *Lun Heng*, 13, 165
   believed body can reveal fate, 13, 178
   denied catastrophies are portents, 13
   astrology individualized in his time, 162
   ability not always rewarded, 174
Wang Fu, 174
Wang Hsü. *See* Kuej Kutzu
Watson, W., 114
Werner, E. T. C., 5
West, the, 7, 111, 113, 118, 120, 125, 126, 127, 136-57 passim
Western body divination, 8
Wilhelm, H., 15
Wilhelm R., 23
world rejection and divination, 122, 178, 188, 191
Wu the Immortal, 30, 63, 78

Y

Yang, C. K., 4, 6, 168-69
Yangshao culture, 114
YinYang principle, 17-18
   importance in divination, 6
   importance in the *Pah Tze*, 7
   an expression of microcosm theory, 17, 123
   used in interpretation of hexagrams, 23-24
   found in Five Planet method, 29
   indigenous to China, 166
Yuan Chungch'e, 9, 12
Yuan Liuchuang. *See* Yuan Chung-ch'e
yung (normality), 130

Z

Zoroastrianism, 138

ABOUT THE AUTHOR

William Armand Lessa, born in Newark, NJ in 1908, earned a BA from Harvard in 1928 and subsequently worked as a research associate at the University of Hawaii in Honolulu, in the early 1930s. It was this period in which he developed a life-long interest in the cultures of the Pacific Rim.

Returning to the US mainland, Lessa enrolled in an MA program in anthropology at the University of Chicago, graduating in 1941. Military service interrupted his studies, but, post WWII, Lessa returned to Chicago to complete a doctorate in 1947. Assuming a lectureship in anthropology at the University of California, Los Angeles, the same year, Lessa remained in this position until retirement in 1969, having in that interim mentored many UCLA anthropology graduate students (including the later-renowned author, Carlos Casteneda).

Throughout his career, Dr Lessa engaged in important field research in folklore, magic and religion in various Pacific island locales. His seminal publications on Oceanic folklore remain standard works in this field.

www.ingramcontent.com/pod-product-compliance
Lightning Source LLC
Chambersburg PA
CBHW020837160426
43192CB00007B/689